How Knowle

Get Things Done

Real-World Adaptive Case Management

Excellence in Practice Series

How Knowledge Workers
Get Things Done
Real-World Adaptive Case Management

Foreword by
Connie Moore

Excellence in Practice Series

Published in association with the
Workflow Management Coalition

Workflow Management Coalition

19 Years of Thought-Process Leadership

Edited by
Layna Fischer

Future Strategies Inc.
Lighthouse Point, Florida

How Knowledge Workers Get Things Done
Real-World Adaptive Case Management

Copyright © 2012 by Future Strategies Inc.

ISBN-13: 978-0-9849764-4-7

Published by Future Strategies Inc., Book Division

3640-B3 North Federal Highway #421, Lighthouse Point FL 33064 USA
+1 954.782.3376 Fax +1 954.719.3746
www.FutStrat.com; books@FutStrat.com

All book titles are available at quantity discounts for corporate and academic education and training use in both Print and Digital Formats.

Publisher's Cataloging-in-Publication Data

Library of Congress Catalog Card LCCN No. 2012949538
SAN: 299-9374

How Knowledge Workers Get Things Done

Real World Adaptive Case Management

/Layna Fischer (editor)

p. cm.

Includes bibliographical references, appendices and index.

ISBN-13: 978-0-9849764-4-7

1. Knowledge Management. 2. Technological Innovation. 3. Case Management. 4. Organizational Effectiveness. 5. Business Process Technology. 6. Management Science. 7. Adaptive Computing Systems. 8. Strategic Planning 9. Business Process Technology. 10. Workflow Management Coalition

Table of Contents

Section 1: ACM Strategy and Business

Section 2: ACM Case Studies

Section 3: Appendices

Appendix

Foreword
The Process-Driven Business Of 2020

The high-stakes hunt for global talent, the consumerization of IT driven by smart mobile devices and the bottom-up push for social and collaboration tool adoption will exponentially increase employee empowerment between now and 2020.

Accommodating the new workforce's expectations may seem premature, given the still fragile business climate; but embracing global talent, new work styles, and a next-generation workforce is high on the agenda for many CEOs seeking to expand into new markets.

This dynamic will put pressure on today's outdated business processes and creaky applications, as companies seek new ways to embed and contextualize collaboration and social tools into applications for a youthful, mobile, and global workforce.

Key trends will be the following:

- **Globalization of human capital.** The race for global talent is strategic for many multinationals as they move into more countries.
  One business transformation executive from a global insurance company said, "Demographics are a large part of what drives our concerns. We are looking at the retiring workforce, the availability of talent five years out— even 25 to 50 years out—and ask ourselves: What is the best use of local talent? Which countries have the right talent?"

- **Mobile workers.** Whether at home, on the road, or in an office, work is something people do, not somewhere people go. In fact, 66% of information workers in North America and Europe already work at least part of the time remotely. This trend will affect everything from the location and design of offices, to IT's provisioning of technology, to how business lead ers marshal expertise and foster collaboration within the context of processes. Enterprises must think mobile first when designing workplace policies.
  Challenges to overcome? Mobile employees spend more time than other workers looking for information to do their jobs, and IT shops struggle to keep pace with demands for more mobility. To capitalize on a mobile workforce, business and IT leaders will need to embed mobility into specific processes, particularly focusing on end to end processes that engage the customer.

- **Ubiquitous and contextual collaboration.** As the enterprise's reach expands and the workforce globalizes, the need for better collaboration tools will move to the top of the business agenda. One business transformation leader told us, "We don't want an information graveyard; we want our business to be dynamic and the culture to be process driven."
  More employees will need anytime access to collaborative, social, and productivity tools to, for example, complete sales, find information, take

---

This research was originally published April 16, 2012 in the Forrester Research, Inc., report "The Process-Driven Business Of 2020" by Connie Moore. Full report at www.Forrester.com

training, and locate experts no matter where they work or what device they use. But we know that collaboration alone—with little business process—doesn't transform the business. Instead, by pairing collaboration with BPM tools, CIOs can deliver contextual collaboration that fits into a sequenced series of steps and tackle processes that are still largely manual.

The business/IT relationship will change radically by 2020. One scenario already playing out is for business-facing IT staff, including relationship and project managers, enterprise architects, developers, and business analysts, to report into the business, creating a smaller IT cadre to focus on legacy renewal and modernization.

As business apps move to the cloud, business technology becomes easier to manage, freeing up more IT skills to be assimilated into the business units. This fundamentally changes the relationship of IT and business stakeholders, a trend Forrester refers to as the shift from IT to BT.

The catalyst fueling the shift is the reality that technology drives every aspect of today's business, no matter what sector, and businesspeople will become more capable of managing more aspects of technology. CIOs, in their existing or evolving role, have an opportunity to facilitate this change by leading strategies for process transformation powered by technology.

Several technical developments illustrate the influence that BT will have on the management of processes and the applications that support those processes:

- **Business-ready technology abstracts configuration from technical complexity.** Technologies supporting the business, including enterprise apps, business process management suites (BPMSes), dynamic case management, and collaboration and mobile apps, are becoming inherently easier to use and manage. This is driven by improvements in end user interfaces, as well as by configuration improvements that present more intuitive (and increasingly graphical) set-up tools.
  As more software vendors deliver business-ready technology, business process stakeholders will become less dependent on IT to design and configure processes and unlock new features of the applications.

- **SaaS and cloud deployment models reduce dependence on IT.** Business stakeholders are increasingly active in procuring business technology directly from vendors, and, likewise, technology vendors are becoming more adept at selling solutions to business buyers. The deployment of these technologies is increasingly cloud-based and provided as-a-service, whether hosted and managed by the vendor or allied third parties. Increasingly, new processes will be deployed within a federated environment: on-premises, in the cloud, and supporting mobile apps.
  The business views IT involvement in these deployments as beneficial (e.g., for integration and security services), but no longer essential in many cases. While most finance applications and some systems of record won't move to the cloud anytime soon, many more processes will, particularly as BPM suite vendors offer process-as-a-service software to help companies (and businesspeople) build and deploy new processes more quickly.

- **Tech-savvy workers and customers become self-sufficient.** Tech-savvy businesspeople and customers are now accustomed to consumer technologies that provide far superior ease of use and manageability than today's corporate systems. More than half of US employees say they have better technology at home than at work, and 37 percent of US information workers solve customer and business problems using technology that they master first at home and then bring to work.

These workers and customers have the confidence to apply readily available cloud and mobile-based apps to address business process requirements. This evolution will result in friction with IT organizations that futilely attempt to limit corporate use of consumer-oriented tools. Resisting this trend will slow your organization's transition to the process-driven business of the future; process transformation depends on the proactive assimilation of technology innovation by the business.

Connie Moore
Vice President and Principal Analyst,
Forrester Research, Inc., USA

How Knowledge Workers Get Things Done

Layna Fischer, Future Strategies Inc.

Highly predictable work is easy to support using traditional programming techniques, while *unpredictable* work cannot be accurately scripted in advance, and thus requires the involvement of the knowledge workers themselves. The core element of Adaptive Case Management (ACM) is the support for real-time decision-making by knowledge workers.

How Knowledge Workers Get Things Done describes the work of managers, decision makers, executives, doctors, lawyers, campaign managers, emergency responders, strategist, and many others who have to think for a living. These are people who figure out what needs to be done, at the same time that they do it, and there is a new approach to support this presents the logical starting point for understanding how to take advantage of ACM.

Keith Swenson points out, "We are seeing a fundamental shift in our workforce, and in the ways they need to be managed. Not only are companies engaging their customers in new ways, but managers are engaging workers in similarly transformed ways."

In award-winning case studies covering industries as a diverse as law enforcement, transportation, insurance, banking, state services, and healthcare, you will find instructive examples for how to transform your own organization.

This important book follows the ground-breaking publications, *Taming the Unpredictable*[1] and *Mastering the Unpredictable*[2] and provides important papers by thought-leaders in this field, together with practical examples, detailed ACM case studies and product reviews.

Contents

Thought-provoking research on how the business/IT relationship will change radically by 2020. One scenario already playing out is for business-facing IT staff, including relationship and project managers, enterprise architects, developers, and business analysts, to report into the business, creating a smaller IT cadre to focus on legacy renewal and modernization.

---

[1] *Taming the Unpredictable, Real World Adaptive Case Management: Case Studies and Practical Guidance*, published by Future Strategies Inc., 2011
[2] *Mastering the Unpredictable:* How Adaptive Case Management Will Revolutionize the Way That Knowledge Workers Get Things Done, published by Meghan-Kiffer Press, April 2010

Section 1: ACM Strategy and Business

THE STRATEGIC BUSINESS BENEFITS OF ADAPTIVE CASE MANAGEMENT
Max J. Pucher, Isis Papyrus

For over twenty years Business Process Management (BPM) has been used as a methodology to improve how a business operates. While that works well for certain processes on a smaller scale, businesses are facing the challenge that half their processes are knowledge-oriented in nature and thus unpredictable. Customer service processes may be simpler and more predictable, but they require a new dynamic for individualization. Overall, all processes should be derived from business strategy and its well-defined objectives and operational targets. Adaptive Case Management (ACM) offers comprehensive BPM functionality and methodology to meet those requirements.

HOW ACM DRIVES BETTER CUSTOMER ENGAGEMENT
Dermot McCauley, Kofax, Inc.

Both routine and unpredictable engagement with customers is an essential part of many critical business processes including customer start-up, account maintenance, transaction management, service fulfillment, incident management, etc. Yet mobile, cloud and social technologies are increasing the power of customers and transforming how they participate with organizations. This chapter discusses the necessary role of adaptive case management in enabling more responsive, flexible and effective customer engagement in an era when the rising power of the individual demands a new architecture of engagement for customers and employees alike.

CASE MANAGEMENT FORECAST: MOSTLY PCM WITH A CHANCE OF ACM
John T. Matthias, National Center for State Courts, United States

Knowledge work may primarily involve routine, repeatable work which constitutes production case management (PCM), but it may also involve problem-solving activities that would benefit from adaptive case management (ACM) capabilities in an application. Work which involves repeatable activities can be defined in advance and be supported by an application designed for volume use. Many jobs involve some amount of routine work but also some amount of problem-solving work. This chapter explores how can this non-routine work be supported.

TYPES OF BUSINESS PROCESS
Keith Harrison-Broninski, Role Modellers Ltd.

Many organizations struggle to improve (and support with technology) critical operational business processes due to poor understanding of the different types of business process. This paper categorizes business process types (and supporting technologies).

This paper also explains how to create a HIM Plan template as a set of Stages in which people play Roles to provide deliverables, and how to use a HIMS server, multiple HIMS servers and/or normal email to carry out a HIM Plan across professional, geographical and organizational boundaries.

DISTRIBUTE PROCESS KNOWLEDGE IN ACM THROUGH MENTORING
Frank Michael Kraft, AdaPro GmbH and Hajo Normann, Accenture

In this paper we discuss two knowledge worker roles within organizations: The expert and the trainee. The expert is a long experienced knowledge worker that has a high grade of responsibility and needs more autonomy in his work. The trainee is relatively new to the organization or to the job and needs guidance and also supervision in terms of quality assurance.

The expert-trainee relationship within the organization is a generic pattern that occurs on many levels of an organization and many areas where knowledge work is done. It is the most important way how knowledge is passed on within organizations. It passes professional knowledge, but also procedural knowledge on to the other workers. It is the prerequisite to professionally delegate parts of work to others. The adaptive case management system affects this work relationship. The paper discusses how the system supports this knowledge transfer and delegation and how this leads to a mid- to long-term advantage of the organization that uses it.

MANAGING STRUCTURED AND UNSTRUCTURED PROCESSES UNDER THE SAME UMBRELLA
Alberto Manuel, Process Sphere, Portugal

There are some companies, highly coupled with structured processes and others where there is a lot of unstructured execution to provide a solution to a customer. Both realities coexist. This means that not everything is black or white and sometimes is grey. BPM as a management discipline must have the capabilities to manage both realities blended together, but alsoto embrace the unstructured paradigm.

NATURAL LANGUAGE PROCESSING, BPM AND ACM IN HEALTHCARE:
Charles Webster, MD

Two great information technology industries, health IT and workflow IT, increasingly overlap. Traditional health IT (HIT) has solved many healthcare information management problems, but not others, especially involving complex processes and workflows. Over several decades business process management (BPM) and case management systems have had great success automating workflow and supporting problem solving that requires human interpretation, creativity, and guidance. Nonetheless, within the BPM community a debate has raged over where and what to automate and how to support Drucker's "knowledge worker." These issues, and their resolution, are central and critical to a parallel debate within healthcare about usability of electronic health records (EHR) and HIT and effects on physician productivity and patient safety. The BPM and adaptive case management debate is reviewed and lessons drawn for creating efficient, effective, and flexible EHR and HIT workflows.

CASE MANAGEMENT MEGATRENDS
SRA International, Inc. & Workflow Management Coalition

This chapter explores the role and interplay of case management within today's most critical emerging information management megatrends, notably mobile, cloud, big data, social technology, as well as the 'appification' or consumerization of IT. Also explored is how Adaptive Case Management (ACM) both builds on, yet is differentiated from other contemporary technologies targeting knowledge worker support, specifically BPM, ECM and CRM.

CASE MANAGEMENT: CONTRASTING PRODUCTION VS. ADAPTIVE
Keith D. Swenson, Fujitsu America, Inc., and WfMC

There are a variety of subcategories of BPM technology -- possibly as many as seven distinct specializations. Two of these are useful for supporting knowledge workers: Production Case Management and Adaptive Case Management. What is the difference? While PCM is developed like a traditional application at design time, and later deployed to workers for use at runtime, ACM has no design-time distinct from run-time. PCM makes use of traditional programming practices of modelling and web service integration, while ACM eschews programming of any form and turns instead to an incremental direct manipulation approach. While both share the term "Case Management" there could hardly be less similarities between the two approaches and an understanding of how different they are is critical in avoiding costly implementation mistakes. This chapter will compare and contrast PCM with ACM to clarify the distinctions, and will use examples from the three PCM case studies that won a mention in this year's awards. The result is that you will be armed with criteria that can be used to distinguish which kind of Case Management a vendor is presenting to you, and also a set of criteria to determine for your own situation what kind of Case Management you need.

Section 2: Case Studies

COGNOCARE, AN ACM-BASED SYSTEM FOR ONCOLOGY
Gold Award: Healthcare

This workdescribes the use of ACM technology, implemented by means of an Artificial Intelligence Planner and Scheduler, to help physicians handle the process associated to the treatment of their patients. The lessons learned come from pediatric oncology treatments due to the previous experience of the company, but they may easily be extrapolated to general oncology or even general practice like the case of chronic disease patients.

VISION SERVICE PLAN (VSP)
Silver Award: Healthcare

Vision Service Plan (VSP) provides high-quality, cost-effective eye care benefits and world-class products and services to eye care professionals, employers, and more than 56 million members. The integration of the OpenText Case360 solution with the Customer Care Portal significantly improved customer service quality by simplifying the creation and processing of critical documents including claims adjustments, complaints, doctor inquiries and fraud alerts while providing over $700K in annual savings on business operations. Additional cost savings are expected as more task types are added.

GENERALI HELLAS INSURANCE COMPANY S.A.
Gold Award: Customer-Facing

Generali Hellas Insurance Company S.A. has become successful largely by making itself the company of choice for agents through its exceptional service. To advance this offering and to streamline processes throughout the company, Generali sought and implemented an enterprise system with the capacity to integrate new and improved workflow processes.

The new system, named *Thesis,* resulted in several improvements. Case handling is now more flexible, with two distinct tracks—one strictly defined for straightforward cases, the other adaptable for cases that are less well defined. Agents gained insight into the policy application process and the ability to respond quickly to underwriter questions and requests. Underwriters and claims handlers, in turn, spend more time doing pure underwriting and claims handling than "paper pushing" and other work unrelated to their core competencies. The company's ability to respond to regulatory requests was greatly improved. In addition, paper and printing costs were dramatically reduced.

FORTUNE-500 BANK, INDIA
Silver Award: Customer-Facing

This case study is about one of the leading Fortune 500 banks from Asia Pacific. Having started operations in India in 1853, the bank has steadily grown in reach and service offerings, keeping pace with the evolving banking and financial needs of its customers.

The bank wanted to automate its Customer Request Management process in India. All the different types of customer requests, complaints, queries, interactive phone calls needed to be processed and routed to the right customer executives (Front/Back Office) based on their skill metrics, experiences and availability. The solution had to be flexible and robust enough to support the growing customer base and different request types.

PANEON GMBH, AUSTRIA
Gold Award: Knowledge Worker Innovation

Paneon GmbH is a two-year old startup located in Austria and currently serving the German-speaking markets of Austria, Germany and Switzerland. As a Network marketing business with a large, decentralized structure of individual sales partners providing contacts to customers, building sales and business relations from informal community relations Paneon faces a number of challenges:

- How to deal with growing and the related rising complexity?
- How to adjust to growth without creating bureaucracy?
- How to quickly adapt to market pull without software development?
- How to stay focused on people and support more engagement?
- How to manage a business with independent individuals?

UWV, THE NETHERLANDS
Judges' Choice Award: Knowledge Worker Innovation

UWV, a Dutch organization delivering employee benefits to Dutch citizens, has been using process management systems from their current vendor since 2001. The system was completely renewed and upgraded to a new version early 2012 to improve the customer experience of a UWV customer that objects to an earlier decision of UWV. These objections are handled by the 1,250 employees of the Objections and Appeals division of UWV.

According to the knowledge workers themselves, their new adaptive case management system offers them the possibility to live up to their customer's expectations. Now they can choose the optimal process path for an individual customer, helping them meet deadlines by giving them access to all necessary information in a structured and efficient way.

MATS NORWEGIAN FOOD SAFETY AUTHORITY, NORWAY
Gold Award: Public Sector

The Norwegian Food Safety Authority's (NFSA) overall objective is to ensure safe food and animal welfare. NFSA's area of responsibility comprises plant health, food and fodder production and handling, water supply plants, cosmetics, animal health and welfare for production animals and pets. Since 2009, about 1000 of NFSA's knowledge workers (veterinarians, biologists, engineers, other professionals) use MATS actively as a decision support system for the main bulk of their professional work; to plan, conduct and register audits. The public (farmers, restaurants, food production plants, food shops, fish exporters, plants importers, butcheries, pet owners) use MATS to register, apply, and view their own case information, resulting in 150 000 communications per year.

QSUPER, AUSTRALIA
Silver Award: Public Sector

QSuper is the superannuation fund (a retirement program in Australia) for current and former Queensland government and related entity workers. As one of Australia's largest superannuation funds, QSuper provides members with access to an extensive range of tools, information and services designed to help members grow their super.

Operating in a highly competitive and dynamic financial services environment, QSuper manages more than $30 billion in funds for over 540,000 members and is committed to working with its members so they can feel more confident they are making the best choices for their situation. QSuper Limited undertakes the daily administration of QSuper and has more than 600 employees.

STATE AGENCY THAT MANAGES SERVICES FOR CHILDREN AND FAMILIES, USA
Special Mention: Public Sector

The State Agency ("the Agency") helps process Daycare and Foster Care applications by collecting and reviewing criminal history review data. The Agency was experiencing increased workloads and mounting storage needs, and the processing of applications was manually-intensive and inefficient. The goal of the case management solution was to implement an automated workflow system to minimize the physical handling of the applications and streamline the overall business processes. The solution enables users—Criminal History Raters, Criminal History Reporting staff, Criminal History Analysts, and Record Keepers—to securely and reliably expedite application processing while meeting legal requirements for processing background checks, enabling validation and audits. The case management platform provides an integrated system that supports processing, maintenance, and distribution of criminal history reviews so that state staff can respond accurately and efficiently. It also provides interoperability with the applications from other agencies and departments.

TOUCHSTONE HEALTH, USA
Finalist: Production Case Management

Touchstone Health faced a momentous challenge with their current Appeals and Grievances (A&G) process. Touchstone was managing 1,500 A&G cases per month through a largely manual case management process. In addition, regulatory compliance requirements required timely and auditable records be provided to avoid potential fines.

The primary users, the A&G case managers, were dealing with a highly manual process that required data gathering from multiple systems and departments. They had to manually reconcile all reporting, and manually generate and track the required correspondence and deadlines. Additionally, the case managers often lost visibility and control when assigning cases throughout the organization.

Touchstone Health adopted a new Adaptive Case Management approach that greatly improved the productivity of the company's knowledge workers and ensured compliance to regulatory requirements. The ACM approach provided an automated system that ensures all correspondence is automatically sent and meets regulatory timing requirements.

Section 1:
ACM Strategy and Business

The Strategic Business Benefits of Adaptive Case Management

Max J. Pucher, Isis Papyrus

1. ABSTRACT:

For over twenty years Business Process Management (BPM) has been used as a methodology to improve how a business operates. While that works well for certain processes on a smaller scale, businesses are facing the challenge that half their processes are knowledge-oriented in nature and thus unpredictable. Customer service processes may be simpler and more predictable, but they require a new dynamic for individualization. Overall, all processes should be derived from business strategy and its well-defined objectives and operational targets. Adaptive Case Management (ACM) offers comprehensive BPM functionality and methodology to meet those requirements.

In ACM, processes are always focused on meeting goals and not primarily on executing flows. Some goals may be achieved using a flow definition, which means that BPMN flow-diagrams can be used within ACM. Ideally, these process goals are aligned with the objectives and targets of the organization's overall business strategy. To make this tie-in of process goals more transparent, high-end ACM systems offer a Business Architecture model for defining a business strategy consisting of value streams, capability maps, strategy maps, and process goals. In principle, it provides embedded business performance management.

Working within ACM templates, management can develop a business strategy by defining business objectives and customer outcomes, and the capabilities needed to fulfill those. Capabilities are defined as a set of process goals that are assigned to process owners. These form a causal network, or strategy map, showing all of these objectives, outcomes, capabilities, targets, and goals. By monitoring this network, executives can verify that goals are fulfilled and processes stay aligned with the overall business strategy.

The use of such a Strategic ACM capability is one element of a System of Engagement (as defined by AIIM) that allows guidance for business performers through a 'Language of Process.' As in Strategic ACM, Gartner Group proposes the use of process templates as a starting point in their definition of systems of innovation and differentiation. A System of Engagement is independent of the company hierarchy and allows business transformation without upfront culture changes.

2. EXECUTIVE SUMMARY

In the past, the focus of Business Process Management (BPM) efforts has been on automating predictable workflows and improving process efficiency. The ROI is achieved by *implementing a process application* that reduces the amount of time and people involved. It cannot be assumed that ensuring a consistent result at lowest cost also improves process quality from a customer perspective, because it removes the ability to individualize and focus on customer perceived value and satisfaction in service processes. Therefore one cannot simply take the cost reductions of small-scale process efforts and translate them into savings for a larger corporation.

One cannot decompose a system into smaller pieces and optimize them individually without considering the whole. Top-down improvement requires expert knowledge of the processes, which means it requires a substantial governance bureaucracy that rather adds cost.

Businesses must further tackle the challenge that approximately 50 percent of all processes are not structured flows, but unpredictable service activity requiring knowledge work. Making the benefits of BPM available to the larger organization thus requires technology to support *unpredictable* processes and the judgment-oriented *knowledge work* that drives business adaptability and success.

Process governance has no other purpose than to translate business strategy into customer outcomes, operational targets and process goals. There is not just a need for better communication but the requirement to make the business strategy transparent and translate it to performance management.

Today, both management and knowledge workers rely on technologies such as email and office tools to do their job and have to deal with the resulting process fragmentation and a lack of contextual functionality. Simply adding social networking capability and mobile apps to those existing tools without a consolidated approach will simply increase that fragmentation between ECM, BPM and CRM.

The most robust such technology, best suited to leveraging the innovative potential of knowledge work in today's fast-changing environment, is Adaptive Case Management (ACM). Based on a Model-Discover-Adapt paradigm, ACM lets knowledge workers create goal-oriented process templates as they work, then reuse those templates and adapt them to changing situations. It does away with the substantial project effort and governance overhead of current BPM methodology using a flow-diagram paradigm.

The ACM approach is offered by differing products, each allowing some or all of the following benefits ("*" indicates benefits offered by strategically-oriented ACM products):

- Knowledge worker empowerment
- Social collaboration and mobile support
- An agile, innovation-oriented environment
- Transparent guidance and monitoring mechanisms*
- A growing, actionable base of process knowledge*
- Advanced decision support*
- Tools for linking processes to overall business strategy*
- In-process handling of business content*

This chapter introduces ACM in more detail, describes all of the above benefits, and discusses how the Model-Discover-Adapt paradigm works at the various levels of the ACM project range, from basic to strategic. Its goal is to help decision-makers differentiate ACM from other approaches and determine which level of ACM technology can best meet their needs.

3. What is Knowledge Work?

Knowledge work relies on the expertise of workers who must make situation-dependent decisions with a potential to strongly affect customer outcomes. From medical caregivers, disaster recovery coordinators, and legal professionals to auditors, insurance claims settlers, customer-support specialists, and product designers, knowledge workers exist across a wide spectrum of occupations. Their value to their organizations and their impact on customer satisfaction are undeniable.

But most importantly, the most relevant type of knowledge work of all is **business management**—turning business strategy into execution through plans, programs, projects, and guiding the work of others. Executives, directors, managers, and other staff members who perform such work are all knowledge workers, and their actions have a particularly strong impact on their organization's success. Technology that supports these managers' strategic, decision-oriented work can make their organizations much more agile and more effective than any flow-diagram can.

In recent years, a new vision of technology-enabled process management has taken hold—one that recognizes the value of highly skilled employees who perform knowledge work and the importance of process adaptability in today's fast-paced information economy. It expands the concepts of case management rather than BPM, because it removes the complexity of analyzing processes.

Previous efforts in process management have focused on upfront analysis and modeling future process flows and automating predictable, high-volume work to improve its efficiency. Now, businesses are looking at how they can use technology to better manage a much less-predictable type of work: the low-volume, high-value *knowledge work* that is key to an organization's ability to adapt and succeed. *Approximately half of all processes are understood to be unpredictable and knowledge oriented.*

4. WHAT BEING 'SOCIAL' IN A BUSINESS REALLY MEANS:

One of the approaches to improve process analysis and execution is to add social networking capabilities to BPM software. It can improve how processes and analyzed and even allow ad-hoc communication during execution. It does not change how processes are implemented and executed. The rigidity of flow-execution remains. There is no improvement in knowledge worker empowerment.

The term 'business process' is predisposed with the concept of the flow-diagram. That definition reduces the ability of many people to imagine that one could describe or perform business processes any other way. But businesses employ higher numbers of knowledge workers than before and they work together in a less hierarchical manner.

Russell Lincoln Ackoff (1919-2009) wrote in 2003:

> "We should no longer treat a corporation as a biological system. We should treat it as a social system. A social system has purposes of its own, as do its parts, and so do the systems that contain it and the other systems they contain.
>
> A social system floats in a sea of purposes at multiple levels with some purposes incompatible within and between levels; and its management must concern itself with all of these. It is for this reason that we are becoming aware of the need to know how to *manage complexity*. There is a growing need to think of the corporation as a community, not as an organism.
>
> Now, the implications of re-envisioning a corporation as a community are huge. First, ownership becomes irrelevant. This notion that stockholders own a corporation is in decline. They

are investors and shouldn't be treated as owners. No one owns a nation, state, city, or neighborhood. But each must take into account the purposes of all its stakeholders.

Communities have an obligation to facilitate the development of its members, to contribute to their quality of life and standard of living, and to enable them *to pursue their objectives as well as they know how."*

Social networking in a process environment is therefore not about ad-hoc, any-to-any communication. It is about better defining and communicating the variety of purposes that exist in the business as strategic goals, operational targets, and process goals. It is about improving top-down guidance and bottom-up reporting. It is about aligning a customer's outside-in perspective with business' inside-out operational management.

This means that a key element of supporting knowledge workers is not to offer either process-less, social communication or dynamic process variations as many suppose, but to make the objectives, targets and goals transparent, therefore providing top-down governance and guidance embedded in the technology. As a consequence it becomes much easier to provide bottom-up transparence in the form of reporting how the processes meet the well-defined goals.

Another element of process management that impacts the usefulness of social communication is the requirement for compliance, which for knowledge work is not achieved by prescribing rigid processes, but by defining compliance rules in a central library that are automatically deployed into the process where necessary. Rules require a solid business data model that they can be linked to.

5.   WHAT A GAME OF GOLF TEACHES BPM

To reduce the difficulty of imagining processes differently, I am using the game of golf as a simile to describe how an adaptive process or case is defined and execut-ed. It is impossible to play a game of golf according to a flowchart. Goals and rules are more important and provide the framework for social interaction.

Golf exhibits all the properties of a well-defined business process:

1. Define a simple and clear goal
2. A few simple rules as constraints
3. PAR gives you a best practice score
4. Ways to restart in case of failure
5. What minimum skill is necessary to play
6. Practice improves the skill to apply within the rules
7. Coaching helps players (performers) to get better
8. Each player uses a different tactic according to skill
9. The most efficient player wins (least strokes)

If all processes were designed like this then work could actually be fun. Golf illus-trate that humans are individuals, and thus different. I propose that golf, as a game, is a great example how to make process management more human.

One might argue that golf is usually not a team game and lacks different roles and thus does not apply to business process. I propose that it teaches us never-theless how to use and improve people skills while reaching the goal each time. To consider process teamwork, *Michael Hammer used the simile of a football game already in 1997.* He said that the coach will assign his players roles according to skill and then train them to execute, but he does not go out on the playing field to tell his players which step to take. Which game to play and which tactic is the decision of the quarterback, who represents the responsible process owner. Hammer says that the team has to understand the general strategy and be trained to apply the tactics. The unpredictable opponent doesn't allow blind execution. *And finally, if you want to win you don't choose the cheapest players and give them a flow-diagram, but the best and rely on their skill.*

6. THE CHALLENGES OF MANAGING KNOWLEDGE WORK

Because knowledge work involves judgment calls and adapting to specific situations, it's impossible to manage with a flowchart-based, automation-oriented approach. In fact, trying to manage knowledge work in this way is counterproductive. Forcing this type of work into predictable steps and decision logic restricts knowledge workers' ability to make expert decisions that satisfy different customers across differing situations and prohibits the development of innovations that improve outcomes. It is impossible to up-front analyze such processes and create all the possible variants that might be necessary.

The opposite of this overly rigid approach—leaving knowledge workers to improvise processes with minimal technological support—is also problematic. They may get some help from products targeted toward specific tasks. For example, they might use budget-setting software, ready-to-fill templates for Balanced Scorecard, or customer service interaction templates in a CRM system. However, such products are limited in scope. They don't address bigger-picture aspects of process management, such as organization of tasks and resources needed to achieve previously unknown customer needs. These products all fail to provide a larger contextual view of the customer situation.

Currently, the majority of knowledge workers rely on general technologies such as email and Microsoft Office to support their work. However, while these technologies can help with the collaboration and content management aspects of knowledge work, they lack crucial process-support capabilities—elements such as decision support, transparency, auditable case histories, and tie-ins to management goals and objectives. These technologies also fail to integrate well-defined processes and data from application silos.

Some propose that the solution to this problem is the inclusion of Social capabilities into BPM products, as it will allow communication of performers from the process environment. Social BPM[1] will solve some of the aspects of knowledge work in terms of communication but it fails to allow the creation of processes by knowledge workers, their retention as future templates and the modification of such templates during execution. It also provides no improvement over how the knowledge worker is guided towards process completion, how to ensure compliance, and the reuse of business knowledge.

7. HOW ADAPTIVE CASE MANAGEMENT MEETS THESE CHALLENGES

So, what type of approach can best address the need to manage knowledge work effectively and leverage its innovative potential? The solution is to take an *adaptive* approach: one that empowers knowledge workers to create goal-oriented process templates as they work, then reuse and adapt those templates as needed to deal with new situations. They do this under the guidance of well-defined busi-

---

[1] Read my chapter "How to Link BPM Governance and Social Collaboration through an Adaptive Paradigm" in the book *Social BPM*, published by Future Strategies Inc., 2011

ness objectives in a capability map. This approach is called *Adaptive Case Management*, or ACM.

Rather than bringing in outside analysts to conduct interviews and build process models, companies using ACM can let those who know the work best handle the process definition and evolution themselves. Free of predetermined steps governed by flowcharts, knowledge workers choose what steps to take, in what order, to best meet the process goals.

With the help of an easy-to-use interface, they simply select resources and content—for example, customer records, and claims documents—and assign to them an appropriate process goal. They can also assign tasks and goals to personnel with appropriate skills. The result of these actions is a reusable, adaptable work template that can link to other templates (by simple dependencies, dependent goals, or user-definable rules) and share data readily with business applications.

The resulting process template represents an AS-IS analysis without a discussion if this is a correct process representation. No one can dispute it as it was executed this way. In the beginning such a process contains no gateways, rules or other restraining entities as that is the way it is currently being executed as well. All resources such as office documents or emails are now part of the process definition. To also use documents as templates and map business data into them they need to be converted from MS-Office to process templates as well. This can also be done by non-technical users but must be considered as effort in creating process templates. In typical BPM products such business content with business data has to be programmed in a project.

By turning those process instances into templates that define goals, sub-goals, tasks, rules and eventually content, the process can be better guided. This work can be done by the business performer or non-technical staff in the process owner's team responsible for process improvement. To link end-to-end value streams and to report to management, both handovers and operational targets (KPIs and SLAs) must be agreed upon on a management level and be added to the ACM definitions.

There is no required, predefined flow for processes in ACM (though optional or implicit flows are possible), so the *goal of the process becomes its driving force*. A process is complete not when a series of steps have executed, but when the process goals are achieved. These goals can take into account human-oriented outcomes as well as mechanistic ones; for example, a goal might involve a rule definition, completion by user input, or achievement of a particular customer rating.

As business conditions change, ACM allows rapid communication among management levels and an agile, coordinated response without the need for process redesign. Knowledge workers can make certain changes to their processes directly, with no need for bureaucratic overhead. The authority to make changes is a means to control which parts of a process are mandatory. Rather than predefining all possible performer actions, ACM frees them to perform as they see necessary within the range of constraining compliance rules. Operational targets such as service levels and maximum cost show if the process remains within those bounds.

8. ACM: A NEW BPM DIRECTION

With its focus on supporting the unpredictable processes of knowledge work to aid business agility and innovation, ACM stands at the forefront of important new trends within the BPM (Business Process Management) community.

At the April 2012 Gartner BPM Summit in Baltimore, Maryland, ideas central to the ACM philosophy came up frequently in Gartner analysts' talks about the direction in which BPM is heading. In particular, analysts made the following points:

- Janelle Hill, Anthony Bradley, Andrew White, and Daryl Plummer discussed the need to expand our view of processes beyond predictable workflows into areas where human decision-making is vital to business success.
- Hill and Betsy Burton noted the need to tie such processes to larger goals and business strategies, rather than simply following prescribed procedures.
- Burton, Plummer, and Elise Olding emphasized the need for innovative thinking and emergent strategies—such as easier process changes performed by non-technical people—to help businesses adapt and thrive in today's fast changing environment.
- Hill and Bern Elliot discussed how case management, social collaboration, and management of both structured and unstructured content are becoming important aspects of BPM

At the BPM2012 conference in September in Tallinn, Estonia many papers referred to the need for an expanded BPM approach. Volker Gruhn and his collaborators presented the concepts of ACM under a new name in "Managing and Tracing the Traversals of Process Clouds with Templates, Agendas, and Artifacts."

As I have proposed since 2009 they discuss the inclusion of business data and content artifacts as essential elements of a 'Process Cloud.' Allowing a performer to create an agenda (which is a checklist of tasks without dependencies) and save it for future use does support knowledge work. While the paper nicely documents the ACM approach, it misses the explicit definition of goals that would substantially improve process quality, while supporting reuse and improvement.

The conference also hosted an ACM workshop with a number of very interesting papers on its relationship to BPMN and how that might be linked to the upcoming Case Management Model and Notation (CMMN) standard of OMG.

From the content of these conferences is very obvious that BPM is evolving away from flow diagrams and that ACM or approaches that derived from it will become an essential part of enterprise efforts to manage processes better. As BPM embraces these new directions—supporting unpredictable, goal-oriented processes and adaptive strategies that combine process management with case management, content management, and social collaboration—ACM stands ready to meet its needs.

The ACM approach is represented by a range of products that complement, consolidate, or replace flowchart-based BPM offerings and leverage the value of knowledge work within companies.

9. THE BENEFITS OF ACM

While the ACM approach encompasses a range of products, some more full-featured than others, the basic idea of ACM is to provide the following benefits for businesses:

- Knowledge worker empowerment
- An agile, innovation-oriented environment
- Transparent guidance and monitoring mechanisms
- A growing, actionable base of process knowledge

At the more full-featured end of the product scale, ACM can also provide:

- Advanced decision support
- Tools for linking processes to overall business strategy
- Social collaboration and mobile support
- In-process handling of business content

Let's look at these benefits in more detail.

10. KNOWLEDGE WORKER EMPOWERMENT

The templates used in ACM empower knowledge workers by giving them authority, means, and goals—without constraining them to use a specific process path to achieve those goals.

As with other types of templates, like the document examples in word processing programs that users can modify, ACM templates make it easier to accomplish process tasks by providing a starting point and some guidance, while still leaving room for creative adaptation and thus *innovation at the knowledge source*. For example, the template might link to an array of resources—such as personnel, documents, and specific automated tasks—even as the knowledge worker remains in charge of orchestrating these resources to reach the process goal.

The future adaptability of the templates they create further empowers knowledge workers, giving them the authority to drive process changes without going through an IT bureaucracy. In large enterprises that already have a central organization supporting process management, these can be a helpful intermediary with the IT department for certain purposes (for example, dealing with application interfaces, company-standard data models, and compliance). However, smaller organizations have the advantage that this bureaucracy is not a must to get a BPM effort off the ground.

Because knowledge workers with ACM systems are able to apply their expertise strategically to meet goals, they are more motivated than they would be if they simply had to follow preset process steps. They feel more valued as they can work autonomously and feel more secure in their job, which is known to improve job satisfaction and thus performance.

11. AN AGILE, INNOVATION-ORIENTED ENVIRONMENT

Knowledge workers using their expert judgment and creativity to develop processes without going through an IT bureaucracy means that the business can respond in an agile and innovative way to changing business conditions and changing customer expectations.

With ACM, developing and changing a process doesn't require a hand-off to IT and a long series of project stages (designing, modeling, testing, simulating, executing, monitoring, and redoing). Instead, those directly involved in the process develop the template as they work, then reuse and adapt it as needed. IT is only needed for new resources, new interfaces to backend systems or changing user authorization models.

Business users also benefit from a common "language of process" based on a well-defined set of terms in business architecture. They encounter these terms in easy-to-use libraries of templates and resources that are already IT-enabled.

As a result of these worker-empowering features, businesses can leverage the innovation potential of engaged process participants and respond more quickly to new situations and customer feedback.

12. TRANSPARENT GUIDANCE AND MONITORING MECHANISMS

When knowledge work is performed within an ACM system, rather than through general tools such as email and office productivity software, participants benefit from both top-down and bottom-up transparency. The top-down transparency comes in the form of strategic objectives, business targets, and process goals that are always visible to knowledge workers, so they fully understand what they are aiming toward, and why.

At the same time, dashboards visible to process owners and other managers give them an overview of how processes being executed. The dashboards show key process indicators such as service levels, cost, customer satisfaction, and how long things are taking. Higher-end ACM products also include voting and rating capabilities that let performers and customers rate process performance directly and immediately, for rapid pinpointing of problems and identification of needed improvements. These bottom-up transparency features keep managers in the loop and allows them to provide coaching and needed guidance to move outcomes in the right direction.

ACM thus provides process governance embedded in the technology.

13. A GROWING BASE OF PROCESS KNOWLEDGE

Another benefit of ACM systems is the growing base of process knowledge accu mulated over time, providing a record of past process actions and outcomes that can provide significant guidance for the future.

Each time a process is conducted, the ACM system retains the complete case history about what process participants did and how well they succeeded at meeting process goals. Because this process data is stored with contextual infor- mation, it builds up into a valuable history of which actions worked well in a vari- ety of circumstances. And because process participants have the power to modify templates and adapt them for future use, the system gradually accumulates a library of templates customized to particular situations.

Where legally required the information about worker performance can be anonymized to prohibit tracking of individuals.

It is important that the casework is organized into goal-oriented work units as this makes the reuse and the optimization of work units possible.

That approach is impossible with current BPM systems as they only follow a flow and can at best add ad-hoc tasks. No record of the actual process is kept except some logging and the process can't be turned into a future template. Processes are rigidly managed as explicit versions or variants of each process. The flexibility to pick process templates from a library does not exist.

14. ADVANCED DECISION SUPPORT

Some ACM systems take performer guidance a step further by making real-time recommendations for process actions based on the records of what has worked well in the past.

Many businesses are interested in figuring out how they can sample and analyze past process data—a technique called "process mining"—to gain insights that will lead to process improvements. However, process mining that occurs separately from process execution can't provide the real-time decision support that is crucial to business agility.

High-end ACM systems combine the analytical aims of process mining with the case-oriented, user-empowered ACM approach to provide something new: automated, real-time process discovery and improvement. Rather than sampling historical data from execution logs and inferring processes, ACM systems are able to work with records that include both process and context information—not just what happened when, but also why it happened, and in what circumstances. By using pattern-matching technology to compare historical process states with what workers are currently experiencing, these systems can propose actions likely to lead to positive outcomes—and they can do so in real time.

This approach takes analytically gained insights from past data and makes them part of a dynamic, human-orchestrated process. Knowledge workers can combine the system's recommendations with their own expertise *in the moment*, making informed decisions and creative process adaptations as they work.

15. SOCIAL COLLABORATION AND MOBILE SUPPORT

As mentioned before, the benefits of social capabilities go beyond the ability to tap into the collective insights of colleagues and customers for timely and responsive decision-making. They must enable the business to support a new approach to business transparency and verification of objectives, targets and goals. In Strategic-ACM products, collaboration and mobile features supporting this type of "social workplace" are not simply an add-on; instead, they are fully integrated within a goal-oriented process framework.

Rather than just adding Twitter-like chat capabilities alongside existing process execution, the ACM user interface provides social collaboration as part of the process creation, execution and improvement, so the collaboration is both goal-focused and adaptive. Participants have defined roles and skills as well as a shared awareness of the overall objectives and intended outcomes.

The result is a more productive and focused type of interaction than would arise from simple chat communication. Rather than following the Facebook and Twitter model, in which communication exists for its own sake, ACM collaboration harnesses the innovative power of social idea-sharing and pulling in additional skills for goal achievement and/or adaptation. Rather than just sending a 'Tweet' one performer can assign a work task to another and attach the necessary information. Searching or subscribing to process-oriented information must in any case be restricted by user access authority. Needed skills for a goal can be broadcast into the social network of performers, but actual execution must happen securely. It becomes transparent if and when that task was sent, accepted and completed and the information remains in the process/case to the archive.

Also the rating and voting features in high-end ACM products use a social framework to provide direct feedback from customers and process participants on the quality of the process itself and more importantly on achieved outcomes.

As they network with colleagues and customers, knowledge workers can adapt their process templates to respond to the insights they gain—and the communications that provided those insights remain part of the case record, as a resource for the future.

To provide knowledge workers with these collaboration resources in a wide range of situations, high-end ACM products provide secure access on a variety of platforms, including tablets and mobile devices. Having remote access to the ACM social workplace helps knowledge workers and their organizations to be even more agile and responsive in reacting to changing situations.

The need for enabling Social capabilities highlights the rationale for another important, but mostly ignored aspect of BPM: It is the content and the related business data that contain the relevant information about the process.

16. IN-PROCESS HANDLING OF BUSINESS CONTENT

The true execution information of processes is not in its flow-diagram, it is rather embedded in the used content. Therefore any BPM system that only deals with simple task management and forms that present business data does not actually manage the complete process. Case Management systems manage content as part of the case history but usually just as a binary file in formats such as MS-Word, PDF or TIFF images.

I have proposed for the last ten years that to truly manage processes, all content—inbound and outbound—has to be managed in terms of its contained process information. That includes structured content that is created such as statements, letters and contracts, or unstructured content such as scanned images or freeform PDF documents attached to emails. The text contained in Social communication must today be included in such functionality. Part of the complexity is that in such documents generic text is intermixed with business data and they have to be merged on content creation and extracted for inbound documents.

Practically all types of knowledge work involve creating or exchanging business content. These processes must use many record types: reports, proposals, offers, contracts, shipments, invoices, MRI images, medical records, to executive or investor reports, maintenance and service agreements, and so on. If the work involves decision-making and person-to-person interactions, whether with colleagues or customers, each instance of a process is bound to require sending and receiving such content on paper and forms, email, faxes, XML files, and social messages.

Because it is oriented toward "cases"—that is, unique instances of more generally defined processes—the ACM approach is ideally suited to monitoring and handling content related to processes. Rather than being focused on the pathway of steps in a process, ACM is concerned with progress toward the process goal, as determined by the state of the process resources—including content.

Case Management products generally deal well with content state, and with storing relevant content with the records of each case. However, high-end ACM goes even further, into rule-, or user-driven content creation from libraries of building blocks and data elements, content tracking and versioning, with final distribution as well as automated capture, data extraction and validation of inbound content.

Strategic ACM systems can perform the following advanced content-handling actions in a process context:

- Capture, classify, and archive inbound documents
- Scan, capture, extract and validate business data in inbound content
- Trigger processes based on the content of documents
- Allow users to assemble documents from templates and building blocks
- Allow users to map data fields into documents and define rules for document processing without programming
- Track document status (including changes and versions) as an element of overall case progress
- Route documents for review and authenticated sign-off
- Link to print and mail-shop production processes for high-volume output, and for tracing and verification of sent documents
- Generate audit trails for actions taken with controlled documents
- Encrypt secure content and ensure non-repudiation

Because these content related actions occur in within process management, there is much better security and integration with processes than there would be with separate software products for process management and content management.

17. How ACM Works

The common approach of BPM methodology uses the project stages of Analyze As-is, Model To-be, Simulate, Implement, Monitor and Improve. Due to the related complexity of BPM software, all stages require the support by technical and/or process management experts.

ACM, by ccontrast, uses three stages: Model, Discover, Adapt. Only the Model stage requires interaction with IT or technical staff. Process management experts can support business performers in the other stages, but that is optional.

There are different ACM-style solutions on the market and they utilize the concept in different ways. Basic-ACM systems do not require a Model stage because the models are encoded for simplicity. In the Discover stage the business users can create the processes/cases on the fly. In the Adapt stage business people can also create case templates, using tasks, checklists (agendas) and forms. These can be further modified by the knowledge workers during the runtime of the process. Most provide a number of real-time reporting and dashboard features to provide management oversight.

In general, Full-ACM systems involve the following additional capabilities:

- Connections to a larger back-end system through data services for record-keeping, archiving, and auditing
- Expanded templates that let users orchestrate roles of business entities and apply business rules to processes
- Social collaboration integrated with case processes and records

18. Model-Discover-Adapt in Strategic ACM systems

At the top end of the ACM product spectrum, Strategic-ACM systems add the following enterprise-level capabilities:

- Integrated business architecture model for defining business strategy and connecting it with process goals

- Decision recommendations based on process mining and analysis of event patterns
- Advanced tools for evaluating process effectiveness, including service-level tracking and performance-rating options for users and customers
- Robust process automation tools, including event triggers, compliance checking, and high-volume content capture and creation

These expanded capabilities fit within the Model-Discover-Adapt cycles for a Strategic ACMS:

- **Model** – In addition to letting architects define case templates and business entities (connected by data services), the Model stage in a Strategic ACMS lets system architects perform professional change management functions (testing the impact of system changes in advance) and define the following advanced process elements: compliance rules, event triggers, content elements, record formats, and a natural-language ontology (for user-understandable entity names and relationships).
- **Discover** – In addition to letting users make the "discover by doing" modifications (working with sub-goals, skill profiles, task delegation, business rules, and social collaboration), the Discover stage in a Strategic-ACMS provides users with decision support (through recommendations they can adopt or ignore) and options for incorporating automated content capture, creation, and output into processes.
- **Adapt** - In addition to letting process owners and managers adapt templates and GUIs for future use—and archive case information for audits— the Adapt stage in a Strategic-ACMS adds the following advanced options for monitoring and evaluating process performance: service level monitoring, voting and rating options (for users and customers to evaluate performance), and automatic evaluation of success at achieving strategic objectives defined in the overall business architecture.

19. MODELING PERFORMS ABSTRACTION

In BPM to model a process means to define the flow-diagram of a TO-BE process. BPM methodology prescribes a governance bureaucracy to manage the analysis, design and simulation of standardized processes before they can be implemented and optimized. Flow-diagrams represent just 20 percent of process functionality, while the other 80 percent (content, user interface, backend connectivity, events and rules) require engineers to create them. That requires both process management and technical experts and reduces the actual agility of a business compared to doing processes by email and office products.

What businesses need, however, is real-world processes that people create and use and not abstract models. In ACM, models are used to define the business entities needed to describe those processes. A business-oriented terminology has to be defined that describes both data and functional elements in terms that non-technical people can understand.

Once an ACM system has been setup there must be no further process implementation stages. If ACM is implemented with orthodox BPM methodology it kills the possible agility. It is essential to let the business start to create their processes as simple lists of tasks without enforcing a standard. Figure out with the business people what user interface functions they need to describe their processes intuitively by picking resources from library menus. Different business units will have different ideas about that. Forget process or user interface standardization if you really want to empower the business.

In ACM systems each user role should be able to have a specific user interface and each department can have their own process templates without adding cost as the business is in control of the changes. Different process templates are not versions as many suppose, but variants that may be useful for different ways to achieve the same goal. Process owners should maintain an eye on these variants to promote the ones that are the most effective and efficient. Over time, process guidance can become more strict using rules to ensure compliance and efficiency.

In ACM, models are used to provide a solid basis that the business performers can understand and use and not a restrictive execution environment.

20. GOAL-ORIENTED PROCESSES DRIVEN BY BUSINESS STRATEGY

While ACM is capable of defining and executing also very strict processes and not just adaptive ones, we can simply look at all types of defined processes as some subset of work that a company performs. Should there be any work that does not need to be performed according to company objectives and management guidance? Especially unpredictable processes should be aligned with the overall business strategy and operational plans. Any work without a clear process goal should be thrown out: WHY would we do it?

Now, if you present a performer with a rigid process, someone else has already thought about (in the governance bureaucracy doing process analysis) how to fulfill business needs with the process flows. The performer just hammers happily away at his keyboard, ignorant to what the point of his work is. Sounds great, but really isn't. Knowledge workers are, however, expected to perform according to their knowledge of what the business or customers need to have at this point. If they use Case Management it just provides a container for all related process information. In what way should that be less aligned with business strategy? They need to work towards it just the same, but unfortunately they are expected to do it without strict step-by-step guidance and without an explicit definition what constitutes a successful completion.

To achieve this understanding, it is essential to create a top-down transparency of business objectives and targets for the value streams and the goals that process owners need to achieve. We define basically WHY we do what we ought to do and make it transparent to the performer. So process optimization in the governance is suddenly a transparent exercise of everyone involved and it happens upfront before you even start to define the process. We still haven't described any of the work, but we know WHY we should do WHAT for the customer. Knowledge workers are experts at the HOW and executives and managers tell them where to apply it and what the outcome of their work should be. *That is the essence of ACM.*

21. KNOWLEDGE WORK: THE ONLY WAY IS UP!

It is rather obvious that the adaptive concept is perfectly suited for corporate change programs, projects, plans, processes and cases. The higher you go in the hierarchy, the less flow-, and more knowledge-oriented work becomes. Adaptive management concepts can be applied at all hierarchy levels and on all time scales. Reuse of easily adaptable project templates can save millions. There were no solutions available that support long-running programs in enterprises. Clearly, a project is not instantiated the same way fifty times, but the entities to describe a project or a program are the same as the ones used to describe a process.

How should such work be described? One can spend a lot of time on abstract term definitions to describe the WHY, WHAT and HOW, but in the end that term definition must be in business language. That is one of the issues that I take with BPMN, CMMN, VSDL, QVT, BDM and other OMG standards considered for business performance management. Business people are unable to use them and the complexity of how they work together is immense.

It is important to use real world concepts such as activity, tasks, goals, documents, notes, times, business events or legal constraints. In terms of describing the work progression one can use events, decisions, calculations, rules, and conditions. Data types should be real world such as time, count, amount, and duration. For people we need skills, roles, hierarchy, and authority. To describe the environment that the user will interact with you have applications, processes, user interfaces, services, and forms. Keep it simple but unambiguous.

While any kind of graphical editor is nice (flow or entity graphs), the whole point is to open the work descriptions of WHY, WHAT and HOW to business people: executives, management and performers. They want an intuitive, real-time representation of the 'things' that drive the business.

Sounds easy, but really isn't. ACM provides the templates to make it simple.

22. GOALS, MILESTONES, TASKS AND MORE …

The term Adaptive means that business people create the work tasks on the fly to achieve defined goals and can reuse those definitions in future when they want to work on those goals again. Goals ought to be linked to objectives and targets (KPIs and SLAs) to ensure that the business performs. Ad-hoc tasks or allowing central changes that are immediately deployed to all processes DO NOT provide adaptive capability! That is still normal process management without user empowerment.

People tend to look at goals as milestones or sub-processes/cases. A goal in the sense of a business guideline is something quantitative, which does not have to be enumerable or measurable. Outcomes maybe quantifiable but are still subjective. Operational targets are usually KPIs but they might still not be measurable. Service levels are typically measurable and enumerable as they are set up this way.

For projects a task could be used as a milestone but I propose to make it an explicit entity. A milestone is a time-line synchronization juncture and might be related to a goal, i.e. completion of all required tasks. A milestone might be a decision point with or without a rule (i.e. once you reach runway speed V1 you must takeoff). It is still not a goal while you work towards it. I use the term objective for goals that are very abstract in the sense of a business strategy. 'Increase revenue by 10 percent' is an objective that can be expressed as a rule. Objectives are mostly achieved when the related targets, goals and rules are satisfied. But they can also be completely subjective and just checked off by the relevant person.

Without a clear term definition for the business users, which I see as part of the Business Architecture, there won't be real world use of ACM or BPM. Most of all business people won't be able to describe their work without that language of process that reduces ambiguity. In the end the business chooses to use the terms they want, but they should not be restricted by the limitation of a system that doesn't allow goal definitions in business language.

23. WHAT DECISION-MAKERS NEED TO CONSIDER FOR BPM

Henry Ford said:

> "A business absolutely devoted to service will have only one worry about profits. They will be embarrassingly large."

To achieve that service devotion, businesses need to support decision-based, high-value processes performed by knowledge workers with technology beyond email and office products. Executives can choose from help-desk software, flowchart-based BPMS, or Case Management.

All of these products fall within the general, evolving category of BPM, and the similarity in the terms used to describe them can make it difficult to differentiate among them. All of them seem to offer some form of dynamic process support, case management, social collaboration, and process analysis and mining. But even those flowchart-based products that include decision points (so process participants can choose from multiple paths) are still following defined paths; they assume process predictability and offer only limited opportunities for process participants to engage with reality and affect the process when the unexpected happens. At that time they step out of the BPMS domain and into a fragmented email/office world. The improvement knowledge is lost.

Even with the best-of-breed BPMS, most large businesses struggle to identify current processes and model them towards some desired end-state. Users perceive BPMS to be restrictive and the offered participation in the governance as *a smoke screen to hide that the ROI is mostly achieved through manpower reductions*. Ultimately, vendors and consultants propose that the savings of small, local BPMS projects can simply be applied to the larger business. According to Systems Theory it is not possible to optimize components by themselves.

The proposition is that BPM—simply by following the methodology—is able to balance organizational assets and resources to provide differentiating services to the customer, ensuring maximum value at the lowest cost throughout the value chain. Achieving long-term viability and success requires organizational resilience to outside change and not just minimized cost. Differentiation and individualization can increase perceived value, but cost money and need manpower to increase revenue and improve the bottom line. It is impossible to cut costs and differentiate and individualize at the same time.

BPM is therefore an investment in the future of a business and ROI can only be considered long-term. Because of the expensive analysis, design and simulation stages before implementation, BPM requires standardization to keep costs at bay. It freezes processes into average happy paths across all departments that then are very difficult to change because of software fragmentation. There is actually no differentiation and individualization possible and it becomes much harder to do as it has to go through the governance cycle. In service organizations, process flow-diagrams or specialized applications only guarantee process completion but not goal achievement or customer outcomes. They enforce rather than empower. They do not save time so that knowledge workers are freed up for more interesting work. The knowledge workers are replaced by less skilled staff to achieve the ROI. Flow-charted BPM reduces overall skill and understanding in a business.

Russell Lincoln Ackoff:

> "Knowledge is transmitted through instructions, which are the answers to how-to questions. Understanding is transmitted through explanations, which answer the why questions. Herein lies a very

fundamental difference. Corporations and corporate managers tend to have a lot of knowledge but little understanding of the complex systems they manage."

BPM flow-diagrams are how-to instructions but not knowledge in the sense of understanding the why. So people who have understanding about the process are replaced with hardcoded knowledge. ACM in difference focuses on organizing knowledge according to goals, which represent the why question. It is in fact the human performer who provides the understanding to execute the processes successfully. Flow-diagrams are meant to control the performer who no longer needs knowledge, while in ACM the performer is provided with more understanding as to why he is doing what towards what goal and towards which business objective.

I propose that therefore the key aspects of implementing BPM successfully are quite different once someone understands the issues of *social complexity, workplace psychology and people motivation.* Revenue, quality and cost are consequences and outcomes, driven by people and can't be enforced. The concept of ACM dramatically improves the ability of the knowledge workers to excel in customer service and experience over the commonly used BPM methodology and BPMS software. ACM embeds a working BPM methodology focused on people.

Because--methodology does not change your business; only motivated people do.

24. SUMMARIZING THE KEY FEATURES UNIQUE TO ACM:

The concepts used behind ACM are based on a broad set of accepted scientific knowledge about systems theory, complex adaptive systems, and behavioral economics.

- **BPM methodology** and 'governance' must be embedded in technology as provided by Strategic-ACM systems. The resilience required in this dynamic age can't be achieved through a command and control attitude.
- **ACM is adaptive, not just dynamic**. Not only can knowledge workers modify process templates dynamically for each case as they discover its particular requirements, they can also assemble new cases as they work without needing process or IT experts. Completed processes/cases can be turned into templates for future use.
- **ACM is goal-driven, not flowchart-driven**. Knowledge workers apply their expertise and creativity to figuring out how best to meet process goals in the current circumstances, rather than being constrained to follow predefined process steps.

ACM's adaptiveness and goal-orientation provide a unique level of empowerment and motivation for knowledge workers. Because these workers are empowered to innovate and adapt processes in response to changing conditions and customer feedback, their organizations become more agile as well—better able to channel emergent knowledge into evolutionary change.

25. SYSTEMS OF ENGAGEMENT VERSUS SYSTEMS OF RECORD

John Mancini, the president of AIIM, created a graph that shows the history of IT in terms of stages of IT development in the content management arena.

He distinguishes between 'Systems of Record' and 'Systems of Engagement.' I consider this a truly relevant perspective, as one of the problems of IT today is the fragmentation of enterprise software by the analyst community. To truly improve how a business is managed requires CRM, ECM, BPM, and several other products that have to be integrated. Executives, management and process performers really need a consolidated System of Engagement.

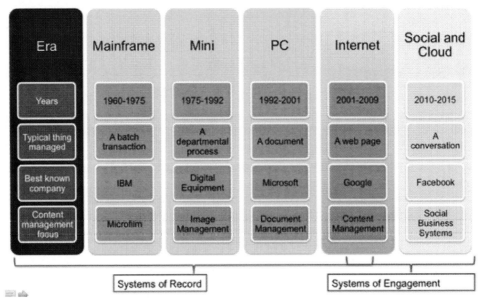

Era	Mainframe	Mini	PC	Internet	Social and Cloud
Years	1960-1975	1975-1992	1992-2001	2001-2009	2010-2015
Typical thing managed	A batch transaction	A departmental process	A document	A web page	A conversation
Best known company	IBM	Digital Equipment	Microsoft	Google	Facebook
Content management focus	Microfilm	Image Management	Document Management	Content Management	Social Business Systems

Systems of Record	Systems of Engagement

Mancini: A Short History of IT

26. SYSTEMS OF RECORD AND SYSTEMS OF ENGAGEMENT

Using Social and Mobile as extensions of ECM, via BPM inside the business and CRM towards the customer, the necessary consolidation of functionality becomes obvious. I proposed already in 1999 to close the customer communications loop with a combined process and content management solution:

> "There is no process without content and content without process is irrelevant."

ERP, CRM and ECM are Systems of Record. Their job is to retain and manage information. ECM software retains archive copies of business content but does not support its creation or process interaction. **A System of Engagement** is both content and process oriented and linked to the SOR to support the knowledge worker and his low-volume, high-value processes. Those knowledge workers take relevant business decisions using inbound content and create high-value content to document and complete the process.

A content perspective leads to state/event-driven processes, which are ideal to support innovation and they are structured in a way that humans can relate to. While it is theoretically possible that the complete process is not creating any content, in reality any kind of people-to-people interaction requires some form of business documents containing data and not just 'documentation.' Business content has no need for version control, but needs embedded business data, related content rules, a state engine, and user authorization.

It is the template that is used to create the business content that goes through versions over time and may need language or departmental variants, but not the business document instance. It is instantiated according to the rules that consider the process context and data and has a state progression that is linked to the process execution. A very similar approach is used for inbound content analysis.

27. HOW TO THINK BIG AND ACT SMALL IN BPM

BPM methodology and process/content functionality must go hand-in-hand in the System of Engagement (SOE). Adequate technology must support the enterprise effort and thus support the methodology, even if it might only be used in the small at first. It is not necessary to create an expansive business architecture and strategy for the first ACM implementations. But to define a process without an understanding where it is positioned within a capability map and what objectives, targets and goals drive its outcomes is to ask for failure.

Executives have to provide the perspectives and principles of the 'Big,' while the knowledge workers utilize their experience to execute and innovate in the 'Small.'

The following checklist will make BPM a success:

- Chose (buy, build or integrate) a homogeneous 'System of Engagement.'
- Create top-down transparency through a business-architectured value stream or capability map visible in the software.
- Define budget responsible process owners and their outcomes and/or handovers. (Authority, goals and means)
- Define with IT the 'language of business (process)' that non-technical users can use to create processes.
- Link with 'Systems of Record' and refine UI's until the business units really want to use the system.
- Define with process owners the targets for 'bottom-up transparency' that enables management reporting.
- Let business units define how to execute and achieve the defined process goals and outcomes.
- Business users collaborate to assemble resources (data, content, rules, forms, tasks) into goal-oriented processes. (NO UPFRONT DESIGN)
- Successful goal-achieving work can be stored as templates and reused and still be modified for each execution. (=ADAPTIVE)
- Motivate business users through autonomy, job security and recognition and forget monetary rewards.
- Enable users and customers to vote and rate each aspect of the process in real-time.
- Continuous improvement is enabled by user empowerment and the embedded project and program management.

How ACM Drives Better Customer Engagement

Dermot McCauley, Kofax, Inc.

1. ABSTRACT:

Both routine and unpredictable engagement with customers is an essential part of many critical business processes including customer start-up, account maintenance, transaction management, service fulfillment, incident management, etc. Yet mobile, cloud and social technologies are increasing the power of customers and transforming how they participate with organizations. This chapter discusses the necessary role of adaptive case management in enabling more responsive, flexible and effective customer engagement in an era when the rising power of the individual demands a new architecture of engagement for customers and employees alike.

You are a changed person; more powerful, more autonomous and also more connected than only a few years ago. To the bank, the supermarket, the department store, the travel agent, the politician, you are a newly-potent individual and a newly-prized and at-risk customer. You have a mobile device, an internet connection, a new generation of software to aid you, and a network of other individuals with whom to share knowledge. The way you engage with organizations—let's call it the architecture of engagement—has radically changed in just a few short years. This has opened new possibilities for you. You know more. You can find out more, more quickly. You can take action faster.

This revolutionized architecture of engagement has also created new opportunities, and not a few risks, for every organization you deal with. How can organizations prosper in this new context? What are the challenges and when can Adaptive Case Management help address them?

2. THE NEW ARCHITECTURE OF ENGAGEMENT

Ok, that's a big phrase—new *architecture of engagement*—so let's start by looking at a simple example of what it has meant in one case in particular. To one person; President Barack Obama.

Before he was elected President of the United States of America, Obama was widely seen as facing a huge funding challenge. How could he fuel his campaign machine and compete effectively against his opponents and their rich war chests of donor funds?

Well, simply put, Barack Obama spotted the potential of a new architecture of engagement. He saw that through a new combination of the Web, social media technology, and more old-fashioned fund-raising techniques, he could bring money flooding into his campaign coffers. This insight helped the Obama campaign committee raise more than $650 million by Election Day, breaking previous records for presidential primary and general campaigns and transforming expectations for future elections. And half a billion of those dollars were raised online[1].

Politicians used to spend years building a network they could tap for funds when they decided to run for office. Traditionally tapped at fundraising events where food is served, the candidate speaks, and wealthy people write big checks, that old-fashioned architecture of engagement was expensive to run, didn't scale well and didn't engage the majority of voters at all. Obama created a flexible and scalable way of engaging potential donors in his fund-raising process. He used online social networks to open up the political process to anyone who cared to join, made it easy to participate, and by doing so, created a fundraising machine that could practically print money.

Obama also spotted that a new architecture of engagement could make a new kind of giving possible—microgiving. And it could make that microgiving possible *quickly and flexibly.* The Obama architecture of engagement was built to take advantage of donors' inclination to engage at short notice. And it worked. On September 4, 2008, the Obama campaign announced that it had raised $10 million from over 130,000 donors in the 24-hour period after Republican Vice Presidential nominee Sarah Palin's acceptance speech. The Republican National Committee reported raising only $1 million in the same period[2].

Obama's donor engagement also made a pattern of repeated contributions a reality. Using the Web, Obama supporters could donate small amounts, $20 or even less, and also have the option of making these payments recurring or donating more later. The impact was huge[34]. Over the lifetime of their participation in the Obama campaign, donors touched the fund-raising process multiple times. Forty nine percent of Obama's supporters' initially donated less than $200 but by the end of that campaign cycle (October 15, 2008), 47 percent had given at least $1000.

By transforming the architecture of engagement, the Obama organization gained a distinctive competitive advantage. Arguably, he could not have won election without it.

Let's draw some lessons from this example and distil some essentials of a comprehensive and effective architecture of engagement that can be widely applicable. We'll then see when Adaptive Case Management helps make this feasible.

3.   Essentials of a Successful Architecture of Engagement

The best organizations have built an architecture of engagement that allows customers to participate effectively in every process they need or want to, anytime, anyplace.

---

[1] Jose Antonio Vargas (November 20, 2008) "Obama Raised Half a Billion Online", The Washington Post

[2] Nico Pitney (September 4, 2008) "Obama Raises $10 Million After Palin Speech", The Huffington Post

[3] David Erickson (January 1, 2009) "Barack Obama's Online Fundraising Machine", e-strategyblog.com

[4] Paul Demko (November 24, 2008) "Obama's army of small donors?", The Minnesota Independent

The necessary components of the architecture of engagement for the fund-raising example we have discussed were already in place (web, social media, fund-raising rules, etc). But it was not the components alone that made the fund-raising successful. Also critical was that those components were effectively combined into a highly responsive, efficient and demonstrably effective means of achieving Obama's fundraising goals. Success depended on the creation of a literally dynamic combination of the components. The Obama campaign's architecture of engagement had the right components and it could flex and respond as the campaign needed it to.

Let's consider three concepts that we see in practice in the fund-raising example and that will appear wherever a dynamic architecture of engagement is needed:

Multiple Touchpoints

Customers are usually engaged with an organization over a long period of time. Even in an election campaign the engagement takes place over at least a few months and often longer. The customer and the organization "touch" on multiple occasions—in our example, the donor and the organization touch many times in context of the fund-raising process. Indeed, the engagement of the Obama supporter transcends the fund-raising process, encompassing engagement in other processes relevant to the political party and its donor/supporter. Sometimes the touch is transactional, sometimes it is a sharing of information only.

For a bank, an insurance company, a healthcare provider, or other organization touchpoints will occur during initial sign-up, onboarding, account opening or registration, and subsequently may involve orders, claims, appeals, service requests, incident reports, complaints, investigations, etc. In the lifecycle of a customer's engagement with an organization, whether in a single business process or many, there will be multiple touchpoints.

Multichannel Engagement

The number of channels available for engagement with customers has grown significantly. And the type of engagement they allow has also changed dramatically. The proliferation of new hardware devices (including tablets, smartphones, wearable internet devices, etc) and software which exploits them to connect people and organizations (Facebook, Twitter, Linked-In, Yammer, etc), is transforming expectations of how customers engage. Face-to-face interaction, paper-based mail, email, fax, etc have not gone away—indeed they, too, are still necessary parts of the architecture of engagement—but they are now supplemented by other channels.

Responsiveness

By constructing a fund-raising machine that could respond to opportunity quickly, Obama capitalized on key moments, outstripping his competitors' ability to fruitfully engage potential donors when they were ripe for engagement. The organization was always ready when the moment of customer touch occurred.

The supermarket, department store, bank, insurance provider; they all strive to be more responsive. To succeed, their architecture of engagement must be more ready to act. More customer touchpoints must become, in fact, "touchless" from the point of view of the organization, requiring no staff member intervention at the time of customer touch. Where the touchpoint requires a staff member in the organization to be engaged, then a similar level of responsiveness must somehow also be achieved.

4. THE CUSTOMER ENGAGEMENT SELF-SURVEY

Each industry sector and each organization has its own pattern of engagement with customers.

Engagement typically begins with an initial sign-up, onboarding, account opening or registration. As the customer lifetime continues it may involve orders, claims, appeals, service requests, incident reports, complaints, investigations, etc. And the customer engagement ends only when he closes his account, elects to cancel her subscription, or otherwise stops the pattern of interaction that characterizes his or her lifetime as customer of the organization.

The diagram below (Fig. 1) presents some examples of processes across the customer lifecycle in different industries.

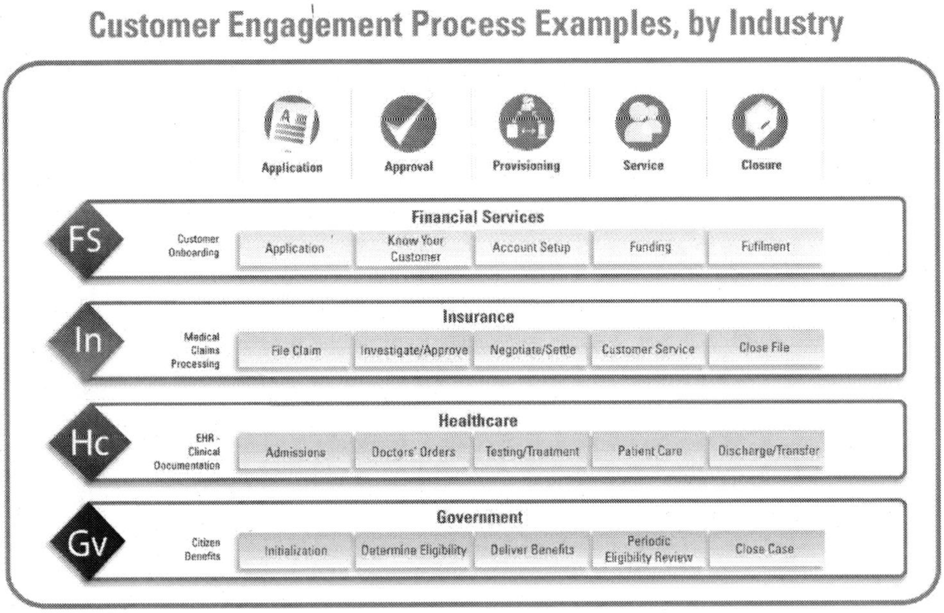

Customer Engagement Process Examples, by Industry

Fig.1 Examples of Processes across the Customer Lifecycle

To help focus your thinking on how your architecture of engagement needs to improve, I suggest that you take a few minutes now to do a simple and fast four-step self-survey that will help you gauge the responsiveness of your organization:

- First, list the most important touchpoints, from a customer point of view, in the lifetime of a customer's engagement with your organization.
- Second, note the channels that the customer would like to use at those touchpoints—some of which may not be supported by your organization today.
- And third, identify which of those touchpoints can today be handled entirely automatically by your organization and which require human intervention by your staff member(s).
- Lastly, from a customer point of view and based on the information in your quick self-survey, give your organization a "responsiveness rating" on a scale of 0 to 10, where 0 means poor and 10 means excellent.

This exercise usually results in some or all of the following conclusions:

- Customers expect fast turnaround, but organizations can only respond quickly if the engagement is highly standard or routine
- Customer engagement that requires unique or case-by-case variation drastically reduces responsiveness
- Organizations cannot keep pace with customer's evolving ability and desire to engage in new ways

Few organizations have as high a responsiveness rating as they need. Can you muster the support of your colleagues to improve your customer engagement, perhaps by asking them to conduct this self-survey and compare results?

5. RESPONSIVE CUSTOMER ENGAGEMENT

Each of us is that changed individual we met at the top of this chapter. Our expectations about how we engage with organizations have changed hugely in a few short years. We will have comparison-shopped before we enter the high street store or begin our shopping basket compilation online. We have researched our illness before we enter the doctor's office. Our engagements with the department store, the bank, the healthcare provider, the government are all quite different now.

We expect to transact quickly when we have made a choice. We expect touchless processing that allows us to act swiftly. If donating funds, if buying a product, if submitting a service request; we want to do it without barrier or delay.

When we need assistance, we also expect to act quickly and, consequently, we want the organization to be able to act fast too. We have lost patience, in this new era of mobile technology, Web-connectedness and instant gratification, with slow organizations. We expect staff to be knowledgeable—about their company, about all our previous interactions, about every contract, policy, transaction, service call and letter that has passed between us. We even expect them to be able to deal, with no loss of pace, with any special circumstances of our case. To be able to make immediate decisions that are uniquely custom to our urgent need.

So, how can organizations be more responsive? Let's assume, for the moment, that we are engaged with the organization at an important touchpoint and in the channel of our choice. The nature of the engagement can be characterized in two types.

Routine Processing

Some customer engagement can be viewed as routine processing. In these cases the customer and organization are dealing with each other in a process that is clearly understood. The purchase of products online, using an online shopping basket, is a simple example. The customer and organization both know what is involved. The organization has automated this to make it possible for the customer to engage quickly and effectively. For the organization this is touchless processing. For the customer it is streamlined, responsive, easy, and predictable. The steps to be taken each time, the rules that apply, the who-does-what are all known before the process begins. It is this clarity of process that allows the organization to make its process so responsive. The shopping basket is fast and simple, just as the making of a donation to an online campaign was fast and simple for Obama's supporters.

To be responsive in routine processing requires highly effective automation across multiple channels. Whatever device the customer uses, we must be able to accept information in whatever format is available and derive from it the information we need to act. For example, if we require a Proof of Identity from a customer as part of an account opening process, we should provide to the customer a way of using her smartphone to photograph and send an image of her driver's license. We must then be able to extract from that image the name, address, Driver ID, expiration date etc., that we need to prove identity. And we should immediately confirm the success of that proof to the customer. The result of this successful highly automated, low-latency processing is a faster new account opening and a sooner-transacting customer.

Unpredictable Processing

Much customer engagement is in fact quite unpredictable. The steps involved in the engagement cannot be predefined. Indeed they are likely to vary on a customer-by-customer, case-by-case basis. There may be rules and policies that apply but even those may need to be altered, again on a customer-by-customer, case-by-case basis.

Consider, in the Healthcare sector, a patient who decides to consult a doctor about their illness—in fact, let's consider two such patients so we can see the impact of case-by-case differences. For one patient, the process of diagnosis lasts five minutes in total and involves nothing more than a brief consultation in the doctor's office. For the second patient, however, the process of diagnosis takes twelve months, involves multiple doctor's visits, blood tests, x-ray, an MRI scan, a hospital stay, two operations and a period of convalescence in a special facility.

Some organizations are in a state of some self-denial, slow to admit to themselves that this unpredictable processing makes up a significant percentage of their activity. A good self-survey of the type we did briefly earlier, usually sheds light on the truth that for many organizations unpredictable processing incurs large costs and is a major source of customer dissatisfaction.

Routine and Unpredictable Processing—Combined

In many touchpoints, we see, in fact, that both routine and unpredictable processing *are* necessary. Let's consider again the Healthcare example.

Blood tests are processed in a routine fashion, but the decision to take one involves the judgment and discretion of an expensive, skilled and experienced medical professional. The need, timing, frequency of tests are unpredictable, but the test when administered is run for very good reason in a highly standardized way.

The path of the diagnosis and cure process is goal-driven, rather than predefined by foreseeable required actions. The Healthcare case worker (in this case the doctor) knows what he wants to achieve, but cannot predetermine what will be needed, who will be involved, when they will be needed, what tests, records, actions or costs will result.

Patient and care records are generated, progress is tracked, test results and the return to health are all made visible, but the complete listing of what records, what reports, what monitors will be needed cannot be known at the outset.

Much customer engagement is precisely of this nature—a necessary combination of routine and unpredictable processing, all of which must be executed in a responsive manner. The health of the customer can depend on it. The health of the customer engagement is undoubtedly impacted by it.

Indeed, successful customer engagement requires that we master both the routine and the unpredictable. Any point of failure, whether in the routine or unpredictable processing, will hurt your customer engagement.

Drawing together our points of discussion so far, we can now envision a complete architecture of engagement (Fig. 2).

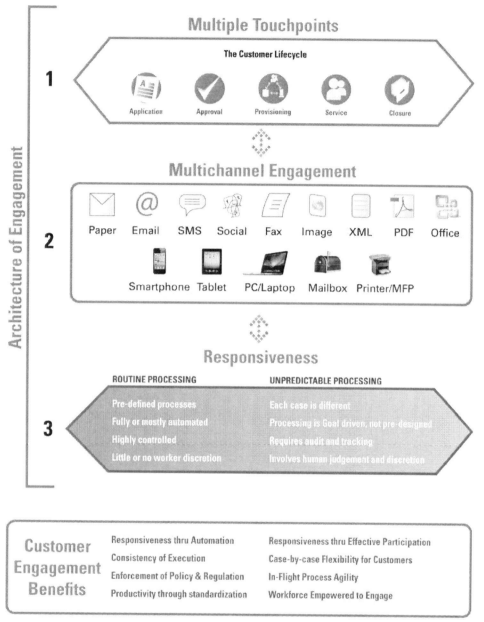

Fig. 2 Architecture of Engagement—Components & Benefits

Responding to any touchpoint in the customer's lifecycle with our organization, we act responsively irrespective of the channel through which the customer engages and irrespective of whether the engagement is routine or unpredictable or both.

6. Mastering the Unpredictable; the Role of Adaptive Case Management

Since the onset of the industrial revolution the forces of efficiency have been on a concerted march; a march in which standardization has opened new paths to increased productivity. Henry Ford famously heralded a new era of productivity by capitalizing on the efficiency promises of manufacturing by production line. Ford cars were not to be hand made by craftsmen. They were to be created at amazing speed by crews of skilled "production workers"; each worker specializing in a small, clearly understood, and predefined aspect of car manufacture. The step-by-step process of car making was broken down into constituent pieces and a production worker would be dedicated and expert in only a few, perhaps only one, of the pieces. Ultimately, this divide-and-conquer approach to the process of car making allowed the job to be so carved into predictable pieces that the production worker was no longer necessary. Automatic machines became capable of the job.

Ultimately car plants became loud with the electronic whirring of computerized robots. Even the initial constraints that standardization forced customers to accept—"You can have any car you want, so long as it's black"—have been eased to allow some degree of customer-by-customer variation—"You can have any of six colors, which one would you like?"

Industry after industry, including service industries, joined the march, automating routine work, reducing the need for worker involvement in the execution of standardized tasks. Business literature, university study courses and most organizations are awash with similar stories of how the challenges of improving routine processing have been addressed.

So, we may say that we have substantially succeeded in mastering the routine. Can we also master the unpredictable?

Focus expanded in the late 20th century beyond only the automation of the production worker's routine tasks to encompass what Peter Drucker termed "knowledge work."

Drucker, widely viewed as the most influential 20th century thinker on business, saw the challenge clearly and raised it to the attention of leaders: "The most important, and indeed the truly unique, contribution of management in the 20th Century was the fifty-fold increase in the productivity of the manual worker in manufacturing. The most important contribution management needs to make in the 21st Century is similarly to increase the productivity of knowledge work and the knowledge worker."[5]

We saw above that much customer engagement entails a combination of routine and unpredictable processing. This unpredictable processing is what Drucker refers to by the term "knowledge work." The staff in your organization doing that work are the knowledge workers whose productivity Drucker believes is "the biggest of the 21st-century management challenges."

Your knowledge workers are engaged with customers in goal-driven work. Their judgment and discretion determines the next best action, the information or document needed to proceed, and its adequacy or shortcoming. They collaborate with colleagues and third parties, often at unpredictable times and with unanticipated information needs. They pick up a customer engagement in mid-flow, where a

---

[5] Peter F. Drucker "Knowledge-Worker Productivity: The Biggest Challenge", California Management Review vol. 41, no. 2 winter 1999

case has been long-running, roles have changed and the goal of the engagement has yet to be met. They cope with unexpected changes in policy or change course due to the emergence of new facts.

Your knowledge workers' productivity is key, as Drucker says. Their responsiveness is vital too. The speed, quality and flexibility of their response can determine the success or failure of your customer engagement.

Adaptive case management has been developed to support the needs of knowledge workers. It enables your staff to be more responsive by providing a means for them to master the unpredictable while efficiently executing the routine. Table 1 outlines the circumstances when responsive customer engagement requires adaptive case management.

Table 1. When Customer Engagement Requires Adaptive Case Management

1	**Goal Driven** — The customer engagement is driven by the need to meet a goal. Standard procedure does not fully meet the customer need
2	**Knowledge Intensive** — The engagement requires the intervention of skilled and knowledgeable personnel
3	**Highly Variable Processes** — While a case may share a common structure (e.g., handling citizen benefits applications), it is not possible to predict the path that each engagement will take
4	**Long Running** — Cases can run for months or years, perhaps changing hands over time, with no single individual having a persistent view of the customer engagement
5	**Information Complexity** — Emails, meeting notes, case documents, and correspondence related to a case must be easily and quickly accessible. Images and the data they may contain needs to be easily captured and readily usable
6	**Highly Collaborative** — Many cases require a team-based approach, engaging people outside the organization, such as clients, third party experts, and loosely interested parties. With the advent of social networking and other community-enabling technologies, the community of parties that a case can engage is expanding
7	**Multiple Participants and Fluid Roles** — People change position or role. Staff members leave or case workers' roles may change in the course of a customer engagement. Multiple parties are likely to be involved directly or indirectly, and they may play different roles in the case at different times
8	**Inter-related Cases** — Outcomes of separate cases may have an impact on each other. Cases can be explicitly linked, or they may need to be linked by inference and conducted with this inferred link in mind
9	**Juggling Fixed and Flexible Timescales** — Cases may vary in how they are conducted but they must meet completion deadlines driven by legislation, policy or service level agreements (SLAs)
10	**Sensitivity to External Events** — The state of a running case can change due to unforeseeable external events
11	**Cross-Organizational Visibility** — It must be possible for supervisors or other case workers to monitor progress, even after handing cases to colleagues in other departments or organizations to undertake specific steps

12	**History** — Every action performed, every decision taken, and every piece of correspondence received has to be tracked, not just for audit purposes, but also to provide guidance for future similar cases
13	**Demanding Security Requirements** — The wide range of case participants and information systems involved results in challenging information security requirements enveloping many pieces of information/data, many documents and other artefacts, and perhaps strict chain of custody management needs
14	**Isolated Pockets of Automation** — The knowledge worker plays an essential role but requires automation to assist in coordinating and orchestrating isolated pockets of information relevant to the case

7. Adaptive Case Management Drives Successful Customer Engagement

We began by recognizing the new power of the individual. Equipped with new devices and new available channels of communication, hungry to engage in new ways, this modern customer is more prized and at-risk than ever before.

We discussed how, in a simple example, Barack Obama outstripped all prior fund-raising achievement by creating a highly effective architecture of engagement, extending the availability of donor touchpoints and making his donation-taking machine highly responsive to critical events in the campaign and to the donors' desire to engage.

Responsiveness of customer engagement requires that your organization master the unpredictable as well as the routine. Whether the processing in question is the onboarding of a new client, the eligibility review in a citizen benefits program, or the arbitration of a customer complaint, your organization must sense and respond rather than only standardize and execute.

In the Customer Engagement Self-survey, you reviewed your organization's ability. Why not review your self-survey again now, with the help of the Architecture of Engagement (Fig. 2) and the tabulated guide to when Customer Engagement requires Adaptive Case Management (Table 1). Can you identify specific opportunity to improve your Customer Engagement?

Organizations that complete their architecture of engagement by embracing an adaptive case management platform will win more new deals, keep more customers happy, operate less wastefully, and capitalize better on opportunities for improvement.

Case Management Forecast: Mostly PCM with a Chance of ACM

John T. Matthias, National Center for State Courts, United States

1. Introduction

Knowledge work may primarily involve routine, repeatable work which constitutes production case management (PCM), but it may also involve problem-solving activities that would benefit from adaptive case management (ACM) capabilities in an application. Work which involves repeatable activities can be defined in advance and be supported by an application designed for volume use. Many jobs involve some amount of routine work but also some amount of problem-solving work. How can this non-routine work be supported?

Court case management is a work environment typically supported by case management solutions designed for routine production work. When confronted by exceptional situations, business users are required to use their ingenuity to create work-arounds, or simply jump through a lot of hoops, to handle problem-solving tasks not addressed by the application.

New court case management solutions may provide ACM capabilities able to modify structured processes using a set of process snippets as a set of building blocks. This chapter explores why and how certain court case types and job roles would benefit from adaptive case management capabilities in a case management solution, and describes the capabilities of a PCM solution with ACM characteristics.

2. Production Case Management Aspects of Court Case Management

Every job has a certain amount of repeatable, routine work. The business processes for routine activities tend to remain stable over a relatively long period of time. A case management solution can be modeled, designed and programmed to effectively assist in execution of routine work for a period of years without significant change—this is PCM. Figure 1 represents the continuum of routine and problem-solving work of some knowledge workers in a court.

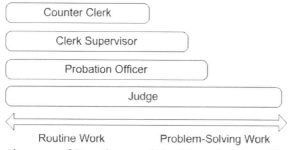

Figure 1: Continuum of Routine and Problem-Solving Work in a Court

Some knowledge workers perform problem solving because of the professional nature of the work, and other workers progress from simpler to more complex tasks as job skills improve and as a worker has a professional responsibility for the result. As problem solving increases, the worker requires more flexibility in performing job activities. A case management solution has more ACM capabilities to the extent that it can support the knowledge worker with a set of tools enabling the worker to adapt the solution "on the fly" to meet the unique circumstances of the case at hand.

There are lower levels and higher levels of an organization, and the trend in recent years is to flatten the organization, giving workers beginning-to-end responsibility for entire activities, and promoting cross training, to make employees more autonomous. This trend requires workers to be more aware of business objectives, process goals, performance targets and customer outcomes. To the extent that technology supports their work by providing workers with information for their jobs, allows them to evolve work processes, and collaborate with other workers, the organization will be more able to achieve its goals.

3. ADAPTIVE CAPABILITIES IN A COURT CASE MANAGEMENT SOLUTION

The criteria used to judge case studies nominated for the ACM Global Excellence Award for 2012 encompass the current understanding of the capabilities that an ACM solution can provide to knowledge workers. No case study demonstrated all, or even a majority, of the ACM award criteria, and no court case management solution yet exhibits all of the characteristics of ACM. This section identifies ACM criteria that would support more adaptive court case management.

Aligning Work with Goals and Objectives

Performance Targets

A jurisdiction's objectives, process goals and customer outcomes are usually found in its mission statement. But, these goals would have more connection to everyday work if business users were able to evaluate alignment of their current tasks with business objectives and process goals, and to verify that performance targets and customer outcomes were being achieved, and to what extent. Current case management solutions provide judges and court staff with little if any reference to the court's performance targets.

A court case management solution with ACM capability would provide clerical workers and supervisors with a process dashboard to monitor work in progress and drive staffing adjustments for particular tasks to meet predefined service levels and customer outcomes. The dashboard could show percentage completion of tasks of all types being worked on as tasks were completed and new ones were added, and if a backlog was developing in certain of those tasks. Similarly, it could provide real-time guidance to switch workers to other tasks if a backlog were developing in higher-priority tasks. For example, notification that a protection order is being issued or that a pre-adjudication defendant needs processing for release from custody, have higher priorities than many other tasks, and a worker would handle them and return to previous tasks after completion. In a courtroom, for example, a process dashboard would gauge availability of attorneys and parties (and an interpreter if needed) for a hearing based on schedule conflicts, and use the parties' case history and the age of the case to suggest a timeline and calendar slots for hearings in the court case.

Terminology/Ontology

Jurisdictions use a customary terminology in case captions, headings of documents, and names of case events, which typically vary by state and even by court within a state. Current court case management solutions have terminology scattered throughout the application, and no systematic ontology can be applied.

A court case management solution with ACM capability would allow an authorized business user to globally set the terminology used to describe cases, tasks, events, templates, states, and semantic relationships between them. This would cause names of court events, and roles of participants that fit the local organizational model, to consistently appear in docket entries and on task lists, on generated documents and reports, and on screens. An arraignment in a traffic case has different legal and operational implications compared to an arraignment in a jailable misdemeanor or felony.

Evolving Processes for New and Existing Cases

Templates

Court cases encompass a range of types including traffic, criminal, civil, domestic relations and juvenile, and a range of auxiliary case types including pretrial/probation supervision services, drug courts and child welfare improvement programs. These case types share basic predefined business entities, content, participant interactions, and business rules. But even these are subject to change as courts adapt to environmental pressures, to become problem-solving (treatment) courts, for example. In addition, techniques in the discipline of caseflow management continue to evolve in the quest to improve processes and help courts manage their caseloads. (Steelman 2000) Current case management systems must either be customized to accommodate new conceptual/operational approaches, or court business users must record a text comment or develop a workaround to handle a new approach within the static framework of the PCM application (usually only partially successfully).

A court case management solution with ACM capability would enable the business user to use a template to add tasks to a standard process to meet unique circumstances. A template to create and assign a task or obligation to someone, for example, would be available for the judge to use when needed to:

1. Request an attorney to prepare a draft decision,
2. Request a special master to prepare a recommendation,
3. Appoint an expert to evaluate evidence,
4. Appoint a mediator to handle an issue in the case, or
5. Any other ad hoc task or obligation a judge needed to create.

The template would include a snippet of process steps with these elements:

- Notification to the assignee of the obligation created by the judge
- Description of duties
- Identify timeline/deadline and set up the tickler for monitoring performance of the obligation, and
- Trigger notifying the judge of a deliverable or result, or of a failure to deliver.

Judges are known for handling cases in unique ways, and for ordering special obligations, to mete out justice in a case. Current solutions are able only to record such things in a comment field or in a docket entry, which contains no business rules and no method of tracking or reporting.

Extending Template

When a court finds that a person is unable to handle his or her own financial affairs, the court appoints a conservator to make financial decisions for the protected person and manage the conservatorship estate. Court staff needs to monitor whether the conservatorship is being handled properly by looking for conditions which will trigger alerts, such as:

1. Occurrence or non-occurrence of events in the court docket, or
2. Anomalies in the inventory and accounting of the estate.

Current case management solutions are incapable of automating this kind of monitoring, and court staff usually has no tools more sophisticated than accumulated personal experience of individual workers, and spreadsheets to analyze data.

A court case management solution with ACM capability would provide templates containing sets of business rules maintained by business analysts/case managers themselves, for flagging questionable conditions occurring within a conservatorship. Such flags could be characterized as follows:

- Relating to the timeliness and completeness of information provided by the conservator
- Relating to characteristics or trends of financial data provided by the conservator over two or more time periods
- Relating to characteristics of the conservator's relationship with the protected person, the conservator's relationship with attorneys employed by the conservator, and actions taken by the conservator with respect to property in the conservatorship
- Relating to characteristics of the conservatorship estate and the conservator, compared to other conservatorships in the caseload of the court (peer group analysis)

Business analysts/case managers would modify and evolve the business rules themselves to flag auditable conditions. The rules would evolve as operation of the rules became more known and refined (e.g., identifying and eliminating false positives), as data requirements of estate accountings evolved hand-in-hand with the flagging criteria, and as the court identified new ploys to monitor to try to stay ahead of fraudulent practices.

Enabling Collaboration

Personal Relationships

Court rules generally limit communication with a judge, and communications with jurors to promote fair hearing a matter, so use of social media is inhibited with a court. A judge, however, often seeks collaboration in handling aspects of a case that require expertise.

Judges and case managers need lists of resources available assist in various aspects of cases, such as interpreters, conflict counsel, guardians ad litem, mediators, drug assessment and treatment service providers, psychological evaluations, expert witnesses, contract court reporters and the like.

A court case management solution with ACM capability would provide a list of resources available to judges and case managers, their organizational relationships, skill profiles, references in other cases to their performance, and performance ratings by judges and court staff that had used the services before. These collaborators would be able to provide input and the results of their services directly into the case record (see "Capturing Data and Content" below). If paid by the court for their services, they would be able to invoice the court, and court staff could review and approve invoices for payment.

Mobile

Public access to electronic case information is fairly widespread, and judges are increasingly interested in using mobile devices to review dockets and case documents from any location at any time.

A court case management solution with ACM capability would enable judges to use mobile devices to perform casework, including viewing documents and signing orders, thereby putting signed orders into the electronic stream of the case process.

Capturing Data and Content

Capture

Courts generally lock down the case record to preserve its integrity (except for service providers as mentioned above), so predefined methods of capturing data and content are required. Data and content are input either on paper and associated data entry, or through electronic filing, which is a form of self service.

A court case management solution with ACM capability would provide e-filing for all parties to a case, and imported data from government agencies and service providers (e.g., demographic data on defendants from the jail, traffic citations from law enforcement, driver's license and vehicle registration information from the state, complaints initiating cases from the prosecutor, collection agency receipts, drug test results, online payments from the credit card vendor, telephone payments from the interactive voice response system), using standardized data formats, enabling data to populate the database automatically (optionally after clerk review).

Exporting Data and Content

Distribution

Depending on the capabilities of agencies they send data to, courts generally export information to government agencies and service providers on paper.

A court case management solution with ACM capability would provide exported data exchanges with government agencies and service providers (e.g., release orders to the jail, warrant issuance and recalls to law enforcement, notice of appointment to the public defender, confinement orders to state department of corrections, convictions to the criminal history repository, violations and reinstatements to the driver's license authority, accounts assigned to the collection agency, revenue transmitted to the local jurisdiction), using standardized data formats, automatically populating the court's docket with a record of such transmittal.

Feeds

People who want information about a case generally have to call a court or look up information online. A court case management solution with ACM capability would allow people to subscribe to cases and be notified of changes in the case as they happen.

Post Data

Courts generally want to provide courtroom location information in the lobby to help litigants find their courtroom, and information on court dockets and other information to the court's website. A court case management solution with ACM capability would automatically post such data to these destinations, ensuring that the data is properly synchronized.

Configuring the Solution In-flight

Schema Extension

As business needs of the court change, traditionally the court must rely upon its in-house case management solution developers or its vendor to change all but the simplest of table entries. Business users are generally able to add and delete court employees, and change user access to screens and data as job roles change, but not much more about the solution can be changed by business users. Additional case types, such as specialty courts for drug, mental health, domestic violence, and veterans' issues, need to be added as courts take on more of a problem-solving role in their communities. Most PCM solutions need to be customized, or users resort to spreadsheets, Access databases or third-party specialty applications to handle these case types.

A court case management solution with ACM capability would allow a non-technical business user to add a new case type with new data fields and new screens or labels for data entry and reporting, and to write business rules that describe process logic, constraints, field validations, and formatting.

Form Extension

Most work in courts is generally driven by the presence of piles of case files on a desk, and virtually no information on work in progress is available.

A court case management solution with ACM capability would allow a non-technical business user to modify that user's own user interface, including the work list and dashboard layouts, the case summary display, subscriptions to case information changes, and reminders set by the user to perform tasks.

Dynamic Access Control

Granularity

Case management solutions generally allow the court to define job roles which give business users access to functions related to their jobs. These are fairly broad categories, and are often limited to separating clerks who handle financial data from those who don't, and judges from the clerical staff. Case types involving juveniles, probate and mental health matters are typically assigned to specific staff for job roles because of the confidential nature of the data. Otherwise, most job roles are fairly open, reflecting a low degree of job specialization and organizational scalability. Social security numbers captured in the system are generally available to all users.

A court case management solution with ACM capability would enable configuring a security level for the following: user work group, case type, document type, task type, event type, data field, query/report, form letter/notice/order when it is to be generated, calendar, user screen, and person on sensitive cases (e.g., attorneys assigned to the case, and no one else outside the court). Security access configuration which is too granular may be difficult to maintain, so a balance of appropriate access and ease of maintenance should be sought.

Providing Business Value

Measured Value and Improvement

Courts have historically measured their activity by the numbers of cases filed and disposed during a year. The CourTool measures published in 2005 for trial courts have provided more granular measures of court performance. CourTool measure 4, for example, identifies by aging category the age of the active cases that are pending before the court. Having a complete and accurate inventory of active pending cases makes clear, for example, the number and type of cases drawing near or about to surpass the court's case processing time standards. This enables the court to focus attention on what is required to ensure cases are brought to completion within reasonable timeframes. Other CourTools measure other aspects of court performance.

A court case management solution with ACM capability would automatically compute all ten of the performance measures, and show changes from month to month through data visualization. CourTool measure 1, in addition, involves a pencil-and-paper survey by court users of the court's accessibility and its treatment of customers in terms of fairness, equality, and respect. If performance measures were more automated and provided real time immediate feedback to process owners, overall performance would be more transparent.

Efficiency—Judicial Control

One persistent issue in courts nationwide is the number of continuances granted by judges at the request of attorneys or parties who are not prepared for a hearing or trial. A judge granting or denying the request needs information on how old case is, the issues not yet resolved by the parties, issues of evidence discovery, and how many times hearings have been held to date.

A court case management solution with ACM capability would automatically provide a judge with this kind of information, motivating the judge to assert judicial control of the case and bring it to quicker disposition.

Efficiency—Workload Transparency

Clerical workers in busy courts generally move quickly from case to case within a type of task, and from task to task during the day. When the amount of work to be completed is determined by a pile of documents or files, work tends to be specialized, and job roles consist of a group of specialized tasks. A clerical worker may not be aware of another unit in the office that is backlogged, or of priority tasks that need to be completed.

A court case management solution with ACM capability would display in a work list tasks that the worker is assigned personally or assigned in a pool to perform, and also links to tasks of other individuals and pools, enabling the worker to perform additional work and be recognized for making the additional effort. This would balance the workload, improve timeliness, and recognize high performance.

Efficiency—Mass Case Processing

Many PCM systems were designed for entering data on one case at a time. This is adequate for low volumes of work, but if the same action is to be performed for dozens or hundreds of cases, the clerk's repetitive actions are very inefficient and the application is not scalable.

A court case management solution with ACM capability would allow a business user to select multiple cases and apply an action with a single transaction, such as the following:

1. Enter the same event in multiple cases with a single transaction
2. Reassign a group of pending events from one judicial officer, courtroom, attorney, or date to another
3. Reassign a group of cases from one judge or judicial officer, attorney, or interpreter to another, to assume responsibility for them
4. Display cases subject to a flagged condition of a certain kind which occurred or failed to occur on a specific date or date range, for mass case processing (e.g., failure to appear, payment or compliance due, bail forfeiture due), including docket entries.
5. Generate individual documents or groups of documents through mass case processing.

Training and Feedback

Most case management solutions provide some amount of context-sensitive help in using the system. Knowing what to do next in performing a task is often a matter of on-the-job training, and this may result in inconsistency of training and the passing bad habits from worker to worker.

A court case management solution with ACM capability would provide in-flight guidance to aid the worker based on the state of the case. Further, it would record for training purposes the types of tasks performed by a worker that may have taken longer-than-average time, based on metrics developed based on the work of other workers performing that task.

Improving Processes

Process Mining

Most case management solutions provide little in the way of data about processes, primarily because most court environments maintain only a system of record listing of documents filed and actions taken. Court workers are unaware of the number and timing of processes that produce those results.

A court case management solution with ACM capability would provide a process mining capability that collects and analyzes internal and external event information, allowing insight into how many times a case was addressed at hearing or chambers review, who was involved in what role, how long it took, what the next scheduled event was to be, and the reason given for not disposing of the case. The information would be available to judges for their own use and to the chief or presiding judge with nominal authority over the judge, as a means of improving performance. Availability of this information among judges has the effect of motivating judges to examine their work methods.

Audit

Most case management solutions have no method of auditing individual cases and user actions for quality control. "Auditing" in current parlance refers to an audit trail to track which user entered specific data in an exceptional circumstance when foul play is suspected. If a case event or document is entered into the wrong case, for example, this is generally not discovered until the case is handled again by the clerk, or until a party or the judge notices it. Current solutions have few or no capabilities to actively monitor data quality by alerting or coaching users of potential errors, particularly in the area of person identity management.

A court case management solution with ACM capability would provide guidance to business users in real time during case record updates and other maintenance activity, based on person identity matching algorithms indicating the probability that a court action involving a person being taken is correct or not. Common identity issues include multiple person records, apparently of the same person, with different information that makes them difficult to identify, match and merge, e.g., alias names, misspellings, dates of birth, identifying numbers, junior/senior suffix omission or mix-ups, and confusion about Hispanic patronymic and matronymic surnames. If two person-identities were merged by mistake, they could be un-merged without IT assistance.

4. CONCLUSIONS

PCM solutions have evolved over a period of years to incrementally provide more functionality to business users. As traditional court dockets, PCMs automated records of transactions as the system of record. They replaced manual counting in providing statistics of filings and dispositions. They enabled generation of documents using case header information. PCM solutions "hit the wall," however, as they have been unable to keep up with business users' increasing demands for changes to business processes, and for efficiency and flexibility in operations. Knowledge work domains like court case management still need to handle routine work, but they also need ACM capabilities to empower knowledge workers to problem-solve. The forecast for ACM is a strong likelihood.

5. REFERENCES

(National Center for State Courts 2011) "CourTools"
www.ncsconline.org/D_Research/CourTools/index.html

(Steelman 2000) David C. Steelman. Caseflow Management: the Heart of Court Management in the New Millennium. Williamsburg, VA: National Center for State Courts, 2000.

(Workflow Management Coalition 2012) "2nd Annual Awards for Excellence in ACM."
www.adaptivecasemanagement.org/images/ACM_Awards_2012_Slide_Presentation.pdf

Types of Business Process

Keith Harrison-Broninski, Role Modellers Ltd.

1. INTRODUCTION

Many organizations struggle to improve critical, high-visibility business processes, due to poor understanding of the different *types* of business process. A direct consequence of the problem is the inability to improve, or support with technology, much everyday work of an adaptive nature. This paper explains the problem using an analogy familiar to everyone.

The following simple yardstick is given for telling the type of an adaptive work process: once it is complete, can you look back and identify what took place as being exact sequences of steps copied from standard templates? Or have the virtual team members used the original template processes as illustrative guides rather than prescriptive instructions—changing, repeating, adding and omitting steps as required by the situation at the time, based on their skills, experience and collective judgement?

If the latter, then the process is not just adaptive but also collaborative, and lies in the territory of **Human Interaction Management (HIM)** and its supporting technology the **Human Interaction Management System (HIMS)**. This paper explains how HIM and the HIMS provide support for adaptive, collaborative processes, illustrating the ideas with a case study from a company whose products are improvement programmes delivered to public sector organizations.

2. THE PROCESS GAP

Let's start with a picture showing how critical processes of a certain type are poorly managed by many organizations.

At the top of Figure 1 is a grid of the different process types within a single organization, showing the technique appropriate to support each process type:Step-by-step work in which the sequence of steps can be predicted—for example, manufacturing, licensing or order fulfilment—is generally described using a flowchart-based notation (such as BPMN) and supported using **Business Process Management** or **Workflow** systems.

- Step-by-step work in which the steps and their sequence adapt to the situation at hand—for example, claim processing, medical diagnosis or invoice discrepancy handling—is generally described again using a flowchart-based notation but this time supported using **Case Management** systems.
- Work in which deliverables are provided through collaboration rather than each person carrying out steps individually, but is nevertheless predictable—for example, laying an oil pipeline or building a power station—is generally described using a Work Breakdown Structure and supported by **Project Management** systems.
- Work that is both collaborative and adaptive—which may in fact represent a very large proportion of organizational activity, since it includes areas such as Research & Development, Marketing, Complex sales, Services delivery, Complex problem resolution, Merger & Acquisition, and Organiza-

tional change—is generally not described in any formal way but rather using documents and illustrative diagrams. As a result, it is not supported by specific systems, but rather left to fend for itself in a minefield of workplace technologies such as email and content management systems.

Figure 1 shows how this problem, and the resulting support gap, exists not only for collaborative, adaptive processes within a single organization, but for collaborative, adaptive processes that cross organizational boundaries—as they typically do.

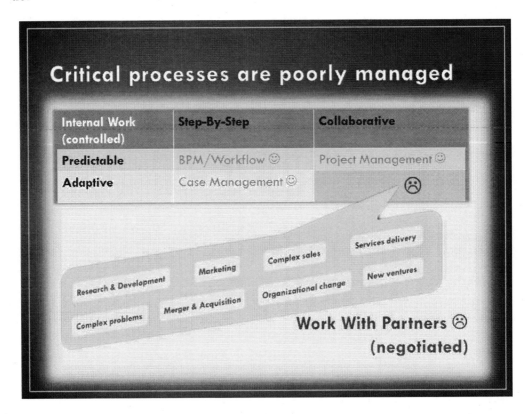

Critical processes are poorly managed

Internal Work (controlled)	Step-By-Step	Collaborative
Predictable	BPM/Workflow ☺	Project Management ☺
Adaptive	Case Management ☺	☹

Research & Development   Marketing   Complex sales   Services delivery

Complex problems   Merger & Acquisition   Organizational change   New ventures

Work With Partners ☹ (negotiated)

Figure 1: The process gap

Human Interaction Management (HIM), and a **Human Interaction Management System (HIMS**, for which the reference implementation is HumanEdj), fill the technology support gap. A HIM Plan template—i.e., a set of Stages in which people play Roles to provide deliverables—is a natural, intuitive way to structure adaptive, collaborative work. Further, people can use different HIMS servers (or even email) to work together in a Plan across professional, geographical and organizational boundaries.

However, for many people it is hard to separate out the different types of work. Where exactly should one apply each type of description technique, and each type of technology? It can be particularly difficult to separate adaptive work processes into step-by-step and collaborative, since even adaptive processes that are step-by-step typically involve multiple people (each carrying out their own set of steps).

So here is an analogy that you can use to classify your adaptive processes as either step-by-step or collaborative. Consider what happens when you build a Lego model as compared to what happens when you cook a stew. When you've completed a Lego model, you can still see the parts—and each part is the same as it was when you took it out of the box. With a stew, you can detect (most of) the ingredients by tasting it—or even just looking at it—but you cannot disassemble the stew into its components.

In other words, the constituents of the stew have been changed by the process of cooking, into something new—something that is quintessentially to do with that particular stew, and the chemical reactions that took place during cooking. A sea change has taken place, into something rich and strange.

It may or may not be possible to repeat the sea change on future occasions—and the ability to do so is part of the learning curve a chef goes through. But one thing is sure—you cannot undo the sea change for a specific stew, and isolate each ingredient in its original form. Making an analogy with human work, collaboration between the people (typically members of a virtual team) who carry out an adaptive process changes the original elements of that process irrevocably.

So this is how to tell the type of an adaptive work process: once it is complete, can you look back and identify what took place as being exact sequences of steps copied from standard templates? Or have the virtual team members used the original template processes as illustrative guides rather than prescriptive instructions—changing, repeating, adding and omitting steps as required by the situation at the time, based on their skills, experience and collective judgement?

If the step sequences are identical to their original templates, your adaptive process is "step-by-step", and you could consider using an Adaptive Case Management (**ACM**) system to support it—as long as it all takes place within a single organization, that is. If on the other hand your process changes the template steps—or involves multiple organizations—then you are in the territory of **HIM** and its supporting technology the **HIMS**.

In a HIM process, as John Seely Brown said [Brown 2005], "processes don't do work, people do." ACM is about tasks. HIM is about virtual teams.

3. HUMAN INTERACTION MANAGEMENT

Drawing from and extending Role Activity Theory, **Human Interaction Management** theory (**HIM**, [Harrison-Broninski 2005]) provides a modelling framework for describing collaborative human working behaviour in process terms, and identifies patterns that underlie any form of human activity (whether collaborative or not). These patterns demonstrate how action learning is the core of all collaborative work.

HIM analyses collaborative work processes in terms of their inner structure rather than from their external manifestation in terms of particular communications. Rather than being based on a specific aspect of human collaboration such as messaging or document sharing, HIM is based on five fundamental features of human-driven processes, the "5 Principles of Human Interaction Management":

1. *Connection visibility.* Successful collaboration requires a strong representation of the virtual team involved—i.e., process participants, their roles and their private information resources. To work with people, one needs to know who they are, what they can do, and what their responsibilities are.

2. *Structured messaging.* If people are to manage their interactions with others better, their communications must be structured, goal-directed and under process control.

3. *Support for mental work.* Management of human-driven processes must recognize the value of the human information processing: the time and mental effort invested in researching, comparing, considering, deciding, and generally turning information into knowledge and ideas.

4. *Supportive rather than prescriptive activity management.* People may not sequence their activities in the manner of a software program, but there is always structure to human work, which must be understood and institutionalized so that it can be managed and improved.

5. *Processes change processes.* Process definition is an intrinsic part of the process itself; it happens continually throughout the life of the process, and the entire virtual team is involved.

HIM suggests that human work typically has five broad stages, which overlap in time and repeat "fractally" (on a smaller scale, at lower levels):

- *Research.* This is about mapping out the terrain of the work; gaining information from external sources, e.g. communities of practice, textbooks, Web search, and turning it into personal knowledge.
- *Evaluate.* Here one steps back to consider and internalize the acquired knowledge.
- *Analyze.* An approach to the problem is decided upon, at least initially.
- *Constrain.* The work is divided into separate chunks and organized. This stage is about laying down the constraints that govern these chunks of work.
- *Task.* As the chunks of work have been handed out to appropriate people, all those concerned can get on with the tasks at hand.

The first stage of the REACT pattern, Research, is further broken down into a sub-pattern AIM, which describes the activities of information discovery:

1. *Access* discovery services. This is about mapping out the terrain of the work; gaining information from external sources, e.g. communities of practice, textbooks, Web search, and turning it into personal knowledge.

2. *Identify* resources required. Here resources of likely interest and usefulness are identified and chosen.

3. *Memorize* information obtained from particular resources. Internalize the ideas in question so that they can be leveraged from a position of knowledge.

According to HIM, the REACT and AIM patterns describe all human working behaviour. The patterns capture the way that people react to the work they take on—e.g., respond to an assignment, fulfil a responsibility, achieve a goal. REACT and AIM help simplify complex situations since the patterns can be repeated, overlapped, and nested in order to reduce any work assignment to the same fundamental stages.

4. THE HUMAN INTERACTION MANAGEMENT SYSTEM

Implementation of HIM in an enterprise environment (i.e., design, execution and management of business processes according to HIM principles) is facilitated by software support from a **Human Interaction Management System (HIMS**, for which the reference implementation is HumanEdj). The aim of a HIMS is to facilitate all stages of human work without forcing people to follow a set of predetermined steps.

A HIMS helps people to see the bigger picture of a process and understand their responsibilities within it. This calls for suggestive rather than prescriptive process description and support: a HIMS provides support and enforces basic control on behalf of the organization, providing an indication to people of what they are expected to do then letting them learn collaboratively how best to meet their assigned goals.

A key aspect of this collaborative learning derives from autopoietic theory, which asserts that communication is founded not on transmission of information but rather on transmission of intent. Research in biology shows that the purpose of animal communication is largely about synchronizing the behaviour of parties. This understanding has been adopted in business via the classic "Conversation for Action" pattern, in which communication between people and organizations is structured in terms of a small set of request/response pairs—request/promise, offer/acceptance, and report/acknowledgement. HIM generalizes this principle by allowing a much broader and less restrictive set of structured communications.

HumanEdj, for instance, provides full support for speech acts theory, according to which a communication act is not only composed of content but also, and at least as importantly, of an intention. For example, the creator of a deliverable can specify its intended usage as a draft for review, as a submission for approval, ... even as having known issues that need to be addressed.

Many business people have found the traditional use of speech acts in the Conversation for Action too rigid for practical use. Hence, HumanEdj permits business people not only to share data and documents, but also to make a wide range of assertions about the status of Deliverables and Stages. More generally, a HIMS suggests actions rather than prescribes them, allows not only for communication but also for action, does not assume that all communication is direct and does not prevent tangential discussion, i.e. unexpected interactions that go beyond the conversation originally expected. This permits processes to evolve via a collaborative learning process.

The HIMS provides helpful structure by modelling work formally as a process, but retains a light touch by allowing people to work according to their judgement at the time. By bringing collaboration tools into a unified and supportive process context, it promises to make knowledge work genuinely more effective.

A key aspect of human collaborative work is the common necessity to include people from multiple organizations, location and disciplines. Hence HumanEdj has a distributed peer-to-peer architecture, more akin to a Multi-Agent System than to a workflow or BPMS engine. Participants in a process, which in HumanEdj is called a "Plan", may belong to different organizations and use different HumanEdj instances. HumanEdj automatically synchronizes the Plan state for all participants via a messaging technology such as email. This makes it possible to participate in a Plan using only a standard email client.

HumanEdj structures activities, messages, documents and data as well as maintains information on who does what, when, where and why. Fine-grained control over who sees what in a Plan is accomplished by grouping all the above items into "Stages", each of which represents a related set of goals and effectively defines a virtual sub-team within the Plan as a whole. Plans may also generate sub-Plans, for instance in order to carry out the details of a public process as distinct private processes.

Plan templates are used to generate Plans for projects, initiatives, ventures, etc.— i.e. executable business processes that may cross organizational boundaries. Each Plan is configured appropriately for the requirements of the situation, and the participants themselves adjust the configuration throughout its life, as they collaborate to evolve the definition of the Plan instance in response to external circumstances and internal progress.

A Plan acts not only as a mechanism for learning but, once complete, as a source of learning materials. Plan instances from a repository show how other people dealt with problems of a certain type, and new Plan templates may be created from successful Plan instances (or parts thereof).

With regard to assessment of learning results, Plan instances are self-monitoring—they include automatic feedback mechanisms both within the Plan and across Plans to higher management levels. Taking part in a Plan instance in itself both measures and provides evidence of achievement. Plans may also use external services to provide:

- Learning materials customized for the Plan instance
- Standardized evaluation of learning progress
- Trusted competency assessment
- User profiles
- Information within a Plan instance automatically has semantic mark-up, as do all communications between participants. This mark-up can be sent to external services to help streamline the results.

5. CASE STUDY

To illustrate how HIM supports adaptive, collaborative processes, consider an innovative company whose products are improvement programmes that it delivers to public sector organizations. The management structure is flat and staff members are encouraged to propose, seek internal funding for, and implement new improvement programmes on a regular basis. While the culture has resulted in innovations beneficial to their customers, and consequently in growth, the company struggled to make its operations profitable. It was not possible to optimize or even obtain the cost of sales, given the complex way in which improvement programmes were created, sold, and delivered. It became necessary to standardize and monitor customer-facing operations.

The company expected to continue its previous success with standardizing back-office administrative processes using traditional workflow techniques. However, standardization of customer-facing operational processes met with resistance from staff, who were accustomed to using their skills, experience and judgement to adapt their working approach to each customer engagement. Hence, there remained wide variance across the organization in the way that core customer-facing and internal processes were carried out.

The solution required a means of process standardization that provided indicative rather than prescriptive processes (i.e. processes that could be adapted flexibly during execution), and that supported the harvesting of innovative ideas into new products (i.e. improvement programmes). The company used HIM to develop Plan templates for core operational processes including:

- *Sales Funnel.* Developing a sales lead into a new customer engagement.
- *Product Delivery.* Implementing an improvement programme for a customer.
- *Non-Standard Product Development.* Developing a custom improvement programme for a customer.
- *Standard Product Development.* Turning a custom improvement programme into a standard off-the-shelf product offered to all customers.

Shown in Figure 2 below is a HumanEdj "Grid view" of the Plan template for the Sales Funnel process. Across the top are the Roles in the process, which in an actual Plan would be assigned to named people. Down the side are the Stages in the Plan template. The numbering is only suggestive, since the Stages may be carried out in any order, and they often run concurrently. HumanEdj Stages are used to represent sets of related goals, helping to ensure that people focus on objectives and thus work effectively.

During the lifetime of a Plan, the Stages are assigned statuses by the Plan owner, such as "Started", "Completed", "Cancelled", and so on. Different Roles belong to different sets of Stages. Any documents, data or messages created in a Stage are visible to all the Roles in that Stage and only to those roles. Here we see the emphasis on mental work that is critical to learning (and a core principle of HIM), via deliverables identified and recognized as a natural part of Plan execution.

Somerset GP Service Q4 2011 :: 31-Oct-2011 14:05:29.390

Stage	Nominated Sales Lead	Lead Owner	Lead Creator	Client	Solutions Team	Product Specialist
1. Generate Lead	View Lead in CRM (-17 days, due 04-Nov-2011)	View Lead in CRM (-14 days, due 09-Nov-2011)	Maintain Lead in CRM	Not in Stage		Not in Stage
2. Qualify Lead	Qualify Lead	View Qualified Lead (-8 days, due 17-Nov-2011)	View Qualified Lead	Not in Stage	View Qualified Lead	Not in Stage
3. Create Opportunity	Assess Client Arrange Follow-Up Meeting Record Change to Opportunity on CRM	View Pre-Meeting Document	Not in Stage	Not in Stage	Not in Stage	Not in Stage
4. Develop Opportunity	Proposal Formal tender Submit Proposal	Approve Proposal Submission	Not in Stage	Not in Stage	Not in Stage	Review Non-Standard Product Offering Initiate Non-Standard Product Development
5. Negotiate Proposal	Send Proposal to Client			Review Proposal		Not in Stage
6. Await Decision	Prepare for Delivery Initiate Delivery Plan		Not in Stage	Not in Stage	Not in Stage	Not in Stage
7. Close Opportunity	Create Contract Close Opportunity in CRM Initiate Resources Allocation For Delivery	View Opportunity Status	View Opportunity Status	Not in Stage	Not in Stage	Not in Stage

Figure 2: Excerpt from HumanEdj Grid View in tabular format of Plan template for sales of improvement programmes

Two Activities in particular are to be noted:

1. "Initiate Non-Standard Product Development" in Stage "Develop Opportunity", which involves the creation of a new sub-Plan for developing a custom improvement programme, if required. The sub-Plan will be based on a standard Plan template, adapted as required. If the standard Plan tem-

plate is adapted, the new version may itself become a standard Plan template for use by others. The creation of the sub-Plan not only draws on organizational knowledge about custom improvement programme creation, but may well contribute to it by addition of a new special case. Here we see how the creation of a particular sales proposal contributes to evolving organizational structure, since the way in which it was done is automatically made part of enterprise knowledge management.

2. "Initiate Delivery Plan" in Stage "Await Decision", which involves the creation of a new sub-Plan for delivering the improvement programme. The Plan template used for this is created as part of the proposal and adapted for each customer engagement. As above, creation of a sub-Plan for a particular Delivery may well result in an adapted Plan template that can be re-used for future Deliveries of the same type. This creation of one Plan from another is typical of HIM, and can be used at any level in an organization to align operations with strategy.

Statistics from the Delivery sub-Plan are used together with statistics from the Sales Funnel Plan itself (shown for an example template in Figure 3) and any sub-Plan for Non-Standard Product Development to generate accurate total cost for provision of the improvement programme to the customer, and hence to create a price that ensures the engagement returns a profit (or a deliberate loss).

		Work To Do	Effort Days	Effort Cost - Total	Effort Cost - Remaining Work	Earliest Activity Start Date	Latest Activity Deadline	Latest Activity Expected Finish Date	Minimum Activity Expected Margin Days
Plan	Somerset GP Service Q4 2011 :: 31-Oct-2011 14:05:29.390	TRUE	11	4,230	4,230	01-Nov-11	17-Nov-11	28-Nov-11	-17
Description	Instances of this Plan template are created via an intranet form that anyone can use. The form enters client details into CRM, then starts the Plan pre-populated with: 1. A link to the client page in CRM; 2. A Solutions Area Director assigned to the Lead Owner Role - this Role may be re-assigned during the Plan if necessary.								

ROLE	DAY RATE	OVERHEAD PERCENTAGE	DAY RATE USED	DESCRIPTION
Nominated Sales Lead	0	0	402	
Lead Owner	0	0	402	All unqualified leads should be assigned to relevant Solutions team Area Director as the lead owner. The Lead Owner Role may be re-assigned during life of the Plan if necessary.
Lead Creator	200	0	230	New sales leads that have been generated that are not yet qualified as being a genuine lead are referred to as unqualified leads. These are expressions interest for our products/services from a variety of sources e.g. simple conversation, email, enquiry in response to marketing/website etc. These leads can be generated and logged by all individuals in the business in this early stage. In some instances the solutions team may ask these individuals to maintain that early relationship and link, until it is appropriate for the solutions team to get involved from a sales perspective. We must be careful that they are leads and not support queries that we log.
Client	50	0	57	
Solutions Team	0	0	402	
Regional Sales Support	0	0	402	Supports Nominated Sales Lead in preparing the proposal
Central Sales Support	0	0	402	
Product Specialist	0	0	402	
Area Co-ordinator	500	0	575	
Business Development Manager	500	0	575	
Defaults	350		15	Defaults are used where not set specifically for a Role

Stage	Role	Activity	Deliverables	Resources	Work To Do	Effort Days	Effort Cost - Total	Effort Cost - Remaining Work	Start Date	Deadline	Expected Finish Date	Expected Margin Days
1. Generate Lead	Nominated Sales Lead				TRUE	0.4	126.4	126.4	01-Nov-11	09-Nov-11	28-Nov-11	-17

Figure 3: Excerpt from HumanEdj Summary View in tabular format of Plan template for sales of improvement programmes

By explicitly associating the different aspects of customer engagement with one another, the organization is making its customer-facing operations and their internal relations visible. This means not only that senior management can learn to manage the processes as a unified whole (and hence improve the way in which the organization operates), but also that new staff can learn what the organization actually does and how they fit into it. These means of learning are fundamental enablers as the organization grows, since geographical expansion means that teams are increasingly virtual and operational staff includes more and more sub-contractors rather than employees.

Further opportunities include passing on the benefits of HIM to client organizations in the form of Plan templates that support their resulting change management initiatives and help to develop their future strategy. The company has effectively started the latter already, by creating Bottom-Up Plan templates for core operations. Next steps include building a Process Architecture to represent their domain of interest, defining vision and mission at multiple levels via a Business Motivation Model, developing understanding of their stakeholders, and creating Benefits Profiles for the changes that they plan.

6. CONCLUSION

Both Lego and cooking may involve multiple model-makers or chefs. The critical difference lies in the interaction between constituent elements (bricks and ingredients, respectively):

1. A Lego model is always exactly the sum of its original bricks—it can be disassembled at any time, since the bricks remain unchanged by usage.
2. Cooking fuses ingredients into something more than the sum of their parts—into new flavours and textures, generated by a non-reversible chemical process.

Similarly, flexible, innovative business processes ("adaptive" processes) are of 2 kinds:

1. An ACM process is a collection of pre-defined fragments—in exactly the same way that a modern software application is a bundle of pre-built components and/or services.
2. A HIM process uses fragments only as a starting point—as the process unfolds, the participants shape the collection of fragments into something uniquely and holistically suited to the situation at hand.

ACM case studies make it clear not only that ACM practitioners typically focus exclusively on the first kind of process, but also that most people only **see** processes of the first kind. Processes of the second kind are the elephant in the room—the hidden bulk of the iceberg, unsupported by mainstream techniques and tools. This hidden bulk conceals a huge amount of business-critical knowledge work, as shown in Figure 1.

The 2012 Gartner BPM Cool Vendors include Role Modellers, whose software product HumanEdj is a HIMS—i.e., based on process "design-by-doing". In its BPM Cool Vendors 2012 report, Gartner Inc. said that "design-by-doing" exemplifies the trend towards social BPM, noting that the ability to "do, then plan"—that is, to alter plans quickly and easily as time progresses and the overall goal evolves, and then reuse plans as new templates—will be useful to teams that need to collaborate on the fly, and then learn from their successes and failures.[1]

Flexible, innovative processes are currently high on many organizations' radar. So it is worth understanding the difference between Lego and cooking, and applying the analogy to adaptive work processes. Buildings are made of bricks, but organizations are made by teams—and modern teams are usually virtual. To support collaborative, adaptive human work, new techniques and new tools are required— HIM and the HIMS.

7. References

(Brocke 2010) BROCKE J., ROSEMANN M., editors (2010). "Handbook on Business Process Management 2: Strategic Alignment, Governance, People and Culture", Springer. ISBN: 978-3-642-01981-4.

(Brown 2005) BROWN, J.S., GRAY, E.S. (2005). "The People Are The Company", http://www.fastcompany.com/magazine/01/people.html.

(Fingar 2006) FINGAR P. (2006). "Extreme Competition: Innovation And The Great 21st Century Business Reformation", Meghan-Kiffer Press. ISBN 0-929652-38-2

(Han 2009) HAN Y., KAURANEN A., KRISTOLA E., MERINEN J. (2009). "Human Interaction Management—Adding Human Factors into Business Processes Management", Helsinki University of Technology.

(Harrison-Broninski 2005) HARRISON-BRONINSKI K. (2005). Human Interactions—The Heart and Soul of Business Process Management. Meghan-Kiffer Press. ISBN 978-0929652443.

(Harrison-Broninski 2009) HARRISON-BRONINSKI K. (2009). "Goal-Oriented Organization Design", Agile Product & Project Management, June 2009.

(Harrison-Broninski 2012) HARRISON-BRONINSKI, K., KORHONEN, J.J. (2012). "Collaboration Infrastructure for the Learning Organization", Proceedings, 15th International Conference, BIS 2012, Vilnius, Lithuania, May 21-23, 2012, Springer, Lecture Notes in Business Information Processing, 2012, Volume 117, Part 5, 120-131, DOI: 10.1007/978-3-642-30359-3_11

(Korhonen 2009) KORHONEN J.J. (2009). "Enterprise BPM—A Systemic Perspective", EDS Finland.

(Lee 2010) LEE J., SEO W., KIM K., KIM C. (2010). "An OWL-based ontological approach to RAD modeling of human interactions for business collaboration", Expert Syst. Appl. 37, 6 (Jun. 2010), 4128-4138.

(McGregor 2005) MCGREGOR M., editor (2005). "In Search Of BPM Excellence", Meghan-Kiffer Press. ISBN 0-929652-40-1

(Sadasivam 2008) SADASIVAM, R. (2008). "An Architecture Framework for Process-Personalized Composite Services: Service-oriented Architecture, Web Services, Business-Process Engineering, and Human Interaction Management", VDM Verlag Dr. Muller. ISBN 3-639087-24-0

(Swenson 2011) SWENSON K., et al (2011). "Social BPM: Work, Planning and Collaboration Under the Impact of Social Technology", Future Strategies Inc. ISBN 978-0-981987-08-8

---

[1] Gartner, Inc., " Cool Vendors in Business Process Management, 2012", Michele Cantara, Jim Sinur, Teresa Jones, Janelle B. Hill, Simon F Jacobson, 23 April 2012, www.gartner.com/id=1992916.

Gartner does not endorse any vendor, product or service depicted in its research publications, and does not advise technology users to select only those vendors with the highest ratings. Gartner research publications consist of the opinions of Gartner's research organization and should not be construed as statements of fact. Gartner disclaims all warranties, expressed or implied, with respect to this research, including any warranties of merchantability or fitness for a particular purpose

Distribute Process Knowledge in ACM through Mentoring

Frank Michael Kraft, AdaPro GmbH and Hajo Normann, Accenture

1. INTRODUCTION

New, and improved, knowledge needs to be captured, enhanced and applied constantly for any organization to adapt and grow. Knowledge harvesting from workshops in business departments and interviewing process veterans is a means of keeping knowledge but not sufficient to survive and thrive. The mine in which the nuggets of knowledge are buried is the place where the bulk of the work gets done every day, where people are finding clever workarounds to cope with an imperfect world. It is their ideas that need to be mined, shared and leveraged in order to adapt constantly and improve as an organization. Thus, Adaptive Case Management thinking should be applied not only towards improving the *knowledge workers* tasks. *Routine workers* in the operational units do have the potential to take on some characteristics of knowledge workers—in the moment they are creative and find new ideas on how to improve their work.

To manage knowledge mining from both knowledge and routine work, organization need to establish a "knowledge creation factory" to ensure that knowledge gets unburied, made explicit and drives the way the enterprise runs its business, constantly improving.

ACM is the right approach to capture this knowledge permanently. It needs to be complemented with a mentoring approach that is discussed in this chapter.

The first sections introduce the concept of living knowledge and are followed by a case study that delves into the details of how to approach it.

2. THE NEED TO EXTERNALIZE KNOWLEDGE WORKERS' EXPERIENCE

One main unsolved problem in companies that employ knowledge workers is that single knowledge workers quickly become bottlenecks in the overall process of work: The individual knowledge worker has special knowledge that is needed in many workstreams.

On the one hand, the company can be proud of employing such good people, and the knowledge worker can be proud of being needed in so many workstreams. But, on the other hand, the knowledge worker is overloaded. Therefore, his work becomes frantically busy. Thus, the reach of his influence is limited, because he can only do so much within a working day. This causes delays in projects and workstreams, if the needed knowledge worker is not available.

To address these issues, there are many efforts to externalize knowledge from the knowledge worker. Organizations build up knowledge in process models, in databases, in portals, in wikis and the like and make it available to everybody in the organization. Often complaints rise: It is difficult to use this knowledge, because it is difficult to find exactly what is needed for a special problem.

3. Mentoring as a Key Tool for Realizing ACM's Aim of Constant, Decentralized Process Improvement

So, how can we distribute knowledge within an organization in a sustainable way? For that, we need process software to support constant, decentralized learning as advocated by ACM on one hand. At management level, a new understanding of mentoring is the most important tool to distribute knowledge across an organization, on the other hand. Mentoring is the passing on of knowledge and experience from one knowledge worker to another knowledge worker over a period of time. This has many advantages:

- There is more capacity to contribute knowledge to a certain workstream
- There is less overload for the experienced knowledge worker
- Overall quality of work increases, because knowledge is where it is needed
- The knowledge can be used actively—i.e. the mentee can combine the knowledge and bring forth new knowledge and experience
- The knowledge can be adapted to current circumstances, while it is passed on
- Knowledge has always been passed on from one person to the next in history—only the means have been different. So it is a successful pattern of knowledge work, which has been successful even for thousands of years.
- But, the most important advantage is, that knowledge, that has been passed on from the mentor to the mentee becomes externalized, "living" knowledge. It is does not reside within the mind of the one knowledge keeper, but starts to become reproduced in different ways and grows organically inside a peer group. Over time, it can be multiplied after that, because the mentee can also become mentor after some time.

4. Between Beginner and Expert: Embracing the Constant Learner

It is important to understand that not all knowledge workers have the same level of expertise. Some are experts with long years of experience and some are beginners. Beginners need more guidance in what they do while experts need less guidance and have the need for more autonomy. Experts, in turn, can provide guidance.

Yet, we see the need to be a bit cautious with an oversimplification that comes with a bipolar categorization of the type of skills of process participants: The mere distinction between "beginners" and experts" we find very often with existing process-supporting software. Here, for a given process step one front end addresses the beginner and another the expert. We want to motivate though, that this is not a feasible approach in many cases: The distinction between a beginner, on the one hand, and an expert on the other misses the point that in reality process participants are not to be found in these extreme spots but in various levels of expertise in between them. A beginner who participates in a given process step becomes gradually more and more proficient: He starts to "know his way", becoming more and more familiar and confident. The task more and more becomes routine for him. His stress level decreases, since the part of his brain which deals with new situations (the pre-frontal cortex), which takes high levels of energy, thus causing stress, gets less involved. (Rock, 2009)

At this point of intermediary expertise, we often observe a very different behavior and approaches to the task at hand, based on the nature of the process participants. Many of them will embrace the sound level of expertise they gained so far and the routine that comes with it and would stop thriving for higher level of proficiency. Most software is currently built for this type of person: The process participant received the training on the software, approaches it over time in his daily work life and is quite happy about it. This type of process participant is the "routine worker."

Some of these routine worker will not be satisfied with accepting a mere passive role. Instead, they constantly think about how to improve the process and get more efficient on it. We want to motivate a new approach towards software creation in which this type of process participant is embraced. This new type of software constantly learns with the process participant.

In this new approach, we do not stop looking at how a process participant as a singular person can achieve higher levels of excellence in his daily work, but look at how a group of people who are assigned to a specific joint type of task can collaboratively achieve higher levels of productivity, quality and proficiency on this task. This group of people understands themselves as taking part in an ongoing journey of constant learning. They organize the passing of knowledge in through mentoring. In this new culture, the relationship between a mentor and a mentee is not strictly hierarchical: A mentee is welcome to contribute based on his common sense to the continuing improvement of the process. Ideas for process improvement are constantly tried out individually of each process participant.

By measuring or by assessing process performance, the best ideas that proved most successful are retrieved by business analysts and baked into "canonical" solutions that benefit all process participants. This bears some resemblance to biological organisms that have the capability to adapt to different environmental circumstances by specializing their appearance and processes and to spread that by inheritance. It also bears resemblance to the century-old method of knowledge transfer that has been proven to be very successful: discipleship or mentoring. Thus, we motivate software that helps the organization as a holistic organism, a system, a knowledge-creating factory in order to learn constantly and improve—with less centralized control. Still, a business analyst department has its place in such a culture as a competence center and guiding entity.

5. WHAT IS "LIVING KNOWLEDGE"?

Adaptive case management helps to solve cases in an adaptive—and not prescribed way. Living knowledge applies the same principle to knowledge transfer. Instead of creating and maintaining knowledge centrally in a business department and then impose it on passive operational units, knowledge is captured where it occurs and adapts while being passed. Tom Debevoise describes this in his blog: "knowledge and the creation of new knowledge" in all its domains and forms are the critical success factors in all modern firms. Knowledge needs to be identified, defined, and incorporated into the decisions that create and maintain agile enterprise structures". (Debevoise, 2010)

To supplement the capture of knowledge in automated forms such as rule engines, BPMN engines or ACM engines, we advocate adaptive mentoring as a means to permanently adapt knowledge while passing it on. This is the essence of living knowledge. This is the key to sustain knowledge work on a higher level within organizations. In other words, cooperative learning by doing is enabled with this pattern.

6. PRESCRIBED PROCESS KNOWLEDGE BAKED INTO SOFTWARE IS STALE KNOWLEDGE

To better understand living knowledge, let's have a look at its opponent, "stale knowledge," as often found in standard software and current "Classical BPM" projects. Here, knowledge is centralized in Business Departments, baked into rigid process and flow models and passed on to process participants who are forced into a rigid corset, leaving no room for creativity and ad hoc process improvement.

The user currently is then forced into a prescribed flow of micro steps that dictate every action, thus making him a passive and externally controlled process participant. This communication style resembles the way how computers like to interact, not humans. They open their task list and are confronted with the same tasks "enter customer data", approve credit", each popping up the same flow of screens every day a hundred times and tomorrow again. They start to feel like a machine. This is fine for them if they do not reflect on their work.

This kind of process design resembles the Taylor-style assembly line; all process instances are structurally identical, can be easily measured and centrally improved - just like the classical factory.

The impacts and drawbacks of this approach can be observed throughout our daily experience:

- Process participants cannot react on corner cases, if they are not baked into the predefined process.
- Process participants feel alienated and helplessly at the mercy of extrinsic forces - control lies in the centralized business department
- Process improvement can not be triggered from the workers in the field but must be achieved solely from the business department in their ivory tower

Still, process beginners will embrace this prescribed flow; routine workers tend to "live with it," while an intelligent and proactive person, who is forced again and again into that same flow of screens and process steps, will soon experience alienation that is associated with a Tayloristic style of work design.

7. USE CASE:

Welcome back Leona—Developer, Constant Learner, Constant Sharer

The use case we have chosen is a similar use case as in (Swenson, et al., 2010) with the key protagonist Leona, the engineer.

Leona is an engineer whose responsibility sometimes is to resolve critical tickets based on customer bug reports. She uses ACM to create templates that allow for tracking the tickets and for constant process improvement for development and testing. However, she feels like a bottleneck and suffers from her workload becoming unbearable; she is the only person who knows how to test a critical component and she finds herself testing into late evenings and weekends. So, she decides to start sharing her knowledge in order to enable her peers to participate in the same task. Also, she hopes for a positive effect on her work-life balance.

Thus, she leaves behind her status of being the sole owner of this secret knowledge, opens the door to her experience for her peer, Steve, and thus forms a team that collaboratively learns on how to improve their telephone solution and meet demanding project goals.

8. THE FIRST STEP TOWARDS LIVING KNOWLEDGE:

Learning by Doing

The tool Leona uses for "learning by doing" is case templates. This has already been described in (Swenson, et al., 2010).

In adaptive case management case instances emerge as they are necessary. This means the knowledge worker can start the work without any templates: Just with the empty ACM system. A knowledge worker enters the first case, just as the working day requires from them. If they want, they can work in that way forever adding case by case. It also has been shown in (Swenson, Kraft, Palmer, & al., 2011) how the timeline can be managed by defining sprints and assigning work to these sprints, and how the performance can be managed by using the burndown diagram. So this is not repeated here.

The problem ticket is created with account details and contact information in the ACM system.

At the beginning with a plain vanilla ACM project, each case looks different than all the others. As work becomes repeated, the individual knowledge worker identifies snippets of cases that he might want to convert into a personal template and reuse. Then, and this is at the core of living knowledge, these personal templates become commoditized, so they can be used by others in the same role.

9. THE SECOND STEP TOWARDS LIVING KNOWLEDGE:

Baking process knowledge into templates

At a certain stage Leona has created a lot of cases and respective templates to solve specific customer problems. Now she finds that some parts of these cases are similar with other cases. Leona finds that the remote software checks are repeated in many cases, because they have proven to be useful. This is the identification of best practices.

Now, a first step towards process improvement is to create a template for these tests, including attachments and links for detailed test instructions. These test instructions are initially simple; some scanned paper notes, because the template is only for Leona. Still it helps her to remember the exact steps that have to be performed when executing the tests. The template has become her process memory.

So from now on, the work for Leona becomes even easier.

10. THE THIRD STEP TOWARDS LIVING KNOWLEDGE:

Sharing knowledge through Mentoring

Of course, it is possible to maintain responsibility within a case for workitems, and, in this phase, Leona holds herself responsible for these tests. She doubts that anybody else has enough knowledge to perform these tests apart from her.

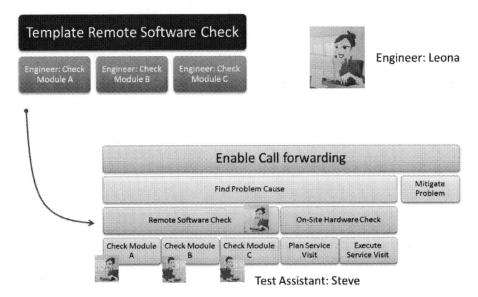

Figure 1 Leona delegates work to Steve

Over time Leona thinks that it makes sense to include Steve in the work—so Steve can relieve some work from her. Steve is her colleague. He does not know as much as Leona, because he is relatively new in the area. But Leona thinks: "If I describe the test steps better, then Steve can do these". So Leona creates some documentation about the test steps and attaches the documentation to the first case, where Steve helps her. She assigns two tests, namely Test Module B and Test Module C to him, because she thinks these tests are easy enough for him to do. The has a meeting with Steve, explains a little bit about the tests, and she tells him, that there is documentation, that she has written attached to the case workitems for the respective tests.

After maintaining the case responsibilities in the ACM software, she uses the "Send To" action of the case; that informs Steve about the case by an email and gives him the link to find the right place and a reminder.

Steve performs these tests, when he has questions he asks Leona, and finally succeeds. Steve has learned something and Leona has somebody else who can help her. From now on, Leona is not the bottleneck any more for Test of Module B and Test of Module C.

11. THE FOURTH STEP TOWARDS LIVING KNOWLEDGE:

Sharing knowledge through a process template repository and assigning tasks to logical roles

"This is great." she thinks. Why not change the template, so that in future Steve or any other Test Assistant can support me in doing these tests, and I can reuse this as a best-practice baked into the software? Said and done—Leona changes the case template in the template library, so that now the responsible role for Test Module B and Test Module C is the role of "Test Assistant"—after she has defined the new role of "Test Assistant" in the workstream. Of course, the roles are shared within the same workstream as well as the knowledge workers. This has already been described in (Swenson, et al., 2010). It is also possible to invite new knowledge workers to the workstream by email and after he has joined to assign to him one or many roles.

As long a Steve is the only test assistant he will be selected, if the template is used in the case, otherwise responsibility determination is done to find the right person.

It is a natural pattern of knowledge work that the assignment of roles and responsibilities to tasks is not fixed once and for all time: This type of constant change is a good sign of a healthy development of an organization. The same applies to the creation of new roles that did not exist before.

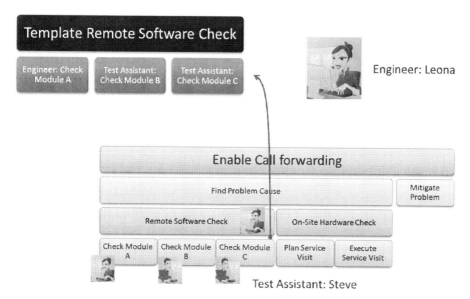

Figure 2 Steve becomes better: Role "Test Assistant" in the Template

12. THE FIFTH STEP TOWARDS LIVING KNOWLEDGE:

Acknowledge the mentees' autonomy

It is important to recognize that autonomy is a key attribute of knowledge work. That is also true in the mentoring relationship. Yes, the mentee is not as autonomous as the mentor, but step by step—of course—the mentee also has to learn to become more autonomous.

In our example, Steve, the test assistant, has his own idea as of how to perform the test he is asked to do. In certain case instances, he decides that it does not make sense to test module B—after he has done it many times without success—but instead—it makes sense to test Module D instead. He—as a responsible knowledge worker—decides this and updates his assigned case.

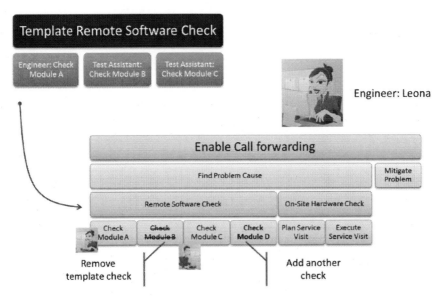

Figure 3 Steve uses his autonomy to decide independently

13. THE SIXTH STEP TOWARDS LIVING KNOWLEDGE:

Review and Consolidate distributed knowledge

Leona does not know about the variations, because she trusts Steve that he performs the needed checks in the area of responsibility that she has delegated to him. So after some time the actual cases deviate from the template.

However, Leona wants to check if Steve does do the work as he should have done it after some time—just as a kind of review. For that, she wants to know all cases where the template has been used and if it has been used in the way it was defined or not.

So Leona can use the "where-used" list of the Template and thus identify all the places, where the template for the checks has been used. ACM helps her to identify where the template had been used as they were (1:1) and where the case has a deviation from the template and how the deviation looks like (difference function). Thus, she can compare the original plan with the actual executions and check, if she is fine with it or not.

A compare function of the ACM system shows Leona which parts of the case deviate from the original template and a statistic function shows how many cases used the same template and how many deviated, also how the deviations were distributed based on quantity (for example, 80 percent add Check D while 20 percent remove Check B). This is very important, because it shows the main path to success—the statistics shows the real best practices. This is a simple kind of process mining, but not in the "fully automated" way as many propose. Of course, fully automated process mining techniques sound interesting, but, in our scenario, it is more feasible to use natural knowledge and discretion of the knowledge worker instead of artificial intelligence or arbitrary algorithms. This is in agreement with the philosophy of the knowledge worker as an autonomous worker, who decides what to do and when based on her goals and within the area of her constraints.

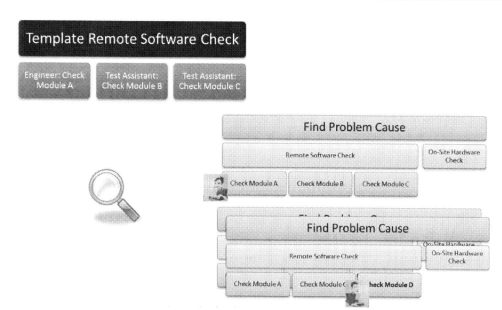

Figure 4 Where-used list of template

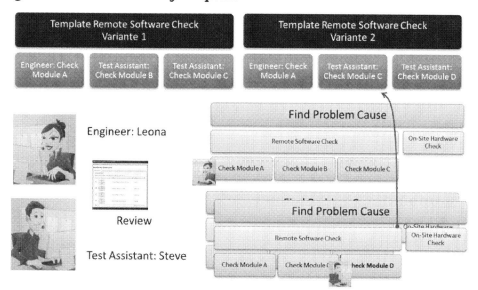

Figure 5 Consolidation of cases to templates

After comparing the case deviations with the templates, Leona can discuss with Steve: "What were the reasons for the deviations?" They might also discuss whether to change the template or not. Doing this, they have different options. One option is to change the original template completely, so that only Steve's new way of doing it is contained. Another option is to create a template variant containing the new way of doing it, while keeping the old template. Another possibility is to change the original template in a way so that it contains both variations and leaving it to Steve to choose which of these he needs in the certain case.

If variant 1 and variant 2 are created in a way that each variant has individual checks, then it is possible after case creation to choose the right template variant. This might be a manual selection or—an important requirement that has been put on ACM many times—selection of the template variant depends on the case type—i.e. on some attributes of the case. For example, if it is a service case or a quality assurance case of engineering or production of the telephone system, then one attribute of the case will be the product—the product number or the product group. The product group may also be a hierarchy, which is defined in the product catalogue system and is imported into the ACM system by means of a user defined case field and value list for the field This makes sure that the application business semantics can be used to choose the right case template. Depending on the product or the product group automatically the right case variant is chosen and thus the right number, and type of check is chosen, that fit to that product or product group.

14. LIVING KNOWLEDGE ON THE TASK LEVEL

We discussed already that we take different personalities of process participants into account. The majority of them has no interest in taking part of or claim responsibility for constant process improvement, but are happy to execute whatever the screen in front asks from them. For this type of process, participants, and for beginners in general, the approach based on predefined screens and flows is perfectly feasible - if we tolerate the potentially low quality of customer service involved: "You did not react on my personal requests".

We could start our design based on screens in the defined way as the default templates for the case. Following the guidelines described in the knowledge worker case study we then add features for more ambitious process participants that allow them to customize, improve and change their templates. A good way to do that is to enable the user to reassemble the fine grained screens on a broader portal as they wish. The result could be a more complex screen that consists of finer grained screens. The flow controller could still make sure to have all relevant data gathered before the customer submits a use case and the data are sent to an appropriate transactional SOA Service.

Additionally the user gets the option to provide feedback for his task in terms of missing functionality or in terms of suggestions for improvement. Examples are:

- Fields that are currently only presented in read mode and the user feels that a write option would make him more productive
- The user needs to copy/paste certain data again and again between different applications and he suggests to auto populate that field.
- The user has come across a variance that is not yet supported by the system and he needed to find workarounds.

We can use the template approach discussed in the previous case story in order to make feedback part of the living knowledge of our organization. Then it becomes not only visible at the business department, but also with other peers in the same role. We can use social media technology to create vivid discussions on certain improvements.

Based on this approach the process participants become parts of a peer group and mentor/ mentee relationship can emerge. The mentor is just a bit more experienced, explains the characteristics of templates and uses the beginner template to start the thought process. Regularly he interacts with the mentee to reflect the learning curve and apply more advanced templates.

We see how this work environment has very different characteristics from the factory kind of routine work.

It allows different ways of interaction styles with the customer or client. Management can begin to think about innovative ways to improve customer satisfaction for challenging tasks. Complex and demanding tasks can be assigned to more experienced agents who use their knowledge to react on more complicated and challenging requests, while more basic tasks are assigned to rather beginner or routine type of process participants.

15. ESTABLISHING SHARED LIVING KNOWLEDGE THROUGH GOVERNANCE

In our knowledge worker case study, consolidation of process improvements takes place while Leona and Steve are meeting and talking about it. In this case, no governance process is necessary. It is not always feasible or practical to meet over the topic. Thus, it is better to include a collaboration function that allows for governance. Consolidation is now an autonomous action of one knowledge worker, and the other knowledge worker merely approves or rejects the changes. In our example, Steve might want to consolidate the changes of cases to the template library, and Leona approves or rejects these changes. Or—the other way around—Leona takes the opportunity to consolidate the changes in the cases to the template library—and Steve is the one to approve or reject.

How is this done? Simply by automatically creating a review case whenever a change to the template library is released. The case consists of two (in other examples many) approval items—one for Leona and one for Steve.

Using this kind of governance is also a kind of mentoring tool. Why? If Leona repeatedly rejects the changes that Steve makes to the template library, Steve might want to ask himself, what he is doing wrong—or better ask Leona. Then he will have the possibility to learn more about the subject, and he feels urged to learn this. At the same time, it is a tool for Leona to give Steve some autonomy, but still be in control of the overall result and thus making sure, that the quality is assured. She identifies learning needs of Steve and thus can teach him what he needs to know.

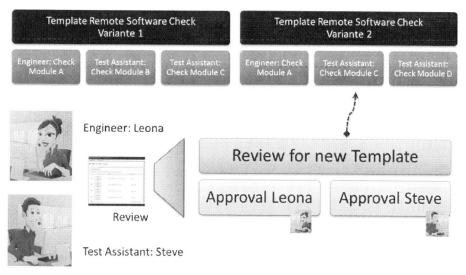

Figure 6 Review case for creating a new template

16. IMPACT OF THE PROPOSED MENTORING APPROACH FOR THE ORGANIZATION

The new style can have a large impact on the success of the organization as a whole. This new organization can excel in customer satisfaction and thorough better quality of work. The question is a broad one: Do we aim for cheap or for quality.

Given we understand the human nature in the described ways, how can we achieve a cultural shift towards collaborative learning, establishing living knowledge that is shared among team members?

Management has a huge impact. Its hierarchies need to be assessed. A classical mechanical management style that is based on a superior boss who micromanages his "underlings" is not supportive for the living knowledge culture. Instead, we need to establish a management style that is based on the mentor/mentee relationship. Then formal power is losing impact while new factual hierarchies emerge through trust in the specific competences of certain team members. Managers begin to think on how they can enable team members in any way in order to excel on each of their jobs.

Each knowledge worker then is encouraged to leave his status as sole owner of knowledge and tools and start forming a team of like-minded peers who collaboratively work on establishing a shared understanding of best practices for an important task and documenting that knowledge.

If we look at the organization that evolves from a systemic point of view, we will be able to observe that work changes to be shaped and done not any more by mavericks or loners who work as isolated cells but by small organisms, a "compound of cells". The chemistry between the participants of such a composite team is pretty interesting and needs to be managed in order to bring the synergetic results aimed for in our new mentoring culture. This type of work organization is requiring team members who are self aware and mature enough to understand the greater goal in order to give up constant self celebration. He still can be rewarded: A major suggestion for improvement in a process template can be associated with its founder and can be advertised as such, generating a culture of competitiveness that is in line with the greater goal of establishing living knowledge.

This new mentoring culture will draw attention from co-workers and management, ideally forming a new momentum that creates a nucleus of attraction. It allows to experiment and experience a new approach that deploys time-proven patterns of success.

17. SUMMARY

Applying ACM principles and tools in a new approach towards mentoring is the key strategic pattern of knowledge work to ensure that living knowledge is distributed across the organization as it emerges, and as it is required.

18. REFERENCES

Debevoise, Tom (2010, November 7) "*Business Agility and a Meta-Knowledge Framework*", blog post at www.tomdebevoise.com, as cited in Fish, Alan

Fish, Alan (2011, December). *Knowledge Automation: How to implement decision management.* Wiley.

Hamel, G. (2011, December). First, Let's Fire All the Managers. *Harvard Business Review* .

Rock, D. (2009). *Your Brain at Work: Strategies for Overcoming Distraction, Regaining Focus, and Working Smarter All Day Long.* HarperBusiness.

Swenson, K. D., Jacob P. Ukelson, J. T., Khoyi, D., Kraft, F. M., McCauley, D., Palmer, N., et al. (2010). *Mastering the Unpredictable.* Tampa, FL, USA: Meghan-Kiffer Press.

Swenson, K. D., Kraft, F. M., Palmer, N., & al., e. (2011). *Taming the Unpredictable.* Lighthouse Point Florida : Future Strategies Inc.

Managing Structured and Unstructured Processes Under the Same Umbrella

Alberto Manuel, Process Sphere, Portugal

1. INTRODUCTION

In the last couple of years, the hot debate has been between two distinct, or more precisely, two conflicting management disciplines. The rise of social interaction is putting pressure on companies to embrace a more empowered style, which means less command-and-control and more dynamic execution.

There is a growing view that enterprises need to shift from the highly-coupled, structured execution, which is becoming considered as old-fashioned. In this structured or "Tayloristic" approach, managers still believe there is only one best way, an optimized way, to execute. Our view is that this approach will not drive the company towards achieving proper results.

Today, we find that the virtual obsession with invoking Peter Drucker's principles can lead managers to feel that they are using an outdated management approach. If we reflect on the fact that Drucker has been teaching this since the 60s, isn't it strange that we are only now applying his management discipline more widely? However, what we do about the routine tasks? Ignore them? Or are we living in a world where unpredictability has become our new standard? Having said that, have we, or haven't we, always lived with exceptions and unpredictable events?

2. THE STRATEGIC ENVIRONMENT FACTORS THAT CHANGED THE WAY WE WORK

Knowledge management, as used today, could not have been implemented in previous decades. Basically, two factors in the modern corporate environment have created new possibilities: the Technology factor and the Social factor.

These changes toward the networked enterprise were sparked by globalization in the early 90s. Globalization, in turn, was triggered by government policies that abolished trade barriers and introduced liberalization in industry sectors. These two inner forces: free trade and liberalization increased information flows between companies. Financial institutions, particularly, were interested in information systems that could promote the acceleration required by stock markets and derivatives.

The Technology factor

As communication costs drop and speeds increase, cost will no longer be a consideration in many parts of the world. Lowered communication costs will radically alter the way business is executed and, combined with different software licensing models, do away with high upfront costs.

As the cost of communication drops, the shift will be towards applications. Combined with increased computer capacity and speed, this will allow users to engage with, and have access to, information in real time. The cloud will free organizations from fixed, and limited, availability and processing power. The way we are used to working will change dramatically.

The Social factor

In leading GDP countries, we face the displacement of "assembly line" people in favor of aspiring workers. Work can be transferred elsewhere for less than half of the cost paid locally. This shift occurs in industry sectors from manufacturing to services. But, in the near future, small tasks will be fully automated and unfortunately, those brave new workers will be obliterated, unless new work opportunities arise, perhaps for more complex work. People will have to push their capabilities to new boundaries. This shift also has a profound implication on the type of people that companies will source in the labor market. As major companies expand and operations are outsourced or transferred to low-wage economies, the future worker profile will be aimed at highly-skilled persons capable of embracing business dynamics.

These factors define the approach that most companies will embrace in the future. Drucker said that, in the future, there will be no developed or underdeveloped countries just educated or under-educated countries [1]. However, raising skills and education levels are only a part of the picture. If countries do not have the companies and business infrastructure to employ these highly-skilled people, they will not develop. We see this already in some countries with a high proportion of highly-skilled workers who cannot find employment.

3. BPM EVOLUTION OVER THE PAST 30 YEARS

The confusion over BPM is due to the many differing views and ideas on management philosophy. Many concepts have appeared in the market, with various different ways to improve a business process. Like an organization that changes and adapts, BPM has evolved and merged with very different disciplines; this is the reason BPM has the capacity to adapt to changing environmental conditions.

Companies that embrace a BPM journey typically start out trying to see the organization as the whole, in other words, the overall enterprise architecture which includes at a minimum:
- The organizational structure, the functions and the roles;
- The business context, what we do, what we sell, with whom we interact;
- The business processes, what we execute and how we execute.

Companies with whom I have worked for the past five years of continuous commitment to BPM keep going a step further each year. Some started out by improving their core business processes and are now moving to different process types. Others defined a clear picture of what they do but cannot control the process effectively and are putting effort into performance measurement on the customer side to see if results are achieved. What can bring BPM discredit is, for example, when a company designs its business process and uses BPM only as a communication tool. This disappoints customers because the process is not capable of changing or adapting to customers' needs and wants. People's commitment, business alignment, and governance are important to BPM.

The problem resides in people not wanting to make change happen. That is the reason for failure. That is not a problem with BPM. It is a problem of human nature. It happens with every change management initiative.

Not every process is from a single type

Today we read in diverse corporate reports about the necessity of adopting Web 2.0 approaches if organizations want to be successful in the enterprise world. Just to name a few: mobile web, the Internet of Things, net-connected objects, big data, cloud, social apps, whatever. Because we live in a continuous-exception mode, we can argue that in this hyper-connected world, these are the tools every company must adopt quickly; better yet if they can adopt them all. However, this argument falls apart if all these tools aren't aligned with the nature of what the company does.

The argument that we are currently living in a continuous-exception mode and we therefore need tools to support how we handle the exceptions also falls apart simply because there is a social tool that has been available for a while: email. I would say that exceptions are an inevitable part of the operation of all types of enterprise. They have always existed and recording began with the use of our email clients.

Fortunately, the two driving forces that transformed the way companies work explain what is behind all the transformation effort. These forces are those presented at the beginning of this chapter: the drop in communication costs, bandwidth increase and ubiquity have transformed the way we access information, backed by the emergence of information systems that automate routine tasks. These factors have led to organizations dispensing with people who perform repetitive tasks. Thus, as the workforce gets smaller, the trend is to attract the highest skilled talent; this is our 'knowledge worker' about whom we hear so much. These combined changes open up the possibility of thinking about executing information-centric, unstructured work. These are the forces that drove the changes. If these two combined forces had not reconciled with the past and current trends of globalization within the corporate environment, maybe we would still be in the workflow era.

Certainly, companies are moving towards becoming more networked organizations and will need to organize work around critical tasks rather than molding it to constraints imposed by corporate structures. Nevertheless, this does not mean that the company of the future will execute only unstructured work, actually it is highly improbable that routine tasks like "approve an invoice payment higher than a given amount," will disappear.

Process definition as we know it needs to be updated, because it has to include the possibility that the activities performed can be structured, unstructured or both.

4.   PROCESS EXECUTION NEEDS TO ADAPT TO INSTANCE MODE

Let us look at a real-world example of the challenges companies need to address. Airport management is one of the most dynamic business environments in existence because there is no common set of rules across the different continents. This means, for example, that if your luggage is lost or damaged, in some countries it is the handler's responsibility but in others, it is the airline's responsibility. Smart airlines have long understood that it is better to handle the lost and damaged luggage service directly with the customer, while settling behind the scenes with the responsible party. With this in mind, let us analyze a process that handles lost and broken luggage.

An angry passenger tweets, or posts on the airline's Facebook page, about damaged luggage which sparks the process. The airline invokes the damaged luggage process, and together with the handler, offers the customer new luggage to be picked up at a local store.

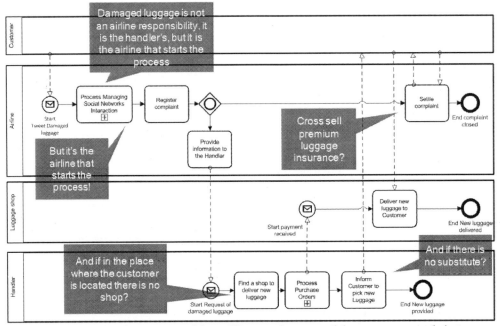

Figure 1: An instance of handling a damaged luggage complaint

This can be a valid process scenario, but next time it is possible to have a different scenario. Imagine, for example, that the customer wants a specific luggage brand or model that is not available and the airline allows the passenger to buy a new one in a favorite store and be reimbursed latter. Hence, there is no point in trying to model all the possibilities because in examples like these it cannot be done. Thus, the point is to provide a way for the enterprise worker to define in real time the activities he wants to perform, without the company losing the capacity to manage what is happening and measuring the KPIs. In this example we can see in the last steps that the process is blended with a "classic" structured by-the-book process: "Purchase Orders." This is particularly what I what to stress: there never was this kind of division of the types of work that are done. What is different is the way we do it. Thus BPM is still capable of handling both process disciplines and helping companies to tackle even more complex business problems.

5. THE CORE OF BLENDED PROCESSES EXECUTION

One of the most cited and perceived benefits of BPM is the breaking down of functional silos, and the increased ease of information flow. The main shift can be characterized as the move from central bureaucracies to the horizontal corporation and that implies that the shift extends to the way processes are connected. When I started to design processes in the early 90s, I remember that process touch points were static. Imagine, for example, a utilities company. Typically, there are two highly-coupled processes: meter reading (measuring your energy consumption) and billing. The end of the meter reading process sparked the billing process. All business processes were designed under this principle. I do not mean that every process end was linked with other process start - actually the middle of a process could prompt the start of another - but the links were static. Today this is not the reality anymore. Interaction dynamics and increased information flow, baked by social technologies and new working habits are having a profound impact on processes as they are being executed. Today it is possible in the middle of a customer interaction about an order, for the customer to request information about an invoice and also to make a support request. The customer expects the same person to be able to deal with all the requests at the same time. This means that multiple process instances are being executed and information must jump from instance to instance to bring context awareness to the next process participant.

For the reasons already stated concerning the changes that are occurring in the way we communicate and work, companies cannot continue to implement an internal operational approach that will not be able to cope with the dynamics of the business environment.

In this sense, it is necessary that companies adopt an enterprise architecture based on the following principles:

- The customer is commanding the business processes and interactions. The company has to adapt in real time to the path that the customer intends to follow.
- There must be alignment between the business strategy, objectives and process vision, supported by technology that allows processes to adapt to real time execution in which processes, business rules and informational entities are embedded and supported by a business ontology[1] that provides meaning to the information that is being accessed.
- Work will be more efficient when it is able to adapt higher-level instructions to their specific application and when it can incorporate feedback into the enterprise. The balance between knowledge work and automation is set to automate all standard processes and to reserve human potential for adaptation and feedback loops.
- Attract the highest skilled talent. The combined shifts opened up the possibility of thinking about executing information-centric, unstructured work. If an enterprise provides the same tools and the same goals to be achieved, there will probably still be differences in performance. The differences come from the way people work and communicate together. A manager needs to understand what is wrong regarding how people are engaged and make adjustments. Business Intelligence will tell you nothing about how people are connected, it simply shows you if things are right or wrong, how many requests were handled and how many are compliant with the SLA[2], because it's not social-oriented.

A claims management process blended with a compensation process

Let us look at another real-world example.

In this scenario, a customer from a telecom company suffers a service disruption and complains about it. The contract sets up a penalty clause and as such the customer wants to receive compensation.

All the work is done with two guiding outcomes in mind:
- Ensure the customer is eligible for compensation;
- Avoid customer churn.

This is important in order that people do not handle the complaint as if it were business as usual.

---

[1] A business ontology consists of: process ontology: identifies all the artifacts that describe a process; domain ontology: defines the company sphere and represents what the company does; organizational ontology: identifies who participates in the work executed and how people are connected through the work and responsibilities assigned to them [2].

[2] SLA – Service Level Agreement

The complaint management process starts with the complaint being recorded and the customer manager obtaining the facts related to the disruption that occurred.

The first two phases are very dynamic and it is not necessary to have any predefined structure, they are completed when a decision is made about compensation eligibility.

Under this approach, the customer manager does not act alone, making an investigation based on point-to-point information exchanges with technical peers.

From the start, he or she involves other colleagues that might help to find a solution. In this kind of approach, there is no predefined path, no task sequence.

Some of the tasks could be:

- Get advice from the legal department in order to evaluate compensation eligibility;
- Analyze with the operations manager if disruption occurred, what was the cause, begin corrective action to prevent the issue reoccurring and improve the knowledge base to better handle these kind of issues.

All the work is carried out by sharing informational entities (documents, emails, service desk records) between people (including the customer, if necessary).

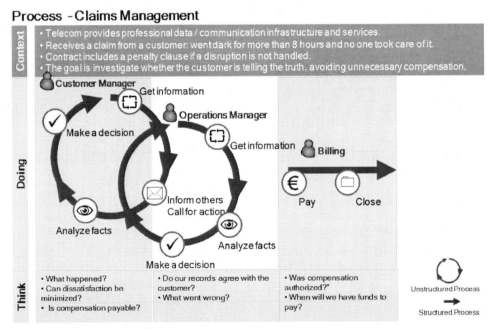

Figure 2: A blended process from claims management to customer compensation

In the end, when the customer manager makes the decision to indemnify the customer, that sparks the compensation process, executed by billing, a typical structured process that ends with a money transfer. To avoid a process silo problem, all relevant information is shared between the customer, manager and billing, hence, the last does not need to go back and read again the contract clauses or make a decision. Billing is in context and just needs to be paid according to business rules and funds availability.

Two important conclusions must be highlighted:

- The scope of the complaint management process does not end with the compensation decision. It ends when the money reaches the customer account. This changes the way we must think and execute processes. This is the truly end-to-end approach. If we concentrate on delivering state of the art complaint management and leave out the compensation process, the enterprise will suffer from a process silo, like any other "classic" functional silo, meaning that if the compensation is not properly handled then ultimately there is a risk of increasing the bad customer experience and losing the customer.
- Under this approach, processes are automatically sparked and discovered at any point of execution. They are linked so as to invoke them in real time as opposed to a classic highly-coupled design, used specifically for a particular purpose that does not cope with today's enterprise dynamics.

6. THE ALIGNMENT FACTOR:

Process types, knowledge types and social network configuration

Managers need to know how the organization can support their workforce and co-evolve with a rapidly changing, uncertain and highly complex world.

Managers need to focus on human activity, because organizations depend on people despite the fact that technology will continue to accelerate new execution possibilities. Technology is headed towards increasing cognitive capabilities, but managers need to understand and provide the right way for people to collaborate according to shifts in multiple knowledge domains regarding the goals and the type of work that must be performed. Thus, it is critical to understand how each individual can better sense, interpret, understand and execute in their complex environment. This means discovering new ways of observing, interpreting and understanding information and co-evolving with the dynamics that are appearing and growing across the business environment.

We often hear that to be successful, companies need to empower employees. Success stories include Cisco and Google, where people work in project teams, make the business case and the opportunity, and are responsible for leading projects to introduce new products and services. I tend to agree with this approach in companies such as those, where each new service/product entails a great deal of research and development, results-people are naturally matrix organized. But if your company's value chain is built on a structured process, for example, accounts receivable or purchase orders, and you let people make decisions by themselves, you will experience a high performance variation (as people deviate from the optimized practice). On the other hand, if, as a manager you put in place a pyramid organizational model, where experiment and intense social connection is needed and each step and decision must be approved by someone, you tend to lose agility and time-to-market. Hence, it is critical to understand the alignment between the process type that is executed and ensuring that knowledge flows properly; and that people are organized to support these two dimensions (process and knowledge type).

Knowledge domains

Below we can look at an approach to categorize the various existing knowledge domains. I concur with the criticism that it does not show the dynamics of knowledge shifts when people are working. Because it is out of the scope of this article to understand how knowledge flow can be identified, let us use this approach particularly to understand the importance of aligning process execution, knowledge domains, and social networks.

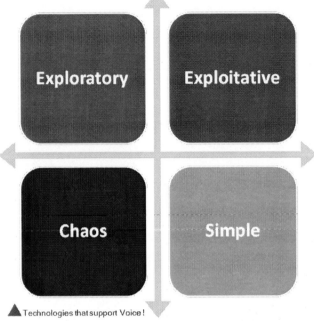

Figure 3 : Knowledge domains

Let us start with the easiest quadrant to understand, Chaos:

- **Chaos domain**: is related to crisis/emergency management. Here, voice is key to coordinating others. It's a sequence of acting first, measure the outcome and acting again until the situation is controlled. When control is achieved[3] it is typical to return to normal operation.
- **Simple domain**: is the knowledge domain that reflects the structured, by-the-book process types. This is the area with a strong correlation between actions and outcome. For example, every time we approve an invoice payment, the money leaves the bank account and it's done the same way, every time.
- **Exploitative domain**: here there is still a relationship between actions and outcome, meaning people know what needs to be done, but they don't know from the start how they are going to achieve the outcome; there is no predefined process (as opposed to the simple domain). In this domain, people use their previous work experience and choose the way that feels best to achieve the predefined outcome. Sometimes they use one approach, at other times they can use a different one. For example, the first two cycles of the complaint management process analyzed in the previous section.
- **Exploratory domain**: here we enter an area where the only thing a person knows is the outcome they want to achieve, but they do not have a predefined approach and need to think and set up a way to do it. Hence typically, actions carried out and the outcome achieved are occurring for the first (and possibly the only) time. Actions are dynamic/fuzzy and

---

[3] See reference [3]

adapted to the circumstances (this can also occur under the exploitative domain but here it occurs with a higher frequency). This is where complexity plays a role. Adaptation occurs in response to feedback loops, and decisions are made according to people's expertise and experience. This is where new alternatives are explored to reach an outcome. Some will turn out to be patterns (solutions) that can be reused in the exploitative domain; others will transform to best practices and can be automated in a predefined manner under the simple knowledge domain.

Social networks

When we look at an organization as a whole, we identify a multitude of flows that are sequences of interaction between physically disjointed positions held by people; process participants play roles that belong to particular social networks. Dominant social structures are those patterns within organizations whose internal logic plays a strategic role in shaping social practices.

Hence, it is important to align the network structure (not your organizational structure that dictates formal authority) to the process type being executed; to evolve and adapt the network type according to the knowledge being played. Let us look at the network types.

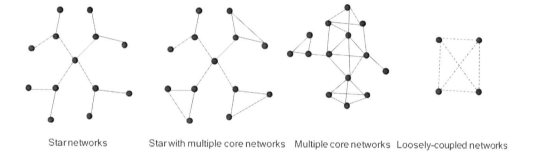

Star networks   Star with multiple core networks   Multiple core networks Loosely-coupled networks

Figure 4 : Network pattern types

- **Star networks:** Characterized by being strongly central and weakly distributed. These kinds of networks are typical of structured processes. People do the same activity one after the other and the same result is achieved in every process instance. This is the simple knowledge domain where concepts are poured into documents, flowcharts and policies (explicit knowledge), where people need to perform by the book.
- **Star with multiple core networks:** Characterized by being strongly central and strongly distributed. Here, someone is responsible for orchestrating others who have their own links in order to achieve an outcome. Feedback is shared, but it is "sent to the network star". Relationships are maintained by authority as in star networks, but communication between other members is maintained and it is improved if peripheral members maintain a close connection, thus these network types must be applied under exploitative knowledge domains.
- **Multiple core networks:** Characterized by being weakly central and strongly distributed. As the process progresses, resources join the quest to find a solution to achieve the outcome. Feedback is shared, but is not centralized. These networks are formed based on tacit knowledge and

trust. Trust is important, because the others believe team members will deliver independent of the circumstances that change in run time mode. This kind of networks can be useful in exploratory knowledge domains.

- **Loosely-coupled networks:** Characterized by being weakly central and weakly distributed. You can find this kind of network in emergency scenarios or under the chaos knowledge domain.

Technology (remember this as one of the factors that changed the way we work) can again disrupt how people are organized, but it is necessary that managers ensure alignment regarding the different process types that shape the knowledge flow and ultimately the network configuration structure. Without this alignment it will be very difficult to execute properly and achieve company objectives. Social networks constitute a company's human capital that is needed to use as leverage to perform and differentiate from the competition. For example, star networks by definition are often negatively related to poor performance, but only if they are deployed into exploratory knowledge domains. In simple knowledge domains they offer the right combination.

Putting it all together

Revisiting again the complaint management process with an end-to-end perspective, the process now starts in incident management, when the disruption that affects the customer is detected. This also implies a change in the mindset in the way the enterprise handles complaints. It is the company that starts the complaint and informs the customer that it is going to find a solution, rather than waiting until the customer perceives that the service level has deteriorated and starts complaining about it. The process ends with compensation payment if it is appropriate.

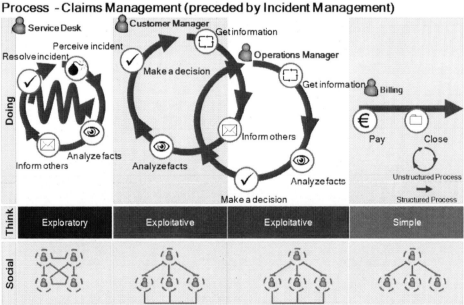

Figure 5: A truly end-to-end process with knowledge types aligned with social networks

The first phase, incident management, applies exploratory knowledge to fix the disruption if there is no clue to a predefined solution. After service has been resumed, the solution is stored in a knowledge base for reference. If in the future the very same solution is again applied, the knowledge type will change to the simple domain, which will have an implication for the way in which it is implemented (it will change to a structured approach) and how people work together (command-and-control style, with someone taking charge and orienting people how to do it, based on past experience).

These shifts in the applied knowledge style, reflect how people apply their knowledge in terms of identifying what they need to achieve and how to use their reasoning. If you do not know how to solve a problem, ideas are generated within a team that has to be connected in a particular network configuration (multiple core) to include people who have the knowledge and experience to solve the problem that must be addressed, as well as letting the ideas flow without a centralizing anchor.

The process type determines the knowledge applied to the situation and also how people relate (socialize) and work together. Technology acts as a facilitator that lets a person make the execution change dynamically as needed, connecting as necessary the different process types.

7. CONCLUSIONS

Much has been said about the capabilities of BPM as a management philosophy capable of keeping pace with constant change and the evolution in working habits, to a point it may not be properly supporting knowledge-oriented work. The problem is not with the BPM framework because it has evolved over time, adding new and revised extensions and methods to handle enterprise change. However, this requires substantial effort, commitment and vision from top management in order to provide a much more dynamic, adaptable and meaningful approach to handling change in the enterprise.

Business processes are not executed in a single flavor anymore; much more is needed to handle current enterprise complexity. Technology is continuously allowing us to do things differently and to achieve higher outcomes, but a lack of understanding about the dynamics between the actions that must be performed, the knowledge to be applied and how people need to work together will not drive the expected outcomes.

8. REFERENCES

[1] (Peter F. Drucker, 1995) Managing in a Time of Great Change, Butterworth-Heinemann Ltd, ISBN-13: 978-0750623926

[2] (Alberto Manuel, 2012) Semantic BPM – epilogue:
http://ultrabpm.wordpress.com/2012/01/17/semantic-bpm-epilogue/

[3] (Bryan Seaman, Gloria Mark, 2012) Technology-mediated social arrangements to resolve breakdowns in infrastructure during ongoing disruption. ACM Transactions on Computer-Human Interaction (TOCHI), forthcoming.

[3] (John P Scott, 2000) Social Network Analysis: A Handbook, Sage Publications Ltd, ISBN-13: 978-0761963394

[4] (Ikujiro Nonaka, 1994): A dynamic theory of organizational knowledge creation. Organizational science, 5 pages 14-37

[5] (James G. March, 1991): Exploration and exploitation in organizational learning. Organization Science, 2, 71-87

[6] (Michael Polanyi, 1966): The tacit dimension. New York Doubleday, ISBN-13: 978-0385069885

Natural Language Processing, BPM and ACM in Healthcare: Memoir of a Radio Interview

Charles Webster, MD

I watched my clock. They watched theirs. The "bottom of the hour" (that's radio industry terminology) approached. I headed into an interview about natural language processing (NLP), business process management (BPM), and adaptive case management (ACM) in healthcare. I'd never given an interview on radio before, even if it *was* Internet radio. I was nervous.

I called in fifteen minutes early. The show's producer told me what to expect and put me at ease. She said, several times, that when the show ended, that was that: simply hang up the phone. (Me: "What? No congratulations? No aural high-fives?") Five minutes before the show the British-accented interviewer rang up and we plotted course. He put me at ease. They were good at that, thank you!

It was great fun. So much so, I decided this memoir was in order. Why memoir? Well, it's not a transcript. It's how I remember it. And it's selective. Section headings correspond to questions from the interviewer or turns in our conversation.

After a bit of conversation about my glut of academic adventures (accounting, industrial engineering, artificial intelligence, medicine, *and* computational linguistics) we started in on the meat of it.

1. WHAT'S THIS ABOUT CLINICAL LANGUAGE UNDERSTANDING AND WORKFLOW?

While I was Chief Medical Informatics Officer at an electronic health record (EHR) vendor, we offered optional third-party speech recognition products to customers. I'm familiar with advantages of speech recognition for EHR data entry. Adding speech recognition can increase EHR usability because it's often more natural to talk-talk-talk than to click-click-click. "Naturalness" is an important usability principle that I'll discuss later.

But there are lots of other interesting connections between natural language processing and workflow technology. Firstly, EHR activities can be performed in various ways: typing, clicking, speaking etc. You have a sequence of tasks, there's your workflow. Speech recognition and natural language processing need to be incorporated into this workflow.

Furthermore, many speech recognition and natural language processing systems are themselves, workflow management systems. IBM's Watson, an NLP system that famously won on the Jeopardy quiz show and is being adapted for clinical use, relies on a workflow system to manage NLP activities. An NLP "pipeline" turns free text into structured database data or answers to questions (in Jeopardy's case, questions to answers).

This is similarly true for the Interactive Voice Response (IVR) systems used for customer service. IVRs have "call flow" definitions, controlling dialogue workflow between customers and automated customer support. So, in some ways, speech recognition and NLP software are ahead of the Health IT community adopting what academics call process-aware information systems. I'm also beginning to see references to speech recognition and natural language processing in business process management and adaptive case management discussions. Cloud-based speech recognition is being integrated with process-aware mobile apps. NLP even generates workflow diagrams.

2.   WHAT'S THE RELATIONSHIP BETWEEN EHR USABILITY AND EHR WORKFLOW?

My interest in usability and workflow dates to graduate studies in Industrial Engineering. I spent one year studying aviation human factors and one year studying workflow and production systems. Those were the research assistant positions available at the time.

Usability and workflow have many interesting connections to each other. In fact, the most important usability issues bedeviling EHRs today are workflow related. I even have a blog about this called EHR Workflow Management Systems, plus the Twitter account @EHRworkflow.

It seems obvious to me, as an industrial engineer, that many EHR usability problems are really workflow issues. If lousy workflow can delay widespread adoption of EHRs, perhaps workflow technology can help increase adoption and meaningful use of EHRs. I've been saying essentially this for over a decade in a variety of venues. Not until recently have I seen such a promising uptick in interest in this angle, from designers, developers, vendors, academicians, and government agencies, even users!

Process-aware information systems—workflow management systems, BPM suites, and adaptive case management systems—are great! You can mix and match and tweak and improve and optimize workflow to improve usability without having to go back the C# or Java programmer. BPM-style and ACM-style tools in the hands of users, or at least super users and clinical analysts, allows folks who know their workflows best to mold their digital tool space to their liking, without expensive programmers.

For example, I know of two pediatricians from the same small hometown, who went to the same medical school and then returned to practice across the way from each other, in that same hometown. One of the pediatricians installed and then customized an EHR. The other pediatrician took a look, liked what he saw, and installed the same EHR. He wasn't happy. He wanted what he saw in his friend's office. We took the first pediatrician's database (with permission) and its heavily customized picklists (lists of symptoms, treatments, and so on), reports, and workflows; deleted patient data, and reinstalled it in the second pediatrician's office.

You'd expect the second pediatrician to be happy. The first pediatrician had already done all the hard work of customizing the EHR. Well, no. The two offices had completely different workflows. This had not been apparent when the second pediatrician looked at the first pediatrician's EHR screens. He liked the picklists and reports, but didn't and couldn't see the workflows. Turns out the first pediatrician intended his physician assistant and nurse to do as much as possible and then for him to check to make sure everything he wanted to be done was in fact done. The second pediatrician wanted to do everything himself. So the second pediatrician still had a lot of workflow customization to perform.

The healthcare IT and EHR market is micro-fragmented. Most of the difference between systems is what tasks are performed, in what order, and who does them. Not only are "happy paths" different, also different are how, when and why users jump off happy paths and when and how to get back on. (A "happy path" is what's supposed to happen, if nothing unexpected happens, when you use a software application.)

3. WHAT'S YOUR ADVICE FOR PHYSICIANS SHOPPING FOR AN EHR?

You're familiar with the real estate saying: "Location. Location. Location!"? Well: "Avoid frozen EHR workflow," "Avoid frozen EHR workflow" and "Avoid frozen EHR workflow."

One of my most popular blog entries is "Litmus Test for Frozen EHR Workflow." You walk up to the vendor booth where they are doing demos, or the demo is over the web, or they've come to your office. Obviously, try to step in and chart a patient yourself. That's fine advice, frequently given. But here's the difference. In most EHRs there are a sequence of screen (or voice) interactions. Whether the sales guy charts the patient or you chart the patient, fine. After the demo say, "I want to change the workflow. Show me the workflow editor."

Workflow editors, allowing non-programmers to edit application workflow behavior, have been around for many years in other industries. They are an essential part of many workflow management systems. These workflow editors are similar to Visio, a popular desktop diagramming application. Sometimes they're simpler checklist-like templates or picklists (to use a popular term in healthcare IT). Change screen order. Change events triggering screens. Change who does what to whom when and why. Users, or at least non-programmers close to real-world workflows, make the decisions, reducing expense, delay, and bugs. Healthcare is substantially behind other industries in use of workflow editors. We're just starting to see them.

By the way, I do not propose EHR users compose EHR workflows from scratch. Even with a visual programming language, which is, essentially, what these visual workflows are, creating a workflow system is complicated. However, if the process definitions are already there, I've seen EHR users up to the challenge of tweaking a workflow: adding, deleting or changing order of steps, or perhaps customizing a step itself (changing a data or order entry form). Most are up to doing this with the help of an appropriately trained clinical workflow analyst. Doing so dramatically decreases the time required to modify EHR or HIT workflow.

Let's get back to my litmus test for frozen EHR workflow. Ask the sales person doing the demo to change something about the workflow—drop a screen, add a screen, switch screen order—whatever! Now you say, "Do the demo again" or "Let me chart a patient again." You should see that EHR change its behavior in exactly the way that would be predicted if a workflow editor actually edited the workflow definition being executed by a workflow engine.

Some EHR vendors say they customize workflow by customizing of data and order-entry templates and picklists. Lots of things are customizable about EHRs. EHRs are, on the whole, more customizable than many other software applications, such as word processors. But, while editing the contents of a picklist or a template may "affect" (influence) workflow, it does not "effect" (determine, bring about, drive) workflow.

Ask yourself, "Who or what appears to be the workflow engine?" If the EHR user manual has hundreds of pages of instructions about user workflow in which the user is instructed on long sequences of clicks or voice commands, then the human user is, effectively, the EHR workflow engine. In contrast, if there's a chapter on workflow instructing how to create a workflow that will execute automatically, in the right context, then the computer is the workflow engine. Many of the usability problems physicians complain about relate to large number of clicks or voice commands required to push a patient encounter from beginning to end. In contrast, a competent EHR workflow system should push tasks to the right people and minimize their effort to perform them. One pediatrician, a great fan of business process management in his medical practice, calls former EHRs "hunt-and-peck" and the latter, "anticipatory" EHRs. Yes, it's hard to believe a solo primary care physician would wax lyrically about BPM. I've got the video interview on my blog to prove it!

4. "AVOID FROZEN EHR WORKFLOW": OK. WHAT ELSE?

I am a fan of five EHR workflow usability principles:

- *Naturalness*—is there a natural fit between EHR workflow and task workflow?
- *Consistency*—do similar activities have similar workflows?
- *Relevance*—does the EHR *not* show you too much data or too many options?
- *Support*—can you see, at a glance, all pending tasks and related information?
- *Flexibility*—can you fix unnatural, inconsistent, irrelevant, unsupportive workflow?

I'll quote from my 2004 MedInfo short paper here. I didn't actually read from it during the radio interview (this is a memoir, not a transcript, I get to add stuff). I might have done so if I'd had it before me. Lucky for listeners I did not!

"EHR workflow management systems are more usable than EHRs without workflow management capability. Consider these usability principles: naturalness, consistency, relevance, supportiveness, and flexibility. EHR WfMSs more naturally match the task structure of a physician's office through execution of workflow definitions. They more consistently reinforce user expectations. Over time this leads to highly automated and interleaved team behavior. On a screen-by-screen basis, users encounter more relevant data and order entry options. An EHR WfMS tracks pending tasks–which patients are waiting where, how long, for what, and who is responsible–and this data can be used to support a continually updated shared mental model among users. Finally, to the degree to which an EHR WfMS is not natural, consistent, relevant, and supportive, the underlying flexibility of the WfMS can be used to mold workflow system behavior until it becomes natural, consistent, relevant, and supportive."

Let's deal with these five workflow usability principles one by one. In each case we'll nod toward cognitive science, but not drive into weedy details.

Naturalness

"Naturalness" is one of the hardest to define usability qualities. It involves conformance, or fit, of a tool to the human, whether it is a glove, favorite shoe, smartphone or EHR. Cognitive science approaches to naturalness range from affordances (handles on coffee cups) to similarity between problems (such as creating accounting statements) and representations (spreadsheets). That discussion quickly becomes arcane. The best judge, of whether an EHR's workflow feels natural, is how it feels to you. At each step of charting a patient, for example, the next thing you need to do should be obvious to you. Of the five workflow usability principles naturalness is perhaps the most subjective. It may also be the most important.

Consistency

From screen-to-screen, are data and order-entry widgets, what and where you'd expect based on prior interactions with the EHR? Consistent screens, voice interactions, and workflows exploit what cognitive psychologists call positive learning transfer.

Does what you learn on one screen, or in one workflow, help you deal more accurately and speedily with other screens and workflows? I am reminded of my Accountancy and Finance courses, where we learned about amortization of cost over multiple time periods. Each interaction is costly, in effort, time, and mistakes. Whatever you learn from one interaction that benefits you on other interactions reduces the total cost of using the EHR.

Support

I'm not talking about calling technical support here. I'm talking about cognitive support. You've got a set of tasks waiting for you. Patient A ("belonging" to physician B) has been waiting ten minutes in Exam Room C for task D usually performed by staff E. Can you look and see those tasks? Can you see their state? What's waiting for whom and for how long? For routine activities, such as all those 30-seconds to diagnosis simple earaches and prescribe standard antibiotics, workflow rules help move things along (automatically print educational materials, send e-prescriptions to preferred pharmacies, etc.).

For less routine, more complicated cases it's impossible to predict workflow in advance ("I've never seen this before: What should I read? Who should I call?"). Adaptive case management systems don't have rules controlling what gets done when and by whom. They say: "These are the goals that need to be done" and "This one is 50 percent done and that one's been completed and the other one has been languishing." That's support in a cognitive sense. Ideally, EHRs should combine aspects of both structured BPM and unstructured case management.

Relevance

Relevance means the EHR doesn't provide *too* much information or too many options. I first encountered "relevance" as a formal cognitive science notion in a book called Relevance (1986, MIT Press) by Sperber and Wilson. A reviewer described is as "one of the most important and influential books of the decade." The Principle of Relevance is this (concentrate now!): "any utterance addressed to someone automatically conveys the presumption of its own optimal relevance."

Of what possible, ahem, relevance could this have to EHR workflow and usability? Well, if an EHR shows a screen to a user, the user is not unreasonable to assume that it's relevant to some task relevant to a goal. The goal might be taking care of an acutely sick child, conducting a camp physical, or perhaps, in one of many visits, tuning asthma meds. One way to make EHRs and HIT systems more relevant, on a screen-by-screen basis, is to use workflow definitions. Who, what, why, when, and where context information can drive which screens, data, and order entry options are pushed to which users. That's the BPM. And if a user cancels, postpones, or forwards a task, that's the ACM. (I know. It's more complicated. But, hey, it was a radio interview!)

Flexibility

Business process management suites and adaptive case management systems are nothing if not flexible, compared to non-process-aware information systems. That said, BPM and ACM vendors frequently debate how to characterize flexibility and whose product is more (or less) flexible. For example, so-called traditional BPM systems are claimed to be flexible in the sense that processes are flexibly designed before execution. In adaptive case management systems, processes are more ad-hoc, flexibly directed and redirected during process execution. "Doing-by-design" versus "design-by-doing" captures the flavor of this debate. In any case, BPM and ACM systems have way more flexible workflows than most EHR and HIT systems. The importance? What if an EHR or HIT system is not natural, consistent, supportive and relevant? Then it needs to be flexible enough to allow users to create natural, consistent, supportive and relevant workflow. In other words, "Avoid frozen EHR workflow!"

Can Healthcare Really Have Both Consistent and Flexible Information Systems?

That does seem contradictory, doesn't it? Healthcare processes need to be both consistent and flexible. Back in 2004 I also wrote:

"Evident throughout this article is a tension between straightforward, predictable, repetitive, high volume episodes of patient care versus more complex, less predictable, one-of-kind episodes, each of which is unique and therefore infrequent, but all of which taken together constitute a significant and important part of the ecology of health care. Traditional workflow management systems excel at what has been called 'straight through processing' (STP) in the banking and finance industries. For example, an order to sell shares in a publicly traded stock should ideally happen in a very short interval (that is, before the stock price changes materially). STP seeks to eliminate the human element that slows down stock trades, to only rely on humans for handling exceptional circumstances, and to reduce exceptional circumstances to an absolute minimum (if not altogether!). However, in health care exceptions happen all the time. Medical care is exception rich because abnormal states are, in effect, normally encountered occurrences."

"Healthcare processes, and especially core patient-driven processes, are rife with exceptions—from the appointment no-show to the abnormal laboratory value to the undeniably unique history of present illness. And yet, these are in a way predictable and therefore categories and rules and workflows can be defined to facilitate execution of core clinical and administrative processes. Workflow management in health care, especially in and around the EHR, will be workflow with healthcare characteristics. While this may seem obvious, it also means that workflow management systems technology and concepts borrowed from other industries must necessarily be considerably adapted to become successful components of the next generation of electronic health records."

Yes. I used to write like that!

Many EHR screens are pixel-perfect. Designers spend time making sure buttons and widgets look great and are positioned just right. They look like jewels. These screens are usually hard-coded in a programming language such as C# or Java.

In contrast, business process management systems use rules, not C# or Java code, to define workflow behavior. These rules make BPM and ACM-based EHRs and HIT systems potentially much more flexible than less process-aware EHRs and HIT systems around today. That said; I do see more-and-more of this technology. Just Google "workflow engine" and "EHR."

Physicians complain about having to hew to what their EHR vendor thinks their workflows should be. It ought to be up to users (or at least someone who knows their workflows) to decide how consistent or flexible they'd like their software to be. Workflow technology opens up the possibility of physicians owning their own workflows. They can make everyone's workflow the same. They can also allow different physicians to have different preferred workflow.

There's a stereotype of workflow systems turning users into cogs, with humans doing what machines cannot, instead of machines doing what humans prefer not. That said, defining and executing workflows is one way to influence user behavior, to get folks to do their work the way *that* medical practice or *that* hospital intends it be done. Instead of making it impossible for users to depart from intended workflows, the best approach is to make it as easy as possible for users to do their work intended ways, ideally ways that have been vetted and discussed and agreed upon by relevant personnel.

Consistency and flexibility are in natural contradictory tension. At one extreme is a physician, working with lots of physician assistants and nurses and staff, who'd like to make sure everyone does it his or her way. In organizational management-speak, customizable workflows enable greater span-of-control than otherwise possible. At the other extreme, multiple physicians can work together and each have their own workflow. Tension between consistency and flexibility is reduced by using rules and process definitions that non-programming users can understand. They, not their vendor, find the best compromise.

Any Other Interesting BPM Developments of Relevance to Healthcare?

Yes! Business process management, adaptive case management, "big data," process mining, cloud, mobile, and social media (naming just a few) are coming together in fascinating ways that will greatly benefit healthcare information management.

Oops! So Sorry! It Looks Like We're About to Run Out of Time!

The radio interviewer: "It looks like we are just about at the top of the hour. Maybe we can invite you back to speak about those interesting topics some other time! That was Dr. Chuck Webster on language, workflow and usability. We've got about thirty seconds or so, any final thoughts?"

I thanked the kind radio interviewer profusely, for allowing me to temporarily share his bully pulpit. And to act so opinionated about these subjects near and dear to my heart! Music welled up. I speeded up. Not sure if anyone heard my last couple words. The same deep-voiced announcer who announced this, now completed, segment, announced the next show, about the meaningful use of EHRs. I looked at my phone for a few seconds. I imagined I heard Peggy Lee singing, plaintively, "Is That All There Is?" and hung up.

Click!

5. Epilogue

Radio is an oral medium, with no possibility for diagrams or illustrations. You do the best you can with word pictures. In fact, I found the conversation, about complicated technical topics, energizing. When you're writing, staring at a blank page (or, more accurately, an empty word-processing document), it's easy to get stuck. Procrastination, writer's block, whatever you want to call it, prevents thoughts from flowing. But when you're on the radio, you can't afford more than a moment or two of dead air.

In numerous venues, on- and off-line, I've argued for combining EHR and BPM technology for years. During this time both the EHR and BPM industries changed dramatically. Computer-based patient records became electronic medical records and, under influence of Federal funding, electronic health records. Workflow management systems became business process management systems and now there's adaptive case management systems too (part of, or not part of, BPM, in current debate). And then there is natural language processing, a linguistic wild card, sure to further shuffle the deck.

Today BPM trends from structured processes toward unstructured knowledge work, but HIT trends from structured data toward unstructured free text. Who knows what will happen? Anything! Exciting! I do have some opinions. But I'm afraid I'm out of space! Right up against that ol' 4,000 word limit. Maybe I'll be invited back to write another chapter or two. I'd like that. In the meantime, I'm looking forward to wonderful developments between two great industries: health information technology and business process management.

Click!

Case Management Megatrends

Nathaniel Palmer, SRA International, Inc. USA
Workflow Management Coalition

1. INTRODUCTION

During election years, there are certain predictable promises presented as new ideas, but they somehow always remain just out of reach. The same might be said of "empowering knowledge workers" which has been the goal of many new technologies for nearly two decades, since Drucker famously pushed this as management's charge for the 21st century[1].

Yet for all the advances seen in the explosive growth of IT over the last 20 years, are knowledge workers today truly more empowered or productive? Have we seen the compression of time spent in decision-making and other "knowledge work" in any way comparable to that seen with the automation of manual work? On the whole, the answer is no. The benefits offered by the vast increases of available information have largely been offset by the concurrent growth of "infoglut"—we simply have more information than we know what to do with. Yet there are promising exceptions that are already demonstrating how Drucker's call for knowledge worker productivity can be realized through an emerging set of technologies focused on enabling adaptability.

This chapter explores the role and interplay of case management within today's most critical emerging information management "megatrends," notably mobile computing, cloud, big data, social technology, as well as the 'appification' or consumerization of IT. While individually these might further contribute to infoglut or information overload, combined with Adaptive Case Management (ACM), they complement a framework for bridging the gap between strategy and execution.

2. THE FIRST TRUE IT REVOLUTION IN 40 YEARS

Since its inception, IT has been defined by the pursuit of data management. Forty years ago, the relational database model was introduced as the most profound and long-lasting evolutionary event in IT design. Arguably all advances since that fundamental shift, even the emergence of Internet architecture, have remained at their essence derivative of the relational database. From monolithic packaged applications, to more lightweight and agile development, all have continued their dependence on this model.

Yet IT as we know it today is amid an inflection point. We are exiting the *Relational Database Era*, in favor of a post-relational model, one that could rightly be called the *"Big Data Era."* Examining the history of "big data," a term that has become omnipresent recently, and like all buzzwords is easily misapplied and misunderstood, it is worth noting that it is not, in fact, completely new. In fact, the core models underlying big data are not unlike the way databases were designed in the pre-relational era. Yet as one of the key shifts in IT architecture it is introducing profound change across virtually all aspects of data management, including our very relationship to information. The move to the relational database model came with a compromise. In order to increase the speed by which data could be retrieved, Ted

---

[1] *"The most important contribution management needs to make in the 21st century is similarly to increase the productivity of knowledge work and the knowledge worker."* Page 116, Drucker, Peter F., Management Challenges for the 21st Century (New York: Harper Business, 1999)

Codd[2] developed applied the concept of relational algebra to data models, so data could be structured in two-dimensional structures and ultimately more easily queried. Yet it is easy to argue (and often was) that this was not the best alternative at the time. The way in which data exists within the relational model has rarely made sense to human beings, and led to a growing schism between "structured" and "unstructured" information. The latter represents the vast majority of information in the world, and is most reflective of how human beings think and communicate. Thus, it is easy to see how the explosive growth of the relational database over the last few decades has done little to boost knowledge worker productivity. In many cases, it has done little more than to relegate knowledge workers to the ranks of disgruntled data-entry clerks.

What if we could manage and use information in a way more consistent with the way it exists in the natural world? Where linkage between pieces of information is reflective of natural relationships, rather than limited to arbitrarily defined relational structures?

This is precisely what is behind the emerging "big data" standards and initiatives, such as Hadoop and NoSQL, which are essentially flat file document databases reminiscent of the hierarchal database model. Although "NoSQL" might sound like it means 'anti-SQL' but it actually stands for "Not Only SQL," and much of it is based on that original hierarchy-type functionality. The critical difference between simply managing data in the older, flat-file file approaches and modern big data is the leverage of semantic meaning of data. Semantics involves discovering the implied as well as the surface meaning—capturing both the explicit meaning of specific pieces of data, as well as metadata or descriptive data which defines the relationship between data itself. In this way, big data transcends the two-dimensional relational structure, by allowing layers of semantic meaning beyond the literal, discrete data values.

3.   MANAGEMENT BY BASEBALL

My 7-year-old son is a member of the big data generation. Like many of his age, he recently developed an interest in baseball and a growing love of the game as a fan. So for his birthday I bought him his first set of baseball cards. As I explained to him about the numbers ("stats") on the backs of the cards and what each represents, he began to understand the basic notion of ratings and even grasped the notion of "parametric data." Whether the term itself holds any meaning, he certainly gets the concept, that in baseball, there is never simply one number that makes a player number one, but rather there are multiple dimensions to the statistics. We can't simply add up these numbers and derive any real meaningful knowledge about a player's likely performance.

Player stats are a holdover of the relational era—they're simply raw averages without context. No manager or team owner uses baseball cards to make decisions about who to trade or who to start. Rather, for the last decade the management decisions around baseball players have leveraged an emergent big data approach called Sabermetrics[3]. Using a very rich set of performance data, Sabermetrics involves examining the interrelationships and the patterns of many different data

[2] Edgar Frank "Ted" Codd was an English computer scientist who, while working for IBM, invented the relational model for database management, the theoretical basis for relational databases.

[3] Sabermetrics is the analysis of baseball through objective evidence, such as statistics that measure in-game activity. The term comes from "SABR" or "Society for American Baseball Research." It was coined by Bill James of the Boston Red Sox, who is also a prominent baseball writer, historian, and statistician.

points, allowing meaning to be inferred and informed decisions to be made. Sabermetrics is big data; the numbers you see on baseball cards is relational data. Thus baseball, while otherwise unchanged in many aspects of century-old traditions, nonetheless offers a real-world example of transformation in the Big Data Era. There is, in fact, a fascinating book called *Management by Baseball*[4], which discusses how the science of Sabermetrics can be applied to many different business scenarios and knowledge worker decision-making.

4. BIG DATA AND CASE MANAGEMENT

One of the reasons underlying big data's increasing popularity is the issue of accessibility. Huge volumes of data are now available in a digitized format, in ways never before accessible. Yet the importance of this approach is not simply the size of the data set, it's the management of data in a way that is actionable. Rather than creating monolithic, integrated data structures, it involves applying semantics and metadata to derive an understanding of the meaning of the data and the interrelationships within it.

This reflects a shift from the transactional view of the world, where "data-centric" means completing a predefined data set (i.e., filling out a form or completing a transaction) to an event-driven model where data informs the process. In the relational world, workflow commonly revolves around completing known sets of data. An order form, for example, will have a predefined set of data needed to be captured, and once done the work is complete. Yet how does this enable me to find the next otherwise unidentified customer? Or to innovate a new product design? It doesn't. It is merely about completing the transaction. Achieving those things is the realm of big data.

The majority of the knowledge worker's day is spent not in completing transactions, but in managing or otherwise responding to complex business events—finding customers, designing products, negotiating contracts, and developing strategies. Each of these has a lifecycle defined in terms of milestones and key stages, and at stage is represented by context defined through various layers of information, largely based on historic event data.

The Sabermetrics analogy applies here as well. Sabermetrics uses the analysis of historic player performance data to make real-time or forward-looking decisions. The fact is that a decision needs to be made, or even the sequence of decisions that can be predictable. Yet each decision itself cannot be automated because it is highly dependent upon the outcome and context of the previous decision. Thus rather than being explicitly modeled out and automated, these knowledge-driven processes are in fact complex business events rather than discrete workflows.

Whether or not it is explicitly identified as such, and whether or not the identified sets of data used are deemed "big," this business event lifecycle is ultimately being driven by big data, as discussed in this chapter. Multiple points of input are correlated against (run against) business rules, policies, computer inference, and from this, dashboards and reports of the results are provided to enable human inference and human decision-making, allowing action to be taken or captured, to which further information is applied informing the next step to take.

Thus, the "process" is not a hard-wired workflow per se, but a template for guiding actions and decision-making through a host of input run against a set of rules and sub-tasks defined within the system.

---

[4] See *Management by Baseball: The Official Rules for Winning Management in Any Field* by Jeff Angus, HarperCollins 2006.

5.   MANAGING OUTCOMES RATHER THAN JUST MANAGING DATA

The longstanding and not largely-outmoded notion of "case management" is based on a folder metaphor. An electronic folder or "case" is opened and information is stored in (and retrieved from) the case until eventually the case is closed. This is still the model in use within many organizations, and there are many products on the market today that offer little beyond this level of functionality.

In this way, previously generations of case management systems are simply an overlay to file management systems. In contrast, adaptive case management involves pulling in streams of information, including both structured information (such as data, file documents, images, etc.) and unstructured information (such as context and comments, time stamps, and information that goes to the audit log) in order to drive outcomes—managing the lifecycle of a business event to the achievement of a specific goal.

Just as a specific transaction—i.e., Sales Order—defined the specific process that is to be followed, it is the goal that defines the case. For example, a customer contacts a manufacturer about a problem with a particular product; the goal is to resolve that specific problem. The starting point from the case is defined by the goal—solving the problem. The exact sequence of steps that follow cannot be entirely pre-determined. Certainly some steps or subprocesses can be, for example the process involved in requesting a refund. Yet exactly when that subprocess is invoked and what will be the entire lifecycle of the business event cannot be predetermined. This will be based on a set of rules and policies, surrounding information, and the application of judgment, which collectively define the case.

The role of big data is to provide as complete a picture of the problem as possible. Having a "360 degree view of the customer" is an expression of big data—offering the ability to see as much about the customer as possible to help drive the decisions which will ultimately satisfy their issue. Much of that information will come from sources outside of internal, transactional databases.

As the ability to manage and infer meaning from big data grows, so does the ability to provide a more precise or helpful solution to the problem. One of the first advances is in what we've commonly called "Predictive Analytics." Think Sabermetrics and the ability to predict *what might happen next* based on analyzing patterns of historic event data. With Adaptive Case Management, however, we are seeing the move toward "Prescriptive Analytics" where data is applied to business rules and policies to help inform *what to do next* at a particular stage in the case.

This is where the notion of "adaptive" comes in. With respect to the labels of "dynamic case management" or "adaptive case management" what you call docs not really matter nearly as much as the ability to facilitation adaptability by situational guidance.

This is a key distinction; ACM it is not simply a matter of supporting ad hoc work, but specifically functions in the delivering of guidance to users in real-time to help identify the next action to take, and presenting "guard rails" to steer users away from erroneous decisions. Information captured at a given point may identify new information required or additional steps to take based on rules are applied to the case.

6.   WE'RE ALL IN THE CLOUD NOW

Modern case management requires the ability to capture and organize information from a variety of sources, typically those residing both inside and outside of corporate firewalls. This often means capturing business context and accessing information from outside of organizational boundaries, such as at a customer site or otherwise while on the road. By providing a secure channel to business data and remotes means for content capture, case management can be a key leverage point for enabling the cloud to function in a business environment.

The notion of the cloud is relatively new. It now tops the list of CIO priorities, and it's at the top of many business priorities too—usually from the perspective of reducing operating expenses, notably by consolidating redundant data centers.

For small businesses, this is less likely to be a hot issue. But for large concerns and government agencies, often the biggest IT cost today is simply keeping the lights on at the data centers. Thus the siren song of immediate cost savings through hardware virtualization and data centers consolidation has dominated many "cloud" discussions, with security risk and lack of local control representing the counter argument. Yet the "OPEX" focus and consolidation equation works only once, and after you consolidate offers no basis for either value creation or cost reduction.

Having more fluid access to the infrastructure—and having a more agile infrastructure, in general—is becoming increasingly necessary. Indeed it's happening fast and is becoming a defining characteristic of IT transformation. How this is achieved, however, is a larger issue than the data center and multi-tenant hosts. We all live in the cloud today because the cloud is all around us—we increasingly rely on public networks and open source information and other dimensions of "the cloud" in the broader sense of meaning. While the manner in which we build systems is going to change dramatically, that discussion is still largely one of infrastructure. The biggest impact the cloud is on our relationship to information and the way we work; allowing us to pull resources from a whole host of areas that were previously unknown or unavailable.

The cloud as we know it is no longer simply a data center running on a virtualized layer (if indeed it ever was). The reality of the cloud includes access to resources from just about anywhere. But how do we manage these resources, and how do we make the access process manageable?

This is where we are seeing the de-materialization of work. The reality of mobile access and social behavior on systems—incorporating social capabilities in addition to specific external social networks like LinkedIn and Twitter—is having a very real material impact on our business.

"Bring your own device" has become the norm for virtually every organization today. The genie is out of the bottle and now it is a matter of how central IT is going to keep up, rather than whether or not they will grant access to mobile device. Had it simply been a matter of cell phones, it may not have been an issue, but one product came along and changed everything—iPad.

Today there are multiple brands and product of mobile devices to choose from, but there's no question that the inflection point of mobile computing came as result of the iPad, leading to more maverick IT purchases than any other product, and completely resetting user expectations. Three years ago the concept of mobile computing was largely limited to the remote field force and sales roles. Today it is executives of all stripes demanding "Why can't I access this on my iPad?" or otherwise bribing their favorite IT geek to set that up for them.

Consumerization has changed and raised expectations faster than IT's ability to keep pace. An increasing number of organizations today have reached an inflexion point where they are no longer the sole provider (and thus "gatekeeper") but rather the shepherd of IT resources. This is the point at which case management becomes a critical element for tying everything together; it provides a degree of consistency across this fluid and, in many cases, maverick access.

7. THE HALF-LIFE OF BUSINESS EVENTS

The most revolutionary leverage point offered by case management with regard to social, mobile, and cloud computing is not simply the fact that now "I can do it at home" nor is it the fact that the work-life demarcation has changed forever (and, perhaps just as importantly, the work-life balance)—yet all these are indeed true. But from the perspective of business value, the greatest leverage point for case management in the context of mobile, social, and cloud computing comes from faster response and resolution of business events.

This is based on the fact that all business events have an implicit half-life—the value represented by the response to an event diminishes over time. Yet of course this based on a utility curve, not a straight-line. Responding twice as fast is more than twice as valuable. The faster the response, the greater the value realized.

Consider the utility curve around any business event to understand why this is so critical. There are hard metrics to this axis because it's going to depend on the specific organization, but what we do know is that every organization has a utility curve. The value of business events is not linear. The faster we are able to respond to it, the greater the ultimate value of acting on and resolving that event.

The ideal point at which to act is in the early stages, where the utility curve is the steepest. So, having the ability to capture an event, to capture data in the field and respond to it at that moment in time instead of having to wait until you return to your office has enormous value. Too often there are still policies in place that effectively require an employee to capture the data in the field, but wait until he or she returns to the office before that event data is actionable and can be managed. The result is a huge loss in value. The greatest value from mobile is derived when we tighten this loop and respond faster.

8. SOCIAL-TAGGING BUSINESS EVENT DATA

The most revolutionary concept introduced by Facebook wasn't that could now post your own embarrassing personal information (something already available in a host of competing networks), it was the introduction of "The Wall" and the ability for friends to "Like" as well as Share and comment about your posts. This same ability has been emulated within a variety of enterprise social tools, as well as LinkedIn and Salesforce.com and why Microsoft bought Yammer.

Whether it is individual users via consumer social networks or businesses via enterprise social tools, underlying this concept is data enrichment through social tagging. It has been said (I believe first by Drucker) that information is the only asset that increases in value through use. Making this practical requires having a feedback loop in place that facilitates the enrichment—the act of adding value through use.

Once again, the operative issue is the notion of the business event lifecycle. Today business computing, specifically the relationship between the knowledge worker and the IT environment, is not sitting in front of a form or a bunch of transaction screens. Of course that is happening, with expense reports or other non-value-creating tasks and activities. Rather "knowledge work" is largely a matter of accessing streams of business events and related information, then applying more context and know-how to them, or otherwise taking action based on what these prescribe. This notion presents the concept of "business event management" which from an IT systems perspective is clearly best represented by modern case management or

ACM. This is not a characteristic of case management in the sense that we understood it ten years ago, or even five years ago. Lacking in those previous generations was the ability to capture and present event data from a variety of sources into a single frame, offering the capability to manage the event throughout its lifecycle, while sharing and enriching the context ("metadata") which defines it.

9. PRIORITIZING INVESTMENT DECISIONS

An underlying question appears to linger for many as to whether modern case management is an outcome of other IT investments (such as in CRM or ECM) or whether it is in fact a separate investment unto itself. To be clear, it is the latter. As much as I want to encourage the practices described herein through any means possible, the fact is that they ultimately require an investment in ACM.

To decompose the decision process, I will step through that made by a recent client experience that involved a large IT investment that was at its core a case management solution. In fact, during a key meeting the client explicitly stated they wanted to support the capability of "dynamic case management."

Yet in this example what the client was actually soliciting (or what they presumed was the case) was something that would have to be delivered through a combination of content management (ECM) and CRM, with a functional requirement for workflow automation. Thus, divining the requirements, as they were written prescribed, was an inevitably brittle mix of ECM, ACM and CRM.

What they really needed was ACM. Working with the client we went through each requirement, developing a granular illustration of how each capability would be realized. As we together evaluated the collection of requirements, for what would be a very representative knowledge worker solution that requires a fair amount of expertise and know-how, emphasizing collaboration and access to the knowledge base, it became clear that while each individual capability could generally be realized through some stand-alone means, collectively there was no single solution that would satisfy the requirements. For example, while integration-centric BPM provides workflow automation, it is not by any means the best solution for ad hoc collaboration.

This seemed to be initially recognized, thus the leap to an integrated kluge of piecemeal parts. Yet the fundamental misunderstanding was that ACM is itself a platform for realizing comprehensive capabilities, not just what might otherwise be deemed "the case management part" but for a complete information lifecycle, as well as business event lifecycle. ACM is (or can be) a system of record, can be a platform for automating workflows, for building and evolving a knowledgebase and customer contact database, for facilitating collaboration.

10. THE FUTURE NOW

ACM is the future for enterprise software. Bold words indeed, but inescapable. ERP is not going anywhere, yet for the vast majority organizations its footprint is frozen. The decision is now whether with ERP, just as with CRM and other packaged applications, you will try to evolve and update them to keep pace with blurring speed at which cloud, mobile, social computing continues to change—and if so—which ones to you update. All of them?

Will you continue to build island of automation or will you seek to simultaneously support truly automated processes, within environments that nevertheless require informed decisions and capture of subject matter expertise?

Sure, we try to do all of this by attempting to cobble together pieces of ECM, CRM and integration-centric BPM, but this would at best be a backward-facing strategy.

The way forward is the generation of ACM that is supporting these dynamic, or adaptive, case patterns by enabling collaborative work, and this is being driven by the cloud, by mobile, and by big data.

One of the few guarantees left concerning the future of IT is that it will continue to change and evolve. A "future-proofed" enterprise IT strategy requires more than simply asking single-purpose questions like "How do we mobile-enable our applications?" *Or* by creating an interfaces tied to a specific access point, such as web app or single device. The reality is that work is already mobile, we're already in the cloud, and consumerization will continue change expectations for how we access and interact with information. Penetration of iPads (or collectively with other tablets) will soon reach the point of saturation where it can longer be ignored, nor can it assumed as the sole means of access.

Whether or not we call it ACM, the need for adaptability, for support of working within multiple platforms, and ability to allow work to follow the worker, rather then relegating knowledge workers to being data entry clerks—these are the immutable challenges of today to deliver on Drucker's charge for the 21st century management, or in the very least to keep up with expectations.

11. MEGATRENDS WRAP-UP: NEXT STEPS FOR BEST RESULTS

ACM represents a compelling platform for making mobile and cloud work for you today and future-proofing your IT investments for tomorrow. Successfully leveraging ACM requires defining the goal-driven processes (or specifically measureable business performance goals) and ensuring that your organization architecture and decision-process supports these.

Beyond the basic ability to make use of ACM, look at information channels you have in place today and how you will leverage them. Ensure you have the ability to manage processes as a business event life cycle, where you're supporting the capture and management of both structured and unstructured information within your environment. The key leverage point for this is standards.

There is no better way to future-proof your strategy than by considering how you're going to take advantage of key standards, like CMIS, XPDL, BPMN, BPAF and others. Central to a future-proof strategy is validating that the assets that you're creating and managing today can be accessible and follow the same evolutionary curve as the systems that you're using to access them.

Understand how you will leverage social technologies for adding value to business events and event data. Many organizations undervalue social tools, but will recognize the value of faster resolution of technical issues or shorter sales cycles.

Finally, look at the state of infrastructure at your firm, where it is being commoditized, and where value can be added through ACM. Server capacity and, in particular storage capacity, is dirt cheap, even though (or despite this) many organizations still place a premium on it by limiting account sizes. Demonstrating the value of ACM will not likely come from virtualization or server consolidation, but can come from its role as a framework for creating, delivering, and managing new capabilities, as well as through accelerating response times and will enable agile, fluid access to information from mobile and remote devices.

Case Management: Contrasting Production vs. Adaptive

Keith D. Swenson
Fujitsu America, Inc., and WfMC

1. INTRODUCTION

While participating in discussions of case management, and while reviewing the submissions to the Adaptive Case Management awards, I see two distinct approaches to case management—one approach called **Adaptive Case Management** (ACM), and a different approach which meets an entirely different need which we should call **Production Case Management** (PCM). This chapter explains the difference, and how these fit into a spectrum of process technologies.

It is important to distinguish these two. If you need ACM, and you acquire PCM you will be very disappointed, and vice-versa. Both are useful in relatively unpredictable situations, but there is one huge distinction that makes all the difference: PCM requires and can benefit from a software developer, while ACM must not. Put another way, PCM must separate the development time from the run time, while ACM must unify these. This may not seem like a big difference, but it affects the very root of what knowledge workers can do, and how they achieve results.

2. PCM IN A NUTSHELL

Production Case Management (PCM) is an approach to supporting knowledge workers. PCM is programmed by technical people (programmers) to produce a case management application. The application is deployed for use by knowledge workers to get their work done. The application offers collections of operations that the knowledge worker can select to use or not use depending on the specific needs of the case.

A PCM application is used when there is a certain amount of unpredictability in the work, and a healthy amount of flexibility is needed, but necessary actions are regular enough, or the volume of work large enough, to make identifying and codifying regular patterns valuable. A worker using PCM will be involved in selecting the actions toward the outcome of a particular case, but will not be responsible for the kinds of actions that might be available.

3. ACM IN A NUTSHELL

Adaptive Case Management (ACM) is an approach to support knowledge workers who need the most flexibility to handle their cases. ACM allows the knowledge workers themselves to create and modify all aspects of a case at any time. There is no distinction between design time and run time: the designing and running are done at the same time by the same people.

This approach is used by knowledge workers who have unique expertise in an area. They don't have a lot of time to transfer this specific knowledge to a programmer, and it is too expensive to hire a programmer for one-off cases. ACM offers a Do-It-Yourself (DIY) approach to process programming. The worker using ACM is responsible not only for the outcome of a case, but also for how the handling of that kind of case improves over time.

4. SEVEN DOMAINS OF PREDICTABILITY

Process technology can be spread across a spectrum to support work with varying degrees of predictability. At one end, you have entirely predictable processes which must be done exactly the same way every time, and that way of doing it will be the same over the course of many years. The other end of the spectrum is complete unpredictability where there is no way to know from moment to moment what will have to be done next.

Predictability and repeatability go hand-in-hand. Any work which is repeated the same way thousands of times, is predictable by definition. Work that is not done the same way every time, that is frequently repeated, is consequently less predictable.

The approach to developing any system will depend on how much change the system will have to respond to over time. Extremely predictable, stable environments can benefit from powerful but inflexible approaches. As the anticipated amount of change rises, it becomes more important to use a technique which offers greater flexibility. More flexible approaches have less precision to match exactly the needs of the situation. The approach depends entirely only on the amount of need to respond to change.

Most job situations lie between the extremes of completely predictable/repeatable and not predictable/repeatable. We can break the field into seven domains according to the technology that might be used to support workers:

1. Traditional Application Programming—If work is very predictable and stable, over time, one can use traditional development techniques (e.g. using any third generation language like Java, VB, PHP, etc.) to create a supporting application. The cost of development might be high, but the benefit of having very precise control of the capabilities, will yield efficiencies that over a large number of cases will pay back the up-front costs.

2. Process-Driven Server Integration (PDSI)—Integration patterns between systems can be quite stable in the short term: months or years. Still, the systems being integrated do change, and business needs change, as well. PDSI usually incorporates a development approach where the key interaction points are depicted on a process diagram is a technique that helps deal with the kinds of change that IT departments experience.

3. Human Process Management (HPM)—Human business processes involving forms routed through a set of people, may also be well-understood routine processes for people in the short term that can be fully designed, but, like PDSI, there are changes in the environment, and having a process diagram as the backbone of this application helps cope with this kind of change. Furthermore, humans have a greater need for flexibility than servers when they are part of a business process. For example, humans change duties much more frequently than servers, and are not identical replaceable units. Thus, HPM has higher requirements for coping with change, and capabilities for addressing this.

4. Production Case Management—PCM is designed to handle situations where there is so much variation between individual cases that it is not possible to set out a single fixed process, and yet there is still a well known set of actions that can be taken. The knowledge worker is actively involved in deciding the course of events for a case, but the range of actions and options is bounded and can be specified in advance.

5. Adaptive Case Management—Cases vary so much that knowledge workers are constantly striving for innovative approaches to meet the needs of new cases. The knowledge worker is involved not only in the case, and picking a predefined action, but is actually helping invent the actions that can be taken. However, there is still enough predictability that a given knowledge worker may want to re-use a process from before, and may want to share and discuss process plans with others.

6. Social Business Software (SBS)—This is collaborative software without a fixed plan. There may be representations of tasks, but they are strictly created on the fly and discarded after use.

7. Email, Telephone, Texting—There is no process at all, no permanent structures, simply communication. This is the default that many current processes are forced to use, but this approach puts the greatest burden on the user, and yields the least amount of analytic data to monitor and improve processes.

It should be immediately apparent that each domain of predictability is distinguished by the amount of investment that must be made up front—the amount of preparation that must be done before you start working. Traditional programming requires a large development project and is useful only once the entire project is completed, and the fully-tested software is installed.

At the other end of the spectrum is email, or phone calls, which need no preparation at all, and can be used immediately without delay. PCM and ACM lie between these extremes; both require a certain amount of upfront investment, but still leaves quite a bit of flexibility to the case manager.

If there is investment up front, then dealing with change means some kind of cycle of improvement. PDSI and HPM have fully defined processes which are regularly updated in what we call the BPM lifecycle. PCM has a less fully-defined process model; the case manager picks from a menu of actions in order to meet the needs of the case. The possible actions are predefined and can change only with the involvement of a developer. ACM takes this a step further by allowing the case manager not only to choose the actions, but to create entirely new actions on the fly as needed. You can think of all of these as having a cycle of improvement that get progressively smaller and faster across the spectrum, and when we get all the way to ACM, the entire improvement cycle is performed by a knowledge worker, making the cycle of improvement fast and effective.

5. WHAT IS ADAPTIVE?

To understand the difference between PCM and ACM, you need to understand what we mean by *adaptive*. Whenever you hear about an adaptive system, you should think about muscles. If you want to increase the size or strength of a muscle, you exercise it. The use of a muscle triggers a response to build the muscle. Conversely, lack of use causes muscle atrophy.

Adaptiveness is not simply the capability to increase or decrease muscle size. Instead, it is more about the ability of the muscle to self-modify to fit the situation; the ability to sense a need, and to respond to it in a kind of feedback loop. Organizations are naturally adaptive if you have experienced people in management and they are getting accurate information about the situation.

Homeostasis is the idea that an adaptive system responds to external changes in such as the way as to keep certain aspects constant. Your body maintains a constant temperature by various mechanisms that respond to temperature change. A retail store that can detect the increasing popularity of an item will order larger quantities in order to keep the item available for sale.

6. EXAMPLES: ADAPTIVE SYSTEM

Human Body—Not just the human body, but all life forms have aspects of adaptiveness. Your DNA specifies how to form all the various muscles, but it does not include complete specifics on size. Instead, a feedback loop is used to find the optimal size. There is no need to predict ahead of time exactly the amount of muscle needed. Each muscle is built with the ability to measure the amount of use and respond by growing, or shrinking, appropriately. This simple mechanism eliminates any necessity to predict up front precisely how much is needed.

Adaptive systems optimize themselves. Take, for example, someone who suffers the tragedy of losing the use of their legs. The muscles that are no longer used will reduce in size, while the muscles in the arms will increase to accommodate the increased use.

There are many such systems in the body. The skin responds to light exposure by varying the amount of melanin at the points that received the exposure. This saves one from having to figure out in advance which parts of the skin should be more and less pigmented. Body temperature is maintained at a homeostatic constant through a number of mechanisms including sweat glands and shivering.

The concept of "practice" pertains exclusively to adaptive mechanisms. Want to learn the piano? Then sit down at the keys and practice, practice, practice. Want to learn to play tennis? Start playing hitting the ball and practice the right moves. Practice only works because the system is adaptive.

The Brain—this complex adaptive system allows a child to learn the language that they hear spoken around them by trying and practicing to improve skill. We study subjects in order to learn them. The concept of "learning" is again something that refers only to an adaptive system.

Ecosystems—The diversity of different organisms that thrive in differing conditions form an adaptive network, each organism dominating different aspects of the ecosystem when the conditions permit. The forest as a whole is extremely robust due to the adaptive nature of the biodiversity.

7. ENTERPRISE AS AN ADAPTIVE SYSTEM

Human organizations have always been naturally adaptive. The day-to-day decisions are decentralized and delegated to front-line workers. Different divisions compete for scarce resources, and good management will shift resources as needed. There may be a centralized view and control at a very high level, but generally this is very much abstracted away from the details of day-to-day operations. Various parts of the organization are sensing and responding to their situation. There is a nested, recursive aspect of this, so that as you get to smaller parts of the organization, the sensing and responding are more finely tuned and detailed.

Organizations are constantly changing and responding to that change. When a person leaves a position, the jobs of dozens of others will change. When an individual is promoted, many people will change their own behavior in response.

Yet the organization is stable. Adaptiveness does not cause constant fluctuation in the organization as a whole. In fact, it is well known that it is incredibly difficult to change an organization once it is in place. Adaptiveness presents a kind of homeostasis that allows an organization to keep its character and form over the years even though people within the organization are constantly coming and going.

An adaptive system is one that effectively senses what is needed, and automatically responds. The knowledge worker is part of that sensing and responding. Without the ability for the knowledge worker to self-modify the system, to adapt to the situation, then the ability to sense and respond at a system level is lost.

Adaptive systems have evolved to conquer complexity. System thinking is the approach to try to understand how things influence one another within a whole. System theory attempts to understand self-regulating systems, which is achieved through some form of feedback.

When we talk about a case management system being adaptive, the complete system includes the case managers. Humans are not excluded from the feedback loop. We talk about a good ACM system facilitating what the professional wants (needs) to do. Professionals (case managers) play active roles in adapting the system to their needs. We can think of this as being self-modification because there is no need for a software developer or process analyst: the professional can adapt the system as needed to meet the constantly changing requirements. For example, when a doctor gets the idea for a new treatment plan, they can institute that new plan without involving a software expert.

There is a feedback loop within a PCM system but it is slower, requiring many weeks or months to get out a new release. This much slower cycle means that a PCM system cannot adapt as quickly as an ACM system.

8. COMPARE AND CONTRAST

There are some strong similarities between PCM and ACM:

1) At run time the most important concept is that of a "case" which is primarily a folder to collect all the information around the case, accepting essentially any format of document
2) Knowledge workers use their own expertise to control the advancement of the case from state to state.
3) The resulting case folder represents a system of record for the work that was done.

The biggest distinction between PCM and ACM is that PCM is not adaptive, and this can be seen by three factors:

1) The programmers use formalism such as modeling or programming to put the application together
2) It uses a standard application development lifecycle: the application is constructed, then tested, then deployed to non-programmers
3) After deployment, there is limited ability for the case manager to alter the structure of the application itself.

ACM is used for what I would call innovating knowledge workers: inventors, creative people, executives, managers, innovators, business entrepreneurs, media producers, doctors, lawyers, etc. These are people who really do need to decide their course of action every day, and the course of action might be to do things that have never been done before. A board of directors does not have a menu of options to pick from when it comes to actions to take. Someone responsible for the merger of two companies will not have a system with all possible actions preprogrammed. A doctor responsible for the survival of a patient may prescribe radical and untested treatment if it seems like the only option.

PCM is for environments where the number of knowledge workers is high, and courses of action on a given case are sufficiently predictable to justify the cost of developing a dedicated application, though not entirely predictable. . Also, those knowledge workers are less responsible for evolution of work to fit new contingencies. For example, while a doctor might be in a position to prescribe a radical treatment, there are many others who work in a health care facility who should not have that flexibility. The routine care of a patient may still be too unpredictable for a fixed process, may still require the judgment of a nurse or clinician, and still the options available may be restricted to a set of known actions.

9. WHEN TO USE PCM

PCM is used when the number of knowledge workers doing the same job is large, and the domain relatively well known, but the process is not entirely predictable. Because the PCM application is developed by programmers, it can make use of more traditional mechanisms for data integration: structured information can be read from some sources, transformed, and written to other destinations. The sources and destinations can be web services or applications with an API. Like a typical development model, once the application is coded, the design rationale behind a particular transformation is not included in the final, produced code, because it is not needed.

There are a lot of service businesses which can make use of PCM. You might use PCM for telecom repairmen. These people need to visit the site, determine what the problem is, and then prescribe a resolution from a menu of well-known operations. It is hard to represent what these people do as a traditional HPM process because it is not predictable enough for a predefined fixed process. The process unfolds at run time because the first resolution might not work, and that tells the repairman more about the situation, possibly leading to further action. Yet the repairman is not in a position to invent entirely new procedures. The phone/TV system is big and complex, and therefore, the repairman's options are necessarily restricted to operations that are well-known not to cause a problem with the operation of the network.

Another example is auto service: the car is brought in and there is a set of things to examine. There are decisions about what to repair or replace. Maybe parts have to be ordered. Maybe components need to be sent to a shop for specialized repair. Perhaps the car needs to stay the night. With luck, it ends with the car being driven home.

PCM is most useful when the number of nearly identical offices is large, and the knowledge worker is a professional but not necessarily an owner of the process, and the process itself is not predictable enough to specify every step in advance.

In this year's ACM Awards, three submissions were awarded a Special Honorary Award for Production Case Management. The case studies were interesting and in their way solved important problems, but they got low marks based on the ACM awarding criteria. It is not that the cases were bad, or that the systems were poorly implemented, but simply that the cases were not "adaptive." We felt that readers would still benefit from these cases, and include them in this book in order to highlight the differences between Production and Adaptive Case Management. The cases are:

- JM Family Enterprise—an interesting interactive records management system that allows flexibility with less prescriptive processes, providing automation of support and reporting processes. It showed an advantage over

BPM for customer support scenario, but no real need to customize on the fly.

- Touchstone Health—a system that can handle a large number (1500) of appeals and grievance cases per month, and shows a documented savings over their earlier, manual system. The high number of cases and inability to customize individual cases both point to PCM.
- New York State Department of Financial Services—another high volume case management system with a very interesting, documented 40 percent reduction in processing time for cases. Like most high volume situations, there is little support for, or need for, customization of individual cases.

All three were quantitative examples of how automation can benefit an organization, but the focus was on automation of the interactions for a large number of workers. Even though a developer was needed to prepare the applications, the cost of this overhead is less than the benefits conferred by efficiencies when the number of cases and the number of workers are high.

10. CAN ONE SYSTEM BE BOTH?

The smart money is betting that in the next year, many systems will be presented as supporting both ACM and PCM. Is this possible? Can a vehicle be both a car and an airplane? Yes it can, but it is neither a good car, nor a good airplane. Can a vehicle be both a car and a boat? Yes it can, but it will be neither a good car nor a good boat. Because cars, boats, and airplanes have distinct needs and requirements, there is no chance to meet perfectly multiple needs at the same time.

To be adaptive, the system must be programmed by the knowledge worker, which necessarily means that traditional programming skill must not be required. Involving a developer would be a barrier to getting the job done.

The Do-It-Yourself (DIY) aspect of ACM puts some significant constraints on capabilities. Consider other DIY products you might see in a store. They must be designed to be put together with no particular skill. An amateur DIY kit will always be more limited than the parts that a professional will use. The "professional" products that require a professional for installation can be higher quality for the same price, because they don't need to be designed to be foolproof.

There are amateur (DIY) kits, and there are professional kits, but one kit is never *both* amateur and professional. A real artist will never use a paint-by-number kit, and a paint-by-number kit will never produce real art.

I have argued that using a two-dimensional graphical process diagram of any sort (i.e. BPMN) is a tool that professionals can use. However, such a language does not provide the kind of fool-proofness that a DIY process system needs. It is easy to drop a few shapes on the canvas and have something that is *syntactically incorrect*. The syntax rules are hidden and must be learned independently. The knowledge worker is too busy with their profession to learn the intricate details of the syntax of BPMN.

For an adaptive system, the right format for a process for a knowledge worker is a simple list of goals. Anyone can add a goal to the list, and there is no possibility to invalidate the syntax. There are no hidden rules to violate.

It seems overly-glorified to talk about a simple list of goals as a *process*. However, this simple approach allows a case manager to complete cases effectively, and repeatedly in the face of changing demands of the situation.

A programmer, designing a PCM process for an organization, will tend to want to use many sophisticated capabilities to do things, such as determining when a task is complete. Or, in hiding particular potential tasks until prerequisite tasks have been completed. All of these are effective in making the PCM application effective in the organization and, because PCM is used in high-volume situations, any small increase in effectiveness is multiplied by the number of cases.

Can't you have both? Have the programmer make the basic process, and then allow the case manager to modify it? This is not possible, because in the act of designing a program, the programmer makes many assumptions that are not apparent in the resulting program. It is dangerous to make even a small change in such a program without careful study of all the assumption behind the program.

While a BPMN diagram is powerful for a process expert to use, it does not make clear the underlying assumptions that went into that program, nor does it provide a way to safeguard those important assumptions, while allowing other things to be changed in controllable ways. Consider process variables: they are not visible in the diagram, nor is it clear exactly all the ways that a process variable is used. Changing the way a variable is manipulated in one part of the diagram might have dangerous consequences somewhere else. Only after careful understanding of the complete diagram can one make a safe change to it, and such effort is not something that a case manager can put into it.

My conclusion, which undoubtedly will be debated, is that if you offer a powerful language for a process expert to make a PCM application, you will eliminate the adaptive capability, and it cannot simultaneously be an ACM system. The two kinds of technology are distinct.

11. REFLECTION

Two approaches to knowledge work imply that there are two kinds of knowledge workers distinguished by "responsibility."

Knowledge worker for hire—someone is trained in a specific field and learns to be an expert, but has little or no ownership of the overall process. A car mechanic must make accurate suggestions on how to repair the car, but does not take responsibility for the repair shop business, and must work within the constraints set by others.

Knowledge worker with responsibility—someone who can plan and be responsible for the course of events. This is defined by Peter Drucker as someone "knowing more about their job than anyone else in the organization." These are the workers who handle the wicked problems and have to think outside of the box, e.g. a board member or someone responsible for mergers and acquisitions.

I am sure there are many more distinctions between types of workers, but for now this seems to be a determinant for whether you use PCM or ACM.

12. SUMMARY

At least two distinct forms of case management have been identified: ACM and PCM. They are similar: both having case folders, goals, and case history. But, PCM appears as an application designed and implemented by a programmer and deployed to a large number of users who face very similar situations. ACM is for less-predictable work situations where knowledge workers need a greater amount of flexibility to alter any aspect of the case at any time. The primary difference is that PCM needs the support of a software developer, while ACM requires case managers to do the work without specialized training.

Section 2
ACM Case Studies

Cognocare, an ACM-based System for Oncology

Gold Award: Healthcare

1. Abstract

This work[1] describes the use of ACM technology, implemented by means of an Artificial Intelligence Planner and Scheduler, to help physicians handle the process associated to the treatment of their patients. The lessons learned come from pediatric oncology treatments due to the previous experience of the company, but they may easily be extrapolated to general oncology or even general practice like the case of chronic disease patients.

2. Introduction

In general, once a diagnosis of a disease has been accepted for a patient, the physician goes into the task of designing a treatment, or care plan, for the patient. The expertise, namely physician's expert knowledge, required to design these personalized treatments relies in evidence-based practice guidelines, a set of recommendations, usually coming from clinical trials of trusted committees or groups. These guidelines fix which drugs have to administered and when, how to calculate the dosages and the administration way, the laboratory tests to be carried out to validate the evolution of the patient and what to do when the condition of the patient is not as expected.

The more complex is the disease, the more complex is the treatment and the more complex are practice guidelines. The issue is that these practice guidelines are very large and complex documents that are not appropriate to be read at the point of care, but this is exactly the point where they are needed. Therefore, the work of physicians is clearly that of a knowledge worker:

- There is no predefined path to follow,
- There is a huge amount of expert knowledge to support their decisions,
- It is an unpredictable environment where the outcomes of many decisions are unknown beforehand,
- They need to react quickly to unexpected conditions, both in the status of the patient and in the availability of clinical and ancillary resources,
- No matter what happens they must keep on maintaining the same goal of healing the patient,
- And last, it has the additional responsibility of having lives in danger exposed to their timely decisions exactly at the point of care.

This hostile environment exposes physicians to a high stress that could lead to important errors like a bad dosage of chemotherapy agents, a bad staging of the risk group of the patient or a missed bad interaction between two steps of the treatment. In addition, there are other relevant but less critical mistakes like a

---

[1] Assembled and written by Luis Castillo, Co-founder and Chief Technology Officer at IActive US Corp. luis.castillo@iactiveit.com

forgotten report that should have been sent to the disease committee or a lab test that no one remembered to schedule.

Happily, most of, if not all, this information is stored electronically, like in Electronic Health Records and even practice guidelines may be represented with structured languages in actionable representations. Therefore, it is time for computer programs to process this information, understand it or propose the path to follow to the physician. These programs can also allow physicians to monitor the evolution of the condition, leaving enough freedom to modify this path according to their preferences and to react quickly to contingencies during the execution of the processes. In other words, this is an excellent field of application for ACM philosophy and technology around the unifying role of the patient as the central case in hand.

3. DESCRIPTION OF COGNOCARE

This is the base of Congocare, an ACM-based Clinical Decision Support System for Oncology that interprets clinical guidelines and expert knowledge, enabling a true dynamic and knowledge-based process generation based on Artificial Intelligence, where these processes are personalized treatments, adapted to each single patient condition. Physicians use it as an assistant to design, follow-up, modify and update fully detailed treatment processes under a very flexible environment.

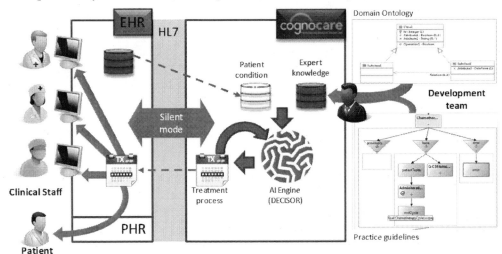

2.1. Architecture

The two most important sources of information for a CDSS like this are, on one hand, the access to clinical information about the patient (to personalize the treatment) and the hospital resources (to optimize their use and align the treatment with their availability) and on the other hand access to clinical practice guidelines (as the main knowledge source on how to build a treatment).

Access to clinical data

This is achieved by implementing a virtual medical record that integrates with external EHR to obtain all the required information. Cognocare does not intend to be an EHR, but to integrate with one of them to provide insightful decision support to physicians. If the EHR provide enough patient data to feed the AI engine (patient profiles, their demographic data, latest blood tests, biochemistry and biometric, as the most important information to personalize the treatment), then Cognocare plugs directly to the EHR by using HL7 [6] interoperability procedures.

Otherwise a local database would need to be set up to store all the information that the EHR is not able to provide. This implies that all the restrictions about privacy and safety of this local data have to be guaranteed by Cognocare itself.

Regarding the access to hospital resources (available rooms, nurses and physicians rosters, etc), if the EHR provides this level of information then it is fed to the AI engine to include several heuristics to optimize the use of resources or to provide warnings on possible future shortage of resources. But if the EHR does not provide support for hospital resources, this capability is immediately ignored and Cognocare does not provide any local database to support its storage.

Personalized treatments are timed processes with a flexible temporal representation scheme known as a simple temporal network [2,7] which encode start and end dates imposed by the guidelines, safety temporal constraints, milestones and deadlines to be met. They are stored in a local database, but since they are rich and structured information, they may be exchanged with the EHR at any moment or downloaded by patient through corresponding patients portals.

These features can also be shared with BPM/ACM suites since they are not intended to be holistic solutions for the whole IT enterprise architecture of a company and therefore, they must provide tools to integrate with legacy software and to be able to extract the required information from there.

The use of external EHR also imposes some "philosophical" restrictions on the use of the Graphical User Interface. In the case of this healthcare area, end users are not comfortable having to switch from their regular screen to "external" screens and require everything to be carried out on the regular EHR screen. That means that, Cognocare can offer its main functions through a well defined Advanced Programming Interface (API), mostly through web services, and let the EHR to interface with the user through its own screen.

Access to practice guidelines

In this case, practice guidelines need to be a structured knowledge representation, that is, an actionable representation that can be understood by the AI engine in order to compose appropriately the processes. In this case we use the freely available Knowledge Studio that fits into our AI engine. But other knowledge representation schemes may also be used if other equivalent AI engines are used to compose dynamically the treatment processes [5]. This family of AI engines and the technical representation of practice guidelines are discussed in section 3.

2.2. A typical lifecycle

A typical cycle of use starts with an incoming patient with a confirmed diagnosis. Then, from the last laboratory tests and biometric and demographic data, Cognocare explores the practice guidelines and elaborates a personalized treatment or process in the form of a calendar (at different hierarchical levels showing the drugs, dosages and all the required information (even administrative tasks).

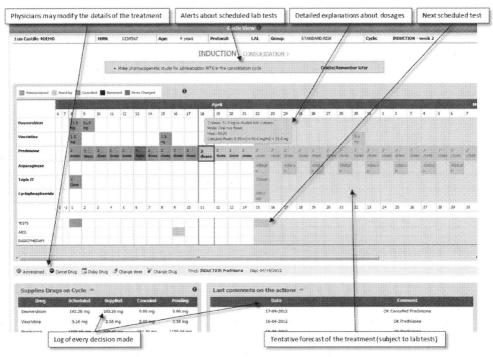

When needed, physicians can modify many details of the treatment, mainly the details about the chemotherapy drugs, their dosage and timing, but respecting the critical backbone of the treatment in order to adhere as much as possible to the practice guideline. Since the outcome of the treatment may not be as predicted, Cognocare notifies (shadow) the part of the treatment that depends on an intermediate evaluation, or tests, of the condition of the patient, therefore it may be considered as a forecast.

Since physicians or nurses can introduce daily values (body temperature) or even data coming from the latest laboratory tests, Cognocare always acts in "silent mode" monitoring these data in background and, in the case of a dangerous deviation from the expected values, it triggers a re-planning process to redesign on-the-fly a new treatment from that day on. This new treatment is always based on the same practice guidelines and on the process executed so far.

This cycle lasts until the patient completes the full protocol of the treatment and it is continued with follow-up sessions.

4. ARTIFICIAL INTELLIGENCE TECHNOLOGY FOR THE GENERATION OF PROCESSES

The kind of AIP&S engine used by Cognocare is known as Hierarchical Task Network Planning [1,2,3] and it focuses on how to decompose a given goal into the subtasks that achieve that goal. All the work described in this section is developed in Knowledge Studio [1] by our own development team and it is completely transparent in Cognocare or any other application built on top of it. It might also be written in any other formalism like the academic language PDDL [2,5] or in Lisp [3].

3.1 Problem Ontology

The problem ontology is usually represented as a hierarchy of categories, each with different attributes, and different relationships among them. Every category, or class, represents an entity of the domain with its own properties, inheritance from its superclasses and relations with other classes. In the case of Knowledge Studio [1] it is represented as a UML 2.0 diagram.

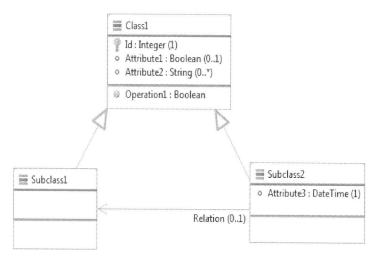

And in other AIPS engines like [2,3] it is represented in a textual representation completely equivalent.

3.2 Goal and processes templates

In this Hierarchical Task Network Planning paradigm, a goal is a high level task that may be decomposed into sub-goals whenever a certain condition holds. The same goal or sub-goal may have different decompositions, each with its own condition, to adapt the decomposition to the current context. There may be atomic sub-goals that cannot be further decomposed, named tasks, but they still contain actionable knowledge to represent the conditions that must hold to execute and how that execution affects their environment. These atomic tasks also contain much information as metadata, like for example:

- Type of administration of the drug.
- Dosage and how it is calculated.
- Its actor, that is, the instance of one or more categories of the problem ontology that is authorized or enabled to execute this type of atomic actions, for example clinical oncologists, surgeons, nurses, etc.
- Warnings detected by the AI engine (justification of steps, values of some variables over predefined bounds)
- Cycle or phase of the treatment to which it belongs.

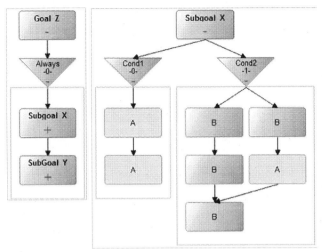

The decomposition of a goal is said to be finished if all its sub-goals have been decomposed into its atomic tasks. This sequence of tasks is the process that achieves the goal for the existing context. In this case, a process is a personalized treatment.

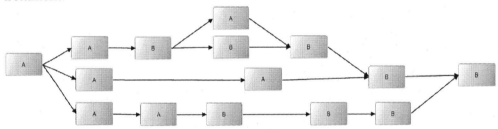

There may be complex decompositions when the same goal also appears in the decompositions of other goals or even in its own decomposition, producing chained (recursive) decompositions, that lead to processes with previously unde-fined length, depending on the conditions of the environment.

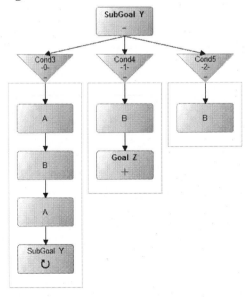

This representation allow for complex nested decompositions like this one.

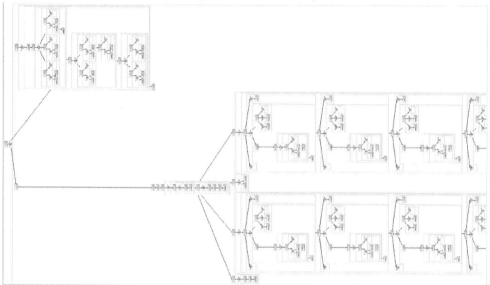

The existing alternative decompositions of goals may act as choice points that allow a certain degree of freedom for the end user to accept alternatives ways to decompose them. Therefore, only those decompositions that adhere to safety rules, legal concerns or any other regulation are allowed, acting as guardrails.

Exponential number of possibilities in a compact representation

Moreover all these decompositions are declarative in nature. That means, this representation doesn't represent a unique decomposition (process), but a very large set of possible decompositions (processes), which depend on the set of conditions that holds in the context of the problem.

Furthermore, the combination of conditions that have to be met to generate a given process might even be exponential: if the average set of alternatives at every level is X and the number of levels explored is Y, this may led to X^Y combinations compactly expressed in the representation with Y rising quickly. Therefore, all these exponential numbers of potential processes are kept in a compact, finite representation.

Searching for the best decomposition

This representation is not only Artificial Intelligence, but also an actionable and compact representation of complex, dynamic decompositions. Once a goal is stated, it is time to find the best decomposition for it, which decompositions are feasible, which tasks are applicable, and this is where Artificial Intelligence algorithms enter the scene. There are several algorithms that can be used for finding the best decomposition of a goal present in classical academic textbooks [4]. In any case, all of the above AIP&S systems are able to carry out this search for the best decomposition, AIP&S Systems like SIADEX [2] and SHOP2 [3] are available as academic software offered as open source license and DECISOR [1] is available as software under a commercial license.

To sum up, we can represent every process template, link them in a compact decompositions tree and, once a goal is stated by the knowledge worker, allow the AIP&S to search for the best process able to meet that goal. All the systems commented in this paper [1,2,3] are able to find processes made up of hundreds of actions in less than one minute or even seconds in any typical notebook.

5. MAIN FEATURES

The main advantages provided by Cognocare are the following ones:

- Knowledge Sharing. All the physicians (knowledge workers) make similar decisions by sharing system's knowledge, in terms of both patient ontology extracted from clinical records and process templates to comply with standard practice guidelines. In addition to this, all the physicians involved in the treatment of the same patient (actors) share the same backbone of information: the treatment stored in the case of the patient.

- Adaptive and Dynamic. Unexpected events are managed on the fly by adapting the current treatment to the new conditions, generating new treatment steps by reusing the previous treatment process, if needed, and sending alerts for validation to physicians.

- Goal oriented. No matter what happens, it always tries to apply correctly practice guidelines, always with the same goal of healing the patient.

- Enables collaboration. Since every action in the process has an associated actor, the plan may be split into the profiles of actors and resources involved enabling a powerful collaborative care approach and increasing the coordination between different teams.

- Powerful reporting capabilities. Since all the information about the evolution of the treatment is logged in Cognocare, physicians may use its reporting capabilities to provided and enhanced situation awareness, like detecting meaningful deviations of the treatment and why, calculating the cost of the treatment beforehand, comparing the evolution of single patients respect to the average behavior in the unit, etc.

- Patient engagement. The whole treatment is available in a structured representation since the beginning. This allows patients to download their treatment thru their patient's portals, integrate them into their personal calendar and make unprecedented decisions regarding the arrangement of their lives to met the scheduled treatment enough in advance (always subject to possible changes in the treatment).

- Productivity. Reduces physician's workload and allow them to focus on more treatments within the same time. An observational study is carried out in Spain in two different Hospitals within the Andalusian Healthcare System: Preliminary results show a dramatic reduction of dosage errors, a cut of time by ¼ and unprecedented higher awareness due to enhanced reporting capabilities.

- Comprehensive. Fully detailed treatments: dosages, clinical tasks, even parallel administrative tasks (automated reports, daily treatment flow-sheets, laboratory reports), are included in the process since the beginning, providing the basis for enhanced alerting and reminding capabilities.

- Errors management. Every decision made by the AI engine (like calculation of doses, changes of chemo cycles due to patient conditions, reminders of scheduled tests) may be shown to the physician, together with a brief explanation, beforehand reducing the likelihood of the errors due to shortage of time.

- Update to new treatments. Practice guidelines are not encoded within the source code, but as a separate file. Therefore, as soon as a new guideline is available for a disease, it is encoded in Knowledge Studio and made it available to physicians without having to reinstall or interrupt the software.

6. Conclusions

Cognocare[2] is the name of the Oncology CDSS described so far and it follows a typical ACM problem statement and lifecycle. Cognocare is one of the main products of IActive Intelligent Technologies[3] and it has been fully developed with IActive Knowledge Studio, a knowledge engineering environment for HTN planning[4], and DECISOR [1] an HTN planner and scheduler. The system is currently implemented in two Hospitals in Spain with pediatric oncology units, integrated with SIEMENS' and HP' EHRs. These are two real testimonials taken from these two hospitals in Spin: a) "Cognocare is the first application ever that takes into account our real needs since the beginning of its development", b) "With Cognocare we increased our care quality and safety, sharing part of the team's workload with an advanced decision support. Dosage calculations and treatment updates are automatically proposed by the application leaving us more time to spend with our patients."

Strengths:

- Adherence to regulation: AIP&S dynamically enforces processes to comply with external rules and applicable regulation as if they were guardrails.
- Processes free of interferences: AIP&S dynamically detects and removes interferences between branches of the resulting process.
- Process scheduling: AIP&S dynamically schedules processes along a continuous timeline even taking into account optimization of time or cost.
- Unpredictable outcomes: AIP&S may re-think a new process, even on top of already existing ones, when the process under execution fails or is no longer applicable.
- Knowledge worker customization: the search process of the AIP&S system may be parameterized with knowledge worker preferences so that it is possible to skip subgoals, or to "personalize" how decompositions are explored.
- Expert knowledge update: since the expert knowledge is encoded apart of the code of the software, it may be updated easily, without having to reprogram the AIP&S.

Weaknesses:

- Determinism: Don't expect AIP&S to generate any possible process, only those processes for which there is a template can be generated.

---

[2] www.cognocare.com

[3] www.iactiveit.com

[4] Freely downloadable at http://www.iactiveit.com/products/studio-knowledge-modeling-tool/

- Knowledge representation effort: To start playing with these AIP&S systems, some knowledge engineering effort has to be made to represent the set of possible decompositions but this is compensated with the efficiency of AIP&S systems, mainly when these processes are continuously being generated and re-generated in the daily activities of knowledge workers.

The AIP&S engines DECISOR [1] and its predecessor SIADEX [2] have also been used in other practical domains achieving several academic honors like in forest fire fighting management (Best Spanish AI Application at conference CEDI 2005, Best Planning Application at conference ICAPS 2006) and the automatic translation of XPDL processes into HTN knowledge representation (Award for excellence in the 3rd International Competition on Knowledge Engineering for Planning and Scheduling at conference ICAPS 2009).

7. REFERENCES

[1] Francisco Palao, Juan Fdez-Olivares, Luis Castillo, Oscar García-Pérez: **An extended HTN knowledge representation based on a graphical notation**. ICAPS 2011Workshop on Knowledge Engineering for Planning and Scheduling (KEPS 2011). Freiburg, Germany. June 2011.

http://decsai.ugr.es/~faro/LinkedDocuments/KEPS2011-PalaoEtAl.pdf

[2] L. Castillo, J. Fdez.-Olivares, O. García-Pérez, F. Palao. Efficiently handling temporal knowledge in an HTN planner. 16th International Conference on Automated Planning and Scheduling (ICAPS 2006).

http://decsai.ugr.es/~lcv/Research/Publications/Papers/ICAPS0602CastilloL.pdf

[3] Nau, D.S. and Au, T.C. and Ilghami, O. and Kuter, U. and Murdock, J.W. and Wu, D. and Yaman, F.. SHOP2: An HTN planning system, J. Artif. Intell. Res. (JAIR), 20, 379-404, 2003. https://www.aaai.org/Papers/JAIR/Vol20/JAIR-2013.pdf

[4] Stuart Russell, Peter Norvig, Artificial Intelligence: A Modern Approach (3rd Edition). http://www.amazon.com/Artificial-Intelligence-Modern-Approach-3rd/dp/0136042597

[5] D. Long and M. Fox, PDDL2.1: An Extension to PDDL for Expressing Temporal Planning Domains, Journal of Artificial Intelligence Research (20) 61-124, 2003.

[6] http://en.wikipedia.org/wiki/Health_Level_7

[7] Dechter, R.; Meiri, I.; and Pearl, J. 1991. Temporal constraint networks. Artificial Intelligence 49:61–95

Vision Service Plan (VSP)

Silver Award: Healthcare

1. EXECUTIVE SUMMARY / ABSTRACT

Vision Service Plan (VSP) provides high-quality, cost-effective eye care benefits and world-class products and services to eye care professionals, employers, and more than 56 million members. The company is headquartered in Rancho Cordova, California, USA.

Adaptive case management has played a critical role in helping VSP improve the quality of customer service, accuracy of information, compliance with government and industry regulations and achieve significant cost savings.

The integration of the OpenText Case360 solution with the Customer Care Portal significantly improved customer service quality by simplifying the creation and processing of critical documents including claims adjustments, complaints, doctor inquiries and fraud alerts while providing over $700K in annual savings on business operations. Additional cost savings are expected as more task types are added.

	Annual Savings
Create Cases	$378,674
Process Cases	$139,554
OA Sorting	$30,240
Letter Review	$65,287
Return Work	$103,645
TOTAL	$717,400

The Complaints and Grievances Unit significantly reduced the time required to review cases to ensure accuracy and compliance.

The case management system at VSP has been very well received by the users. VSP invited users from the various areas to design sessions to discuss requirements and design a product they could use. They held focus groups to solicit feedback and received additional feedback during pilots. Status meetings were held monthly so stakeholders could review deliverables. VSP assigned Change Managers from the two departments, Customer Service and Claims Services, to educate users and facilitate change management and adoption. They also identified team champions who were responsible for raising awareness and promoting the case management approach as a positive step towards improving customer service.

The case management system is heavily used across VSP's Customer Care Division, which includes various work groups responsible for processing claims adjustments, complaints, doctor inquiries, fraud alerts, and more.

The key users of the system, by role, include Customer Service Representative knowledge workers who create the case and can add tasks that trigger collaboration with the Processor knowledge workers who receive the case and process the necessary activities on the case. This type of case handling has enabled VSP to better serve customers. A management dashboard provides Supervisors with visibility and access to active work.

2. OVERVIEW

The project utilized a co-located team that had been formed previously to upgrade the Customer Service desktop application. The team used Agile methods to deliver on the project goals and objective.

VSP started out by identifying all workflows within the Call Center. They reviewed the existing processes and then prioritized each process based on complexity and business risk. Since they were implementing new technology and had to bring in other work areas since their workflows touched people outside of the call center, VSP chose to implement simple processes that did not involve compliance.

The second phase took on the Complaints and Grievance process. This approach minimized VSP's exposure, allowed for change management activities and learning the new tool and technology.

VSP created a change management team which included management and staff to help with the transition and engaged the front line staff not only in identifying requirements but actually sitting with developers for testing. This created buy-in and generated excitement.

VSP's challenge was not with technology but with the people side. First, their call center was very used to giving requirements and coming up with suggestions. The claim processors had not been involved in a project of this kind and often asked for the system to replicate what they had today.

Additionally, the claims area was going through another project that was introducing another type of technology and process change. They struggled to handle both at the same time. It took an analyst and lead developer sitting back and listening, then re-architecting the process, then presenting options to the front line staff.

Also, when the processors sat with the project team to test, the project team noticed system changes that could improve claim handling which had nothing to do with the project. VSP implemented those small enhancements which helped create buy-in as well.

VSP implemented a pilot for six weeks and integrated feedback and completed the rollout of Phase 1 without any system incidents and with complete buy-in to the changes.

VSP followed the same methodology for Phase 2 in the Complaints and Grievance process. This is a heavily-regulated activity and tolerance for issues is low because a system change is not acceptable. VSP again included additional users, completed a pilot and rollout finished up within months.

VSP is seeing benefits in several areas. CSRs are completing forms more accurately reducing returned work. The previous process was very linear. VSP now routes specific work types to multiple locations at the same time. Their claim area manually used to distribute work, now they have eliminated approximately eight hours a day of the manual distribution process. CSRs can now complete the forms in less time saving handling time. It took several minutes to complete the mainframe form, now we are seeing less than one minute in some cases to complete the new forms.

3. BUSINESS CONTEXT

VSP's workflow tool was over 20 years old. CSRs used this mainframe-based workflow system to create and route Research Inquiries (RIs) to various work groups in the organization for claims adjustments, complaints, doctor inquiries, fraud alerts, etc. Each workflow type had its own steps required to complete the RI. If a CSR did not follow the process correctly or provide all the required detail, a processor could return the RI for correction thus affecting claims timeliness.

Distribution of the work was also very manual. Supervisors distributed work by running daily reports and passing them out to their teams, sending emails or using whiteboards.

For Complaints, generation of acknowledgement letters and resolution of complaints had to be completed within specific timeframes to stay in compliance. The C&G Unit spends significant time reviewing RIs to ensure accuracy and compliance.

4. THE KEY INNOVATIONS

Integration of OpenText Case360 with the Customer Care Portal significantly simplified the creation and processing of workflow. Now when CSRs create tasks, most of the detailed information is carried over into the case thus reducing returned work for missing or incorrect data.

Tasks are now routed into work queues eliminating the need for manual distribution of work. When tasks are due, reminders are sent to the user's workflow through the Customer Care Portal.

Supervisors also have visibility to active work through the Supervisor Dashboard.

4.1 Business

VSP's call center takes calls from its members who utilize our vision benefits and providers who may need assistance with payment reconciliation. The project improved the employee experience with tools to do their job; this is translating into improved documentation and follow-up. CSRs are now documenting more information and using it to improve call handling if the customer were to call back. Flags are reminding CSRs to meet deadlines, which is helping them meet commitments and compliance.

It was important to collaborate with business partners, users and stakeholders as the workflow affected so many areas of the business. They were engaged throughout the project to ensure the solution met their needs, improved processes and gained efficiencies.

4.2 Case Handling

How VSP handles cases is the crux of what makes theirs an adaptive case management approach as opposed to a more structured traditional BPM approach. A generic case template has been defined that contains key fields (member id, doctor id, claim id, etc) to aid in finding cases. Customer Service Representative knowledge workers create the case using the template and can add tasks to the case as needed to initiate the required work activities. Each task represents a co-operating process. Adding tasks triggers collaboration with the Processor knowledge workers who receive the case and process the necessary activities on the case. This approach allows a nice balance between ad-hoc workflow with any combination of tasks, but still provides some structure for specific task types.

- An auditor reviews a subset of cases to look for coaching and compliance items.

- A Customer Care analyst team manages changes to the UI, workflows and queues. As corporate projects are initiated, they are responsible for identifying requirements and including changes to case handling.
- An operations support team identifies internal process improvements and works with the analyst team and IT for any changes needed.

The case template has remained unmodified.

4.3 Organization & Social

Case was very well received by the users. The implementation of case has streamlined their processes and improved efficiencies. VSP eliminated administrative steps which improved employee engagement.

5. HURDLES OVERCOME

Management

Management in the call center now has a tool to review returned work and aging of cases. While they had to learn a new tool, the change was simple and welcomed.

Claims management had a much more impactful change to go through. They were implementing another tool at the same time. That tool was changing processor standards and how they would manage staff.

The project set up a change management team that included management and front line staff from both areas. They were responsible for championing the change with their peers. Front line staff was brought over to the project team's co located area and were able to test and provide feedback. Pilot teams were established and a pilot was conducted for six weeks. Feedback was tracked and updates made based on direct user input.

Demonstrations to management also occurred throughout the project.

Business

The project was heavily internally focused to the Customer Care Division. VSP's goal was to improve the tools that the business areas utilize. Employee engagement along with process improvements were their key considerations.

Organization Adoption

VSP invited users from the various areas to design sessions to discuss requirements and design a product they could use. VSP held focus groups to solicit feedback and then got more feedback during pilots. Sprint Reviews were held monthly so stakeholders could see deliverables. VSP had Change Managers from the two departments, Customer Service and Claims Services, to help with change management and adoption. VSP also had team champions who were responsible for raising awareness and promoting case.

6. BENEFITS

6.1 Cost Savings / Time Reductions

	Annual Savings
Create Cases	$378,674
Process Cases	$139,554
OA Sorting	$30,240
Letter Review	$65,287
Return Work	$103,645
TOTAL	$717,400

(Savings does not represent all RIs. Additional task types will be added.)

6.2 Increased Revenues

The project focus was to improve VSP's internal processes and manage administrative costs.

6.3 Quality Improvements

VSP is seeing quality improvements in several areas. CSRs are completing forms more accurately; reducing returned work. The previous process was very linear.

VSP now routes specific work types to multiple locations at the same time. Their claim area manually used to distribute work, now they have eliminated approximately eight hours a day of the manual distribution process.

CSRs can now complete the forms in less time saving handling time. It took several minutes to complete the mainframe form, now they are seeing less than one minute in some cases to complete the new forms.

7. BEST PRACTICES, LEARNING POINTS AND PITFALLS

7.1 Best Practices and Learning Points

- ✓ *Engage users to find out what's working and what's not*
- ✓ *Ask why? Be aware of "it's always been done this way"*
- ✓ *The project team being 100% allocated and co-located made a significant difference in speed of execution*
- ✓ *Don't underestimate change management. The human side is the biggest hurdle.*

7.2 Pitfalls

- ✗ *Not spending enough time understanding existing processes and knowledge worker needs*
- ✗ *Change management leader wasn't experienced enough*

8. COMPETITIVE ADVANTAGES

Because competitive advantage wasn't a goal of their project, VSP didn't measure how they have moved competitive goal posts for the insurance industry. However, improving the quality of service to its members can be viewed as a competitive advantage in keeping current members and gaining new customers.

9. TECHNOLOGY

The OpenText Case360 application is running on the WebSphere 7.0 platform. This provides high-availability to the application through JVM clustering.

Also, since VSP is heavily invested in using OpenText Case360 as a service via the WebService API, WebSphere provides a nice facility for identity propagation to enable authentication of the user from VSP's web app without requiring users to rekey their credentials.

10. THE TECHNOLOGY AND SERVICE PROVIDERS

OpenText Business Process Solutions (BPS)

OpenText BPS provides process management, case management, and business architecture solutions that increase efficiency and effectiveness through a highly individualized user experience that empowers the people that do the work. OpenText BPS is supported by a strong global partner network including SAP®, Microsoft® and Oracle®. OpenText BPS's industry leadership has been recognized by global IT analyst firms including Gartner, Forrester Research, IDC and others. Visit www.OpenTextBPS.com or our blog www.BecauseProcessMatters.com.

Generali Hellas Insurance Company S.A.

Gold Award: Customer-Facing

1. EXECUTIVE SUMMARY/ABSTRACT

Generali Hellas Insurance Company S.A. has become successful largely by making itself the company of choice for agents through its exceptional service. To advance this offering and to streamline processes throughout the company, Generali sought and implemented an enterprise system with the capacity to integrate new and improved workflow processes.

To enhance the development phase and gather business requirements, the IT team created a steering committee that consisted of IT and end user personnel. The users who were part of this committee embraced the new system enthusiastically, while others took longer to adapt.

The new system, named *Thesis,* resulted in several improvements. Case handling is now more flexible, with two distinct tracks—one strictly defined for straightforward cases, the other adaptable for cases that are less well defined. Agents gained insight into the policy application process and the ability to respond quickly to underwriter questions and requests. Underwriters and claims handlers, in turn, spend more time doing pure underwriting and claims handling than "paper pushing" and other work unrelated to their core competencies. The company's ability to respond to regulatory requests was greatly improved. In addition, paper and printing costs were dramatically reduced.

Already competitively positioned because of superior agent service, Generali built on this capacity by offering greater efficiency, updated processes, and options for mobile interaction.

2. OVERVIEW

Generali differentiates itself from other insurance providers by offering excellent service to agents. In an effort to improve its service offerings and streamline processes at the home office, the company sought an enterprise system to implement new, improved processes.

Key innovations to come out of the implementation process included agents having better insight into application and claims processes. As a workforce that commonly works outside of business hours, 24x7 access to this information is a significant benefit. Another innovation was the automation of processes that were previously manual. This change has increased the accuracy of such processes. Case handling has also become more streamlined, with two models of operation: the "application" model, which does not allow exceptions, and the "offer" model, which is largely unrestricted. The history of each case is much more transparent now that all related documentation is in one place.

Organizational acceptance of the new system has been mostly positive, largely as a result of many staff members participating on a steering committee to determine the goals of the new system. Other than some resistance to the new system, primarily by those not involved in its development, problems were limited to the typical adjustments needed with any new system and workflow.

Benefits of the new system were noticeable in cost savings and quality improvements. Specifically, a reduction in the need for paper and printing has reduced costs for Generali significantly. The time it takes to issue a new policy has dropped by 70 percent. Quality improvements have come partly in the ability to respond to government compliance demands—a process that can be cumbersome for many companies—and partly in the ability to provide enhanced service to agents.

Best practices noted through this process include making end users feel included from the beginning planning stages, defining business processes in as much detail as possible, sticking to the decision to move forward despite implementation challenges, and having dependable local IT assistance. The one pitfall the IT team noted was paying too little attention to the definition of use cases.

The new system has built on Generali's competitive advantages. The already excellent service the company has provided to agents over the years has improved, leading to the likelihood that agents will choose Generali over other insurance companies for their customers. In addition, processes are now clearer and better defined, so the home office is able to respond more readily to agent requests. Another advantage is Generali's use of mobile technology, which started with the new system: Agents can begin the policy application process using their mobile device. Generali plans to maintain its competitive advantage by extending the new system into more areas of the company's operations.

The technology used for the new system includes a web portal for agents and offsite staff, an enterprise capture tool for integrating documents into the system, a business process engineering (BPM) engine, business activity monitoring, service-oriented architecture (SOA)–based integration with back-end systems, PDF conversion tools, barcoded applications and cover letters, the ability to use both legacy and new communication methods, and two aspects for addressing various lines of business (LOBs)—strict workflow for standardized packages and collaborative workflow for complex proposals.

3. BUSINESS CONTEXT

Providing exceptional service to its sales force differentiates Generali from other insurance companies, so the organization wanted to improve this aspect of its operations. Examples of service include helping the sales force, which includes partners, brokers, and agents, to sell Generali products; providing the ability to track information needed for offers to become agreements; and other forms of assistance.

Mr. Elias Mandouvalos, assistant IT manager at Generali, explains: "Prior to adopting the new tool, processes were left up to the reasoning of the individuals [who] implemented them. So, they were performed differently by different people in different departments or on different days. We wanted to streamline internal processes to make them more trackable, defined, measurable, and standardized."

In addition, many of the processes the sales force was using were outdated. Rather than putting old data and processes on top of a new system, the IT team intended to develop entirely new, automated processes to replace those bogged down by paper.

The changes were set to affect both end users (the sales force) and internal users at Generali headquarters. The needs of the two groups were different and required different levels of security and rules.

The implementation was based on the IBM Rational Unified Process methodology. Because of the high complexity and innovation of the project, a prototype was implemented initially to get business sponsor approval and ensure the correctness of technological choices.

4. THE KEY INNOVATIONS

Several key innovations came about as a result of implementing the new system.

4.1 Business

Although the end customers of the company's products are policy holders, Generali views as its direct customers its agents, who have been positive in accepting the new system. Agents are positively affected, because they now have the ability to check on their cases and interact through the tool on a 24x7 basis. This access is highly convenient, because many agents regularly work outside of normal office hours, including evenings and weekends. They need certain documents to serve their clients, and now they have access to them at any time.

In addition, many processes have been automated. For example, cases that involve issuing internal certificates used to be manual; now, the information is submitted electronically, and the system responds. Official certificates can also be generated, such as motor stickers, which are necessary for driving a car in Greece.

4.2 Case Handling

Figure 1 represents the basic roles and processes managed through the system.

The key roles within the application are (1) the agent, or external user; (2) the underwriter, or case handler; (3) the underwriter supervisor; (4) the claims handler; (5) the claims supervisor; and (6) the data entry workers and dispatchers.

Data entry workers and dispatchers are responsible for handling incoming paper documents and bringing them inside the domain, performing scanning and other functions for different documents. These workers primarily do document type classification, but they also initiate workflows when handling specific types of documents. For example, they would start an insurance application workflow if they received a paper-based application form or a claims flow if they received a fax that includes a claims announcement.

Claims handlers can include physicians, claims experts, or companies involved in information exchange. These users, who become part of the process on an as-needed basis, help insured parties fill out paperwork, provide photographs, and communicate with Generali. They also help underwriters and claims handlers access cases, such as a physician who provides health history information for a prospective medical insurance customer or a claims surveyor who drafts a report to determine the size of a claim following a fire.

Key roles are assigned when new people come into the system. New user credentials are created and updated automatically.

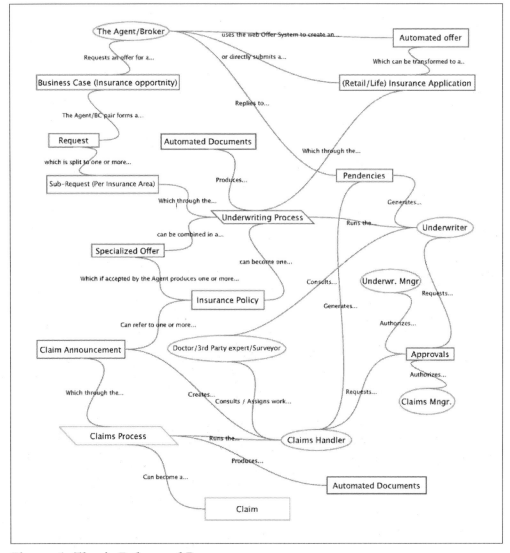

Figure 1: Thesis Roles and Processes

The main business entities correspond with different types of insurance, such as corporate, individual life, and group life. One entity is the insurance application. Mr. Mandouvalos explains: "As soon as the application is approved, it becomes an insurance policy that contains terms and conditions, letters, forms, and issued bills, all kept together in the system." Another entity consists of claims brought against a policy that has been created. This entity may contain reports from experts, invoices for compensation, and records of checks that have been issued.

A case manager can approve or reject the case instance. The normal process involves an approval portion and a payment portion before the payment is completed. In this case, the system knows who the immediate supervisor of a claims handler is, so it sends a notification to the supervisor, notifying the manager that the claims handler wants to make a payment and is asking for approval.

The process is similar for down payments—also handled by the system—which identifies that there should be a down payment, creates a subcase (a dependent task that must be completed before the case can reach the next stage), and opens a case with the accounting department. When the accounting department receives it, department personnel must complete the subcase.

The system can handle unanticipated roles, as well. Two workflow models are built into the system. The first is standardized and immutable. There are well-defined specifications, rules, and fields. The other model accommodates situations outside the norm and creates a specific, unique business agreement for each case.

The latter model allows for negotiations; nothing is predefined. The system keeps track of different versions of the offer as the case progresses, including all communications from the agent. This process allows underwriters to request more information by creating a subcase within the system. When the agent responds to the subcase, the underwriter is notified. All activity is tracked within the case, until acceptance of all, part, or none of the offer is recorded. It is possible to keep track of the case as a whole or as individual parts.

4.3 Organization & Social

Prior to adopting the new tool, notes Mr. Mandouvalos, "seeing the specific transactions in each case was a challenge. It was hard to see what the decisions were, what the offers were, and how they were negotiated, especially after a long time. Now things are a lot more organized. We can see the details of what has happened in specific cases, even if a long time has passed or if the case handler has changed. It's easy to understand what has happened in each case."

The sales force has gained a level of transparency that Mr. Mandouvalos compares to "being given a seat next to the underwriter and internal users." Whereas in the past agents would submit an application, and then have no idea where it was in the process, now the communication channel is open, underwriters can quickly request additional information, and the application process is visible to all involved.

Users now have better systems and more specific ways to do things, enabling constancy, consistency, and measurability. All information related to a case is in one place, and nothing is missing as a result of lost paperwork.

However, along with the positive changes came some challenges. Internal users had to change the way they sent items into the system, requested and granted approval, retrieved information, relied on printed documents, and integrated systems. Mr. Mandouvalos explains, "It took some time; it was uncharted territory. For some people, the rapid transformation was a big shock. It took time to standardize how processes should work. There was some resistance to change, but it could have been worse."

When the change was first being considered, the IT team assembled a group of employees to help determine and maintain the new direction. Mr. Mandouvalos says, "During the design phase, we heavily involved a lot of users. We created a steering committee [that] consisted of vendor resources, internal IT resources, and actual would-be users of the system, who all took an active role. This committee defined what the project needed to be. Those people who had been a part of the process ended up as fans and followers of it. Rather than being imposed on them, it was their own brain child. The committee continues to meet to address challenges and changes that need to take place within the system."

5. HURDLES OVERCOME

The primary hurdles occurred during system adoption.

Business

An ongoing challenge is the fact that Generali has no control over the infrastructure or equipment that brokers and agents use. Many still use fax, so the capacity to use a variety of communication methods had to be accommodated within the system. Some users were resistant to moving toward a paperless environment. In addition, some users remain technically out of date, so the system required an intuitive process and a simple user interface to address these users. At the time of the new system launch, the business had to determine fixes and workarounds for these and other issues that arose with the new functionality.

Organization Adoption

Staff that were not part of the steering committee were more resistant to the change. However, as the system has become integrated into Generali's workflow, staff have seen the benefits it can provide. Mr. Mandouvalos notes, "We handled the transition as we would handle any other big project. We had milestones, progress reports, and steering committee meetings to keep things on track."

6. BENEFITS

The new system has benefitted Generali in several ways.

6.1 Cost Savings/Time Reductions

One highly measurable change that has materialized is the reduced need for paper. The previous process required three copies of each policy: one for Generali, one for the agent, and one for the customer. The new system eliminates the agent copy, saving more than 1 million printed pages per year, which translates into significant savings in paper and printing costs.

The time it takes to process information has also been reduced. Underwriters now have all the information for an application together and so do not have to spend time compiling it. They can get replies from agents on pending issues much faster and so can process applications and policy transactions quickly. Consequently, the time needed to issue a policy has dropped by approximately 70 percent.

6.2 Increased Revenues

Although the condition of the Greek economy has stifled revenue growth, Generali has the potential to increase it when the economy rebounds. This potential is the result of being able to process applications and claims more quickly and move on to the next customer. The new system has given the company the capacity to serve more customers.

6.3 Quality Improvements

A positive impact has resulted from an increased ability to respond to government compliance demands. Mr. Mandouvalos explains: "For the claims process, we need to have all files and everything related to claims documented. In the past, these items have been scattered. Now, we have them all in place, so we can easily locate them when needed for reporting. We are one of the very few companies that can respond efficiently by the deadlines imposed from the ministry and be 100 percent compliant."

7. BEST PRACTICES, LEARNING POINTS AND PITFALLS

7.1 Best Practices and Learning Points

- ✓ *It is crucial to involve users from "time zero" and make them feel that they own the project.*

✓ It is important to define your business process in as much detail as possible. Think of exceptions and document them, as well.

✓ Stick to your decisions, and don't be tempted to backtrack. Even if things
are missing, move forward; if you have a basic structure, go ahead and address challenges along the way.

✓ It is essential to have people on hand who know what they are doing technically. You need good, local IT resources to support the project.

7.2 Pitfalls

✗ Avoid paying too little attention to the definition of all use cases. They
should be defined down to the smallest detail and documented carefully.

8. COMPETITIVE ADVANTAGES

The new system has led to a competitive advantage for Generali, because the organization is now able to provide better service to its agents, who are the primary
selling channel for Generali's offerings. As a result of this better service, agents
are more likely to offer their clients Generali insurance above offerings from other
providers, leading to increased market share.

Processes are now clearer and more defined, and internal employees know where
to find information, so workflow and efficiency have improved. The system provides benefits whenever processes are incorporated into it.

Another new competitive advantage is the ability to comply with emerging legislation in a timely manner. Mr. Mandouvalos observes, "When a company is not able
to comply, this can be a huge problem. We have seen situations in which other
companies haven't been able to comply, which was very challenging for them. For
us, it has been easy." This ease of compliance is made possible by the flexibility of
the underlying infrastructure, which allows rapid changes to processes and rules.
The system can be used as a platform for building any new functionality that the
state requires.

Generali has also developed a mobile component as part of its solution. A mobile
version of the system is used to create quotes from an Apple iPhone or Google
Android device. The same application can be used to gather and submit data from
customers via PDF documents. This step is the beginning stage of creating an
insurance policy and the starting point for adding the policy holder in the system.
In development is another application that customers can use to view billing information as well as terms and conditions for their policy.

A new level of service to agents combined with higher efficiency, the ability to easily respond to new legislation requirements, and a mobile component have shifted
the competitive goalposts for the insurance industry. To maintain this competitive
advantage, Generali plans to use the new platform as a strategic tool for handling
all unstructured corporate information as well as a strategic choice to implement,
monitor, and enforce business workflows and processes. Mr. Mandouvalos states,
"We want to expand the use of the system to cover all business functions and departments and empower our employees to better serve our agents in all aspects of
their collaboration with us. We also want to maintain transparency in our operations and expand [them] to ensure that our agents feel they are dealing with a
robust, serious, and trustworthy partner that they will favor over other insurance
companies."

9. TECHNOLOGY

The technology infrastructure of the new solution consists of the following components:

- A web portal for agents and roaming staff
- An enterprise capture tool for integrating documents into the system
- A BPM engine that supports both structured workflow and collaborative flows
- Business activity monitoring for tracking process metrics and trends as well as generating notifications and alerts
- SOA-based integration with back-end systems:
    - In-house–developed insurance system
    - In-house–developed insurance rating and offer-creation system
    - Server (integrated with the email client) with mailbox polling and workflow triggering through email
    - Access to several publicly accessible web services offered by government and insurance industry agencies for verification of tax status, motor vehicle data, etc., as well as provisioning of web services for consumption from peripheral systems
- PDF conversion tools for generating documents that the system requires
- Additional functionality:
    - Application for filling out forms (This feature is intuitive for end users and decouples form-specific data from application logic.)
    - An enterprise capture tool for barcoded applications and cover letters that provides automatic classification and indexing
    - Ability to use both legacy (fax) and new (email, direct online) communication methods (Users experience faster processing time when using new methods.)
    - Aspects for addressing various LOBs:
        - Strict workflow for supporting standardized insurance "packages"
        - Collaborative flows for facilitating tailor-made or complex insurance proposals

Figure 2 shows the high-level workflow process.

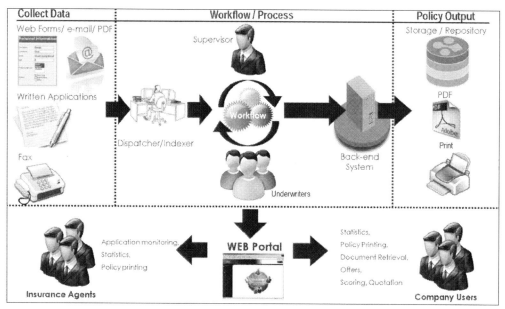

Figure 2: Workflow Process

Figure 3 shows the solution architecture components.

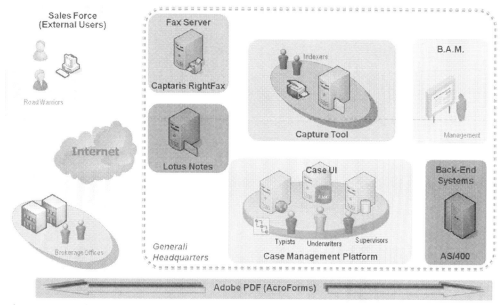

Figure 3: Solution Architecture Components

Figure 4 shows the solution architecture flow.

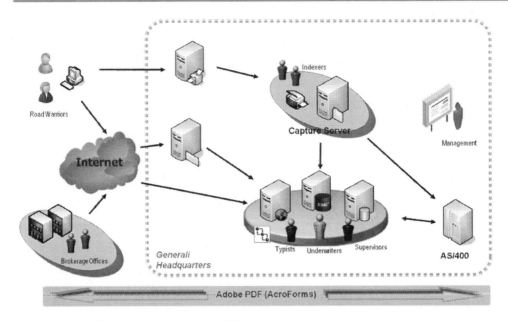

Figure 4: Solution Architecture Flow

Benefits for brokers and agents include real-time access to information related to their customers. They no longer need to keep paper copies and have a consolidated view of all information related to customers, including policies, claims, and applications. They also have the ability to track the life cycle of each application and claim, with no need to call Generali headquarters to inquire about an open case. Another benefit is fast turnarounds following the submission of electronic applications.

Benefits for internal Generali users include the elimination of paper, streamlining of processes, immediate access to each customer's files, a lifting of the "data entry" function for underwriters, the ability to easily define key performance indicators, and the ability for managers to view all open cases and determine whether service level agreements are met.

10. THE TECHNOLOGY AND SERVICE PROVIDERS

Generali turned to Uni Systems (http://www.unisystems.gr), the largest non-multinational information communication technology systems integrator in Greece, for proven business know-how. The excellent technical team demonstrated a solution that fully addressed Generali's business requirements.

EMC (http://www.emc.com/xcp) provided the technical infrastructure for the solution, including EMC Documentum xCP for Case Management, BPM, and BAM, and EMC Captiva for enterprise capture. EMC was selected based on its reputation as an industry leader and the completeness of its platform. EMC's local branch was supportive and responsive.

Fortune-500 Bank, India
Silver Award: Customer-Facing

1. EXECUTIVE SUMMARY / ABSTRACT

This case study is about one of the leading Fortune 500 banks from Asia Pacific. Having started operations in India in 1853, the bank has steadily grown in reach and service offerings, keeping pace with the evolving banking and financial needs of its customers.

The bank wanted to automate its Customer Request Management process in India. All the different types of customer requests, complaints, queries, interactive phone calls needed to be processed and routed to the right customer executives (Front/Back Office) based on their skill metrics, experiences and availability. The solution had to be flexible and robust enough to support the growing customer base and different request types.

Newgen provided the Request Management Solution (RMS) built on its Case Management suite. More than 3000 users (Front Office and Back Office) are using the solution with various roles assigned to them. According to the request type, the request management solution auto-disseminates tasks amongst those users. The Case Management solution for RMS supports request initiation from multiple channels and departments like

- Call Centers (Phone)
- E-Mail requests
- Centralized Complaints Team (System log screen)

Also, customer requests are initiated by scanning customer letters/documents at all the branches of the bank, NRI Centers, and Customer Contact Centers. The Request Management System cuts through almost all the departments of the bank, Pan-India. Some of the NRI branches also use the RMS solution. Almost all the banking products and services are intertwined with the RMS solution and more than 30 business areas are reaping benefits from it. Some of those key business areas are:

- Retail Banking products & services
- Corporate & Commercial Banking products & services
- Other areas include: Clearing Houses, ATM, Wealth Management System, Credit Product divisions

Every day 8000+ cases are raised on the RMS system. The system supports more than 470 case request types and enables addition of new request type or a new subcategory of request in the RMS system which becomes an integral part of the solution. Other key highlights:

- Scenario based multi-level escalations for turn-around time; TAT-burst
- Auto-routing of the requests

2. OVERVIEW

With its ever burgeoning customer base, the bank felt the need to employ a comprehensive Customer Request Management Solution which would not only cater to their large customer base but also streamline the entire process and integrate disparate systems and several departments which used to work in silos.

The bank had three major departments namely

- Call Center (CC)

- E-Mail Management Team (EMT) and
- Centralized Complaint Team (CCT)

These departments would take care of all the customer requests coming from different channels like phone call, e-mail, SMS, website portal etc. However, they were working in silos that resulted in duplication of the same customer's requests that came via different channels like phone, email, website portals. Multiple processing of the same customer's requests in three different departments was making it extremely difficult for the bank to meet the SLAs of customers. Also, it significantly increased the process cycle time which made customers less than happy.

The bank would cater to a variety of customer requests and hence wanted to build specialized task force groups where each group would have clearly defined core competencies in servicing a specific set of requests. Group personnel would be mapped to each group depending on skill sets and respective requirements. In this way, the bank would become more efficient and achieve faster turn-around time (TAT) in processing various kinds of requests. Now, the challenge was to get a comprehensive Case Management solution that would streamline the entire request management process and automatically distribute the customer requests to the right task force and to the right user with appropriate skill set and experience. Also, to keep pace with scalability requirements, the case management solution had to be flexible enough to serve any kind of request and in case of a new request type the case management solution should be able to make it an integral part of the system for future references.

To monitor the request management process, the bank required a business activity monitoring tool with a report dashboard that would provide complete process visibility. The tool must show drilled down reports with live data on the monitoring screen so that the business users can take faster and accurate business decisions. For exceptions like bottlenecks of a user group or TAT-burst, the system had to show pro-active alert signals on the screen send alarm messages for escalations.

The bank implemented Newgen's Case Management suite to automate and streamline their RMS process. The case management solution comprises a comprehensive workflow automation tool, dynamic work allocation with load balancer toolkit, rule engine, process templates and Business Activity Monitoring tool. The workflow based RMS process created a common process platform for all the three complaint departments namely Call Center (CC), E-Mail Management Team (EMT) and Centralized Complaint Team (CCT). A single integrated user interface is created so that users can view the customer history data, past requests, documents on the single screen. For instances where a customer has made the same requests via multiple channels, it should be displayed on the user interface and viewable to the person who is processing the request.

The work allocation tool and load balancer provided the flexibility to configure filters and check points for routing requests to the right users based on the request type, user skill set, core competency, user experience and customer profile. Load balancer optimized the entire process of task allocation so that there were no bottlenecks in addressing customer requests.

End-to-end tracking and monitoring was envisaged in the workflow right from the time the request was logged onto the system till the time the request moved to the exit. It also tracked the dispatch and delivery status if some deliverable was required to be couriered to customers. The BAM tool showed customized reports on the dashboard which gave complete process visibility and helped make quick changes in the business process as and when required.

More than 3000 users are using the case management solution. Every day 8,000+ cases are raised and more than 20,000 requests are processed on the RMS process. The system supports more than 470 case request types and enables addition of new request type or a new subcategory of request in the RMS which becomes an integral part of the solution.

Some of the key benefits experienced by the bank are:
- Scenario based multi-level escalations for TAT-burst
- Auto-routing of the requests to the right users
- End to end tracking of requests
- Faster TAT results leading to improved customer experience
- Adherence to SLAs
- Automatic notifications to customers via multiple channels like email, SMS
- Interoperability with disparate business systems and banks core processing applications

3. BUSINESS CONTEXT

With an ever increasing customer base, the bank felt the need for a customer helpdesk department very early on. Initially, customer requests were serviced via phone calls and couriers. With the advancement of technology, the bank started serving customer requests via multiple channels like email, SMS, phone banking, letters, web site portals etc. So, a department that started small grew drastically. For the sake of operational dexterity, it was divided into three departments. These three departments were Call Center (CC), E-Mail Management Team (EMT) and Centralized Complaint Team (CCT) that used to take care of all the customer requests coming from discrete channels.

Even though the departments were created to serve customer requests, they used to work in silos as there was no technology that could integrate them on a single platform. The CC department took care of all the phone calls and SMS, EMT used to process all the emails that came to the helpdesk address and CCT department used to process all requests that came via courier.

The major challenges, faced by this business model were:
- It lacked complete process visibility
- Poor resource utilization
- Higher process cycle time
- Difficulty in SLA management while addressing different kinds of service requests
- Addressing a new kind of service request was a major concern as there was no process or resource pre-defined for that
- No provision for optimum resource utilization facility for work distribution amongst the users, caused bottlenecks and decelerated the entire service request process
- No pool of knowledge workers with core competency for different kind of service requests caused variations in customer service and hence in customer experiences
- Since the three departments lacked interoperability, It was difficult to identify instances where a single customer sent the same request via dif-

ferent channels and hence more than one resource processed the same request

- Since, no drilled-down reports were available, the business owners were unable to monitor and track the request management process

This was the scenario when the bank decided to opt for request management process transformation which would bring complete process visibility and continuous process improvements by eradicating all the above business challenges.

4. THE KEY INNOVATIONS

4.1 Business

The case management solution provided by Newgen for Request Management, essentially addressed the requests/ complaints of customers coming via different channels. The solution provided a unified interface which would help the users to not only verify some basic details of the customer but also help the users to raise multiple requests simultaneously. The interface shows all the relevant customer information and documents on the screen so that no discrepancy might arise at a later stage as a result of an incorrect request raised. Users were given the freedom of filling up the customer request form online while interacting with the customer or at a later stage after call. The system automatically populated customer data in the form which provided even more time to the user to interact with customer over a phone call to understand his/her problems.

There were scenarios where a customer would raise more than one request at the time of making call or writing e-mail. In that case, each request would be treated as a different request, and hence compete data was available with each request for successful processing at the Back-office. This brought a lot of visibility to the back office users to understand what the requests were and who were working on those requests.

The task distribution system had a load balancer engine. The load balancer made sure that there were no bottlenecks for a user. Unlike before, now the request types defined the flow of tasks to the user groups best fit for the particular requests. Automatic dissemination of tasks or service requests in a group was based on user skill sets and experience in handling similar kinds of requests. Also, customer profile details determined the flow of request. Requests from high profile customers were automatically directed to the senior officials as per hierarchy defined in the case management solution.

The system gave the flexibility to the bank's customers to raise multiple and different kind of requests from a single email, SMS or phone call. Unlike before, where a customer received feedback from various channels for the same request, he/she got a single consolidated answer from one channel.

The business owners got complete process visibility. System escalated the cases on burst of TAT as per the defined escalation matrix. Business owners found alert messages and signals from the Business Activity Monitoring (BAM) dashboard to take pro-active actions on upcoming opportunities or threats.

4.2 Case Handling

In the previous RMS system, requests were logged in an application called the e-Diary. There was a manual follow up by the department to close the request. There was no facility to monitor the requests and ensure they were getting closed.

Three departments, namely- Call Center (CC), E-Mail Management Team (EMT) and Centralized Complaint Team (CCT) were created to take care of all the customer requests coming from various different channels. Even though the departments were created to serve customer requests, they used to work in silos as there was no technology which could integrate them on a single platform. The CC department took care of all the phone calls and SMS, EMT used to process all the emails that were received at the helpdesk address and CCT department used to process all the requests that came via courier. There was no case flow template available. Logged in requests were assigned to users and followed up manually. At the time of TAT burst there was strict hierarchy of manual escalations. And since the escalations were not case specific, it caused delays and unsatisfied customers.

After the case management solution implementation for RMS, the process flow became dynamic and non deterministic as it was controlled by several constraints like type of the request, profile of the user, desirable user skill set and experience, core competency of a user group and availability of the user. In case of TAT burst, the level of escalation was defined by the margin of missed SLA.

The work allocation tool and load balancer provided the flexibility to configure filters and check points for routing requests. The work distribution engine associated with the rule engine ensured that every request had to reach to the right user to achieve the best possible process outcome in terms of TAT, SLA and customer satisfaction.

End-to-end tracking and monitoring was envisaged in process flow right from the time the request was logged into the system till the time the request was completed and exited from the workflow. It also tracked the dispatch and delivery status if some deliverable was required to be couriered to customers.

Overall system architecture.

The case management solution is a multi-tiered, platform independent solution built using robust server-side Java technologies. Its scalable architecture can be applied from small-to-medium workgroup usage, to truly enterprise-wide workflow management requirements. The case management solution comprises of a comprehensive workflow automation tool, dynamic work allocation with load balancer toolkit, rule engine, process templates and Business Activity Monitoring tool.

The users in the front office log customer requests in the RMS. Once the requests are logged onto the system the request then gets routed automatically to the appropriate back office for processing. The routing is determined by various constraints like type of the request, profile of the user, desirable user skill set and experience, core competency of a user group and availability of the user.

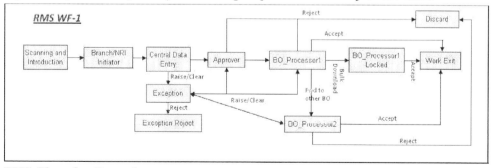

RMS Flow for Branches

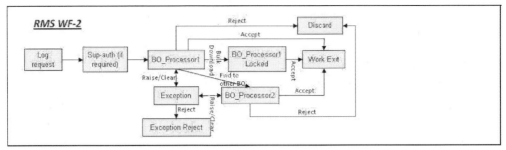

RMS Flow for Call Centre & Customer Connect

All the requests that were logged in through

- Call Center (CC)
- E-Mail Management Team (EMT)
- Centralized Complaints Team (CCT)

The case management solution had been running in the front offices and back offices. All the requests, captured by the three departments were sent across to the back offices for further processing. Users in the back offices were classified by their skills, experience, core competency, history etc. and that data was supplied to the case management solution which helped determine the process flow on-the-fly depending from case to case.

Process Manager was a module component of the case management solution, used to define the case templates. It provided the flexibility to configure filters and business rules at server level for routing tasks to different users. This setting maintained the uniformity and optimization of the entire process. This feature was highly critical in the case management solution because there were a number of back offices which were supposed to process various request types. All these back offices would be mapped to one work-step in the process and filters would be configured accordingly so that a specific back office would view only those request types that matched its expertise.

When a new request type arrived in the system, the process manager would create a process template for it. If the constraints were too new and different than usual, the system generated alert messages. Then the business user had to intervene in the process to define the case template which eventually became an integral part of the solution for future references.

Escalation feature of the solution was used extensively throughout the process so that users finished their work within the Turn-around Time (TAT) and if failed to do so then it was able to identify and define the gap in performance. Process Manager & dashboards would provide the process view with respect to tasks completed, pending & in-process to operation mangers for them to take appropriate action on a given day.

End-to-end tracking & monitoring is envisaged in the workflow right from the time the request is logged onto the system till the work item exits the workflow. It also tracks the dispatch and delivery status if some deliverable is required to be couriered to customers.

The key roles

There were request initiator (Front Office), Request resolver (Back office) and business owners, involved in this project .

Initiator could be Call Center, Branch, Customer Connect or Email Management Team. There were around 60+ groups within the back office team.

Depending on the request type and subcategory, requests were assigned to an appropriate team member in the back office.

There was a hierarchy of business owners. At the incident of TAT burst, depending upon the severity, the request was escalated to the right business owner. Then the business owner took control of the request and reassigned the request to some other user or solved it himself.

The main business entities and how they are maintained / lifecycle.

- RMS is used for many businesses of the bank. Few example -
- Wealth management, Credit Card, Retail Assets, Consumer Finance, Treasury and other banking products

The case template

- Each request is considered as a separate case. The case templates were defined as per the request type / subcategory in the system. Selection of Template is dynamic. The selection of process path takes place at multiple levels. The request type and its subcategory are defined at the time it is logged on to the system. In the first level, according to the request type and sub category, a particular case is automatically forwarded to the right user group.
- In the second level, the case manger looks into more details of the case to determine what will be the suitable user profile to process the request. The user profile is selected as per the case type, skill and competency required, years of experience and the customer profile. The case manager forwards the task to the best fit user in the group. If the best fit user is busy and might create a bottleneck then the case is forwarded to the next best person and so on. The group heads of every user group is notified about the case distribution amongst the users in their group. Each user can only view the cases assigned to him. The business owners are allowed to view all the cases that are distributed amongst all the users.
- For a new request type that arrives for the first time, a case template is generated and the filters are set in the server level. And after that, it becomes an integral part of the solution.

4.3 Organization & Social

There were significant changes in the way employees of the bank executed their tasks. Before RMS implementation, all the requests were logged in an application called e-Diary. There was a manual follow up with the department to close the request. There was no facility to monitor the requests and ensure they were being closed. The customer request capture process was manual and error prone.

After implementing the RMS process, the process flow became dynamic and non deterministic. The right employees used to get the right kind of cases which matched their core competency and skills. Unlike before, the employees did not have to perform data entries. The RMS solution automatically fetched the right customer information from the core HUB application of the bank and auto populated the data in the customer request form. Employees were rid of the tedious data entry job and spent more time talking with customers over the phone to better understand their problems. Also, the employees were given the freedom to fill up the customer request forms later after finishing their conversation with customers. This ensured better case understanding and more accurate data entry (for the few fields which were left after auto data population). The customer satisfaction level was improved significantly as they found the helpdesk employees more attentive and consultative.

The unified solution screen showed not only the case data and request forms but also customer history and other related documents on the screen. The employees did not have to toggle between screens or search for customer records which significantly saved their time and made their job much easier than before.

The bank also formulated a Center of Excellence (COE), a cross-functional team, which worked towards continuous process improvement and growth in terms of servicing new requests.

5. HURDLES OVERCOME

Management

The bank pursued a strategy of rapid expansion both vertically and horizontally. The bank wanted to expand the number of branches and at the same time to provide more services to its customers. So even though the solution solved all the major business concerns, initially the management was concerned about how the solution would align with their business strategy. However, at the time of UAT, the RMS system was able to earn enough trust of the management. Within a few months after going live, the management became confident that the solution was scalable and flexible enough to align with their larger business strategy.

Business

The solution demanded changes in the way business was done. A lot of manual hand offs were required after implementing the new solution, which became a major concern. However, after a few months of going live, better business result began to materialize.

Organization Adoption

The bank was looking to set best-in-class operations and productivity standards. However shifting people from paper to images was a major hurdle. Initially employees of the bank took some time to understand how the solution worked. At the beginning, there were several instances where employees were unable to complete the task as described in the process. But with time, all the employees were able to adopt the new system and started enjoying the benefits of automation.

6. BENEFITS

6.1 Cost Savings / Time Reductions

- More than 3000 users of the bank are using the solution
- Solution supports request management for more than 470 different types of requests.
- Everyday 8000+ requests are raised and the scalable solution serves 20000+ requests every day
- Adherence to SLA to 99%
- Significant improvement in process cycle time and TAT
- End to End tracking of requests i.e. from the time a request is logged into the system to tracking the delivery details of a request
- Reduced customer call holding time as the system helps the users in logging in requests in a more quicker and efficient way
- Business Activity Monitoring dashboard for complete process visibility
- Seamless integration with core banking applications and various departments which used to work in silos
- Knowledge and competency based work distribution resulted in better business results in terms of higher number of satisfied customer

- Continuous process improvements

6.2 Increased Revenues

The bank has experienced top-line growth considering all the tangible and intangible benefits that were accrued.

6.3 Quality Improvements

Skilled Based Dynamic Work Allocation and Tracking:

Work allocation and tracking of those tasks had been a major challenge for the bank. The BPM solution provided a work distribution console that made sure that there would not be bottlenecks in job allocation and equal distribution of tasks. Work was distributed as per employee skill sets and furthermore, the solution supported complete audit trail of all the tasks and activities that could be monitored and tracked whenever required.

Improved customer experience:

The employees of the bank were given the freedom of filling up the customer request form online while interacting with the customer or at a later stage after the call. The system automatically populated customer data in the form which provided even more time to the employees to interact with customers over the phone to understand their problems. This significantly improved the quality of the customer service process.

Faster Exception Resolution:

The bank had an exception management process which was manual, time consuming and error-prone. The BPM solution provided an exception management mechanism which required minimal manual intervention.

7. BEST PRACTICES, LEARNING POINTS AND PITFALLS

7.1 Best Practices and Learning Points

- ✓ Automation as a facilitator and not as a dictator for the resources working on it
- ✓ Simplicity, flexibility and robustness should be the prime focus
- ✓ Simple, lesser and similar interfaces across modules
- ✓ Case management solution is a relatively different way of handling business challenges. The users and the management should be given enough time to adopt it.

7.2 Pitfalls

- ✗ Complex user interface may cause delay in adopting new technology platform
- ✗ Phase wise implementation may be slow but more effective in the end

8. COMPETITIVE ADVANTAGES

- Single sign-on: Every user while logging into their system is automatically and simultaneously logged into the RMS process
- Auto Population of fields from HUB: Integration will core banking system helped verify the user details before initiating the process
- Multiple Request Initiation: The Initiation interface included a feature to raise multiple requests for the same customer.
- Modify/Cancel Request: A request initiated may need to be discarded or re-opened

- Re-open Cases: 'Initiating Department' user has the option to reopen the closed request in case of certain requests that have been unsatisfactorily closed by the back office during processing.
- TAT and escalation: TAT was defined for every request that entered into the system and Escalation features were used extensively throughout the process so that users could finish their work within the defined Turn-Around-Time (TAT).
- Attachment: Front offices have a feature to attach documents at the time of logging in requests.

9. TECHNOLOGY

The bank has procured the case management suite from Newgen. The case management solution is comprised of a comprehensive Business Process Management suite- OmniFlow™, dynamic work allocation with load balancer toolkit- rule engine, process templates and the document management system - OmniDocs™.

OmniDocs™ It is an Enterprise Content Management (ECM) platform for creating, capturing, and managing, delivering and archiving large volume of documents. OmniDocs™ provides highly scalable, unified repository for securely storing and managing enterprise content. It provides a centralized repository for enterprise documents and supports rights based archival. It supports both centralized and distributed scanning with policy based upload. The platform manages complete lifecycle of documents through record retention, storage and retrieval policies. It supports exhaustive document and folder searches on date, indexes and general parameters as well as full text search on image and electronic documents.

OmniFlow™ OmniFlow™ is a platform-independent, scalable Business Process Management engine that enables automation of organizational business processes. Built using open technologies, it has seamless integration abilities allowing it to be introduced into any IT infrastructure.

Newgen's Business Process Management Suit offers the following tools:
- Business Process Modeler: Used by business users to define the business process. Process is defined as set of activities in sequence, parallel, or loop.
- Process Manager: Enables efficient process management and administration using various people and process oriented real time reports.
- Process Client: Enables manual intervention in business processes through web.
- Business Activity Monitoring Component: Consists of a set of reporting tools for process owners, senior management, and other business users. eg: Real Time & Historic Reporting Tool and GUI Reports Builder

10. THE TECHNOLOGY AND SERVICE PROVIDERS

The solution has been implemented by the Newgen Implementation team and no third party team was involved in it.

Newgen consultants proposed a solution to the bank as per the best practices followed. The system study, solution design and implementation was carried out by Newgen professionals

Paneon GmbH, Austria

Gold Award: Knowledge Worker Innovation

1. EXECUTIVE SUMMARY / ABSTRACT

Paneon GmbH is a two-year old startup located in Austria and currently serving the German-speaking markets of Austria, Germany and Switzerland.

As a Network marketing business with a large, decentralized structure of individual sales partners providing contacts to customers, building sales and business relations from informal community relations Paneon faces a number of challenges:

- How to deal with growing and the related rising complexity?
- How to adjust to growth without creating bureaucracy?
- How to quickly adapt to market pull without software development?
- How to stay focused on people and support more engagement?
- How to manage a business with independent individuals?

Clearly, as a business that prides itself in promoting ecological, natural and social balance as its business principles, a post-modern management style and strategy was required. Customer satisfaction and quality are the core objectives with revenue and profits being a consequence rather than a target.

What kind of software can support such a management style?

One option was to buy off-the-shelf warehouse, accounting and CRM solutions or use for example Salesforce.com. After an analysis it was found that none of these could handle necessary functionality:

- People network structure representation
- Account transition processes assigned to partners
- Special views for office and sales partners to assign work tasks
- Extended network structure with transitions and hierarchy changes
- Order extensions e.g. order mask extensions
- Purchase-to-pay stock order tracking until payment (JIT ordering)
- Stock management UIs as cases
- Products and articles management processes
- User defined tasks and delegation according to role/skill profile
- Twitter sentiment analysis and customer care processes
- Interfaces to banks, logistics, warehouse, commissions, ...

Solution overview:

The solution consists of an ACM goal-oriented case management system for customer care and warehousing and logistics services, task-oriented collaboration derived from business objectives linked to goals.

Two independent organizations have to be supported; one for the social interest, the other for business operations. A challenge consists in transiting users between roles: member-customer-partner-coach.

- Sign in, sub-domains, orders, management, frequent changes.
- 1000 web users 2012, planning for 5000 in 2014.
- Content creation for customer on-boarding into ACM case.
- Fax and email inbound order document capture into ACM case.
- Webforms interface for direct customer orders into ACM.

2. BUSINESS CONTEXT

Many businesses adopt a management or planning method because "everyone does it." With Balanced Scorecard, Business Reengineering, or CRM, too often no one involved can explain the principles that are driving the method and why changes are being made and how they will affect them.

As a startup, Paneon could not afford to build a large customer and partner care organization and the related management hierarchy according to orthodox CRM principles. Customers must all be treated equally and not grouped according to revenue into A, B, or C types, each with less service focus than the previous.

Using the concepts behind Strategic ACM, Paneon was able to make the relationships between strategy, people, roles, authority, goals, tasks, customers, and means (formerly rigid budgets) transparent and understood. 1911 Taylorism was about power, control and monitoring in organizations, ACM is about dynamics and empowerment.

Because organizations are human and social structures, self-organization in complex adaptive systems (a business and its boundary to its customers) is natural. A Network Marketing business has a fuzzy edge of the organization, where 'employees' are both partners and customers, requiring constant adaptation to keep the organization in sync with the market.

Leadership has to be focused on making the system work and not by controlling and enforcing certain work or behaviors. Because Paneon partners participate out of their free will and can leave at any point in time, policy enforcement is not usable. Ethical principles of behavior and common goals are the only binding forces.

Key principles of guidance:

Pay is per individual results of each partner and his team.

There are no budgets to keep or targets to reach.

Compensation favors long-term customer satisfaction.

Customer satisfaction is monitored case by case and not statistically.

Payment is structured hierarchically but identically bottom-up.

Participation and innovation is rewarded and not target incentives.

3. THE KEY INNOVATIONS

4.1 Business

Information is like oxygen. Without it the business will suffocate. But this information is not about gathering huge amounts of senseless data, but providing all information (data and content) in business (process) context and thus ensuring top-down and bottom-up transparency

Easy access to real-time process and financial information is like turning on the light in a dark room. Transparency not only creates understanding but also trust; top-down and horizontally between teams. In fact, the network structure is only hierarchical in terms of the time-line how teams grow but not in terms of command and control.

Rather than centralized functions and departments, Paneon grows as a lean and organic network of independent teams, which each work as fully accountable business units. This requires a fundamental change the way the business organizes itself. Collaboration rather than functional decomposition is the key.

In network marketing the business goes where the market pulls and each team can grow its own structure of members to support the possible revenue or motivate new partners to build more revenue. All teams are in constant healthy competition, but cross-team support and coaching is an ethical principle. The compensation structure supports win-win cooperation.

A networked marketing structure is like a living organism. A single cell (team) must never outgrow a sound size that ensures communication among team members. When teams get too large they are being split and as a result a new hierarchy level can appear. The support software must be able to deal with such changes in 'business organization' ad-hoc and without any delay or development effort.

The key innovation is that there is no rigid process organization. There are teams and each team can have any number of members with certain roles and skills (some members are physicians or veterinarians).

4.2 Case Handling

Before the solution was installed, ordering was by fax and phone, requiring large manual overhead for processing. Because there was no well-defined process description available from Paneon (mostly as they did not know how they and their partners would operate with the software) the solution was built over time by discovering the processes by adding additional case templates and adapt them until satisfactory. As Paneon has no IT team and no process management skills, this was done by the software vendor and a CRM partner company. The solution is actually hosted at the software vendor and is planned to be moved to Amazon Cloud once large enough. The most complex parts for IT were to create the stock management database modeling, the bank payment interface the document capture definition for incoming paper, fax or email orders, and the calculation using rules for the commissions.

ACM cases and goals:

- Users and performers can only be added by authorized staff. For security reasons there is only a registration request but no self-registration. LDAP is possible but not used by Paneon as the ACM system manages all users.
- The only fairly strict process is the customer order process that is presented as a sequence of forms (Desktop, Browser or Mobile) and passes then to logistic fulfilment. This process goal is instantiated inside the customer case.
- A case can be started by receiving an order form by fax or email, which is then captured and the order data extracted. While all attachments of an email are kept in the case, Paneon does not use the content capture for ad-hoc data extraction at this time.
- While stock availability is checked during the order data entry, it is possible that some shipment conflict requires order postponement and additional work steps to complete the process are needed. These tasks can be added by authorized user roles from a simple menu.
- The BPMN view is not needed to manipulate the case tasks. Dependent and prerequisite tasks with rules can be added in the case view.
- There is no need to create all possible variants and relevant logic, but simply a few constraining rules to ensure correct completion.
- Should a customer open a complaint for the shipment, it is added as a new goal to the same case, to which new work tasks can be added ad-hoc for resolution.
- Emails and SMS messages are sent from the case.

- A library of letter and email templates is available and partners can modify and use the templates at any point in the case and attach them to a task for processing, i.e. including email or SMS send.
- Chat messages can be sent to any other person in the network from within the case.
- The complete team can see all cases for the team and accept the tasks.
- Case tasks can be delegated to new roles or individuals. Only the resources attached to that task are visible to the delegate.
- Because the payment is a task in the order process that sends the request to the bank interface, the payment data incoming from the bank have to be consolidated to change the payment task state.
- There are a number of customer payment and shipment resolution templates as goals that can be used and reused by the support staff or by the qualified partner coaches.
- A team member can see all cases and the complete history of this customer and reference any historic elements in the current case.
- Natural Language Rules can be used to search cases and to set notification triggers so that partners can be notified when certain orders or events take place. The rules can trigger cases or messages to be sent.
- For the warehouse orders a 'purchase-to-pay' set of case templates was created. They are also goal-oriented and help Paneon to ensure that only invoices are paid when they match the actual deliveries to stock.
- Several dashboard views were defined to see open cases, time overruns, error states, revenue, commissions, and partner network structures.
- A Gantt chart view can be used to see the complete case timeline.
- A number of regular reports were created that print the above.
- A Twitter/Facebook interface was installed and tests are running that open service cases if Paneon is mentioned on social networks.
- Customers and interested parties can request service cases on the web or via incoming email.
- For partner management a number of templates exist already that allow the assignment of tasks inside coaching and training cases. This will the next focus for the use of ACM.

4.3 Organization & Social

Paneon does not intend to create a center of excellence as it sees that as an outdated artifact of hierarchical organizations. Knowledge must be spread as wide and deep as possible because that makes the organization as resilient to change as possible. To ensure common approaches, the business knowledge must be embedded into case templates and they too allow the reuse of prior experience.

Knowledge is not just text or flowcharts that can't be executed but actual previous cases that can be reused as new templates. Coaches support learning processes and support team members when cases run into obstacles. Coaches will start to use training programs defined as ACM projects, to improve the understanding of values and attitudes towards customers.

The new management paradigm requires that work and performance consideration have to be reassessed. In a team, partners have to be entrepreneurial, whereas coaches in these structures advise on objectives and principles. A networked structure does not need traditional roles of commanders.

4.4 Hurdles overcome

Management

While being small and very entrepreneurial, a better understanding from Paneon management what processes will be required would have simplified the project start. The main problem was not the creation of the case templates, but that all the data entities and the related backend interfaces have to be modeled before the cases can be practically tested. There was no time for a more formal business architecture approach at the project start. That also made the creation of rules for case control and commission calculation a lot more time-consuming.

It was also difficult for Paneon management to understand that they received a consolidated CRM/BPM/ECM functionality with order entry and warehouse processes supported through several SOA and REST interfaces with banks and social networks. So the overall effort was misjudged.

Business

The initial cost and time of creating the interfaces to other systems was misjudged. Several bank interfaces had to be tested to manage to create a semi-automatic payment step in the ACM case. Banks basically only allow file submission and not transaction-oriented interfaces. This added complexity of merging/decoupling order files and account statements.

The usual problems appeared related to comparison with orthodox software and/or management concepts by the individual partners. These could be resolved when changes and requirements could be provided much quicker than with programmed solutions. It took some time until people are willing/able to utilize the ability to add new tasks and content to define work steps for problem resolution. People would send emails and attach a print file rather than delegating the task to the same person. Some of it had to do with adoption issues.

Organization Adoption

As the organization grew with using the ACM solution there were no change-over issues from other solutions. One of the few 'green lawn' situations...

The main problem of adoption was user interface issues. Because the original requests asked for as much data to be shown as possible in just a few screens, including live data from stock, that slowed down presentation and made the forms and related rules more complex. Over time the forms were simplified and finally the most important order process was also enabled in a simple set of fairly rigid HTML-forms, substantially improving speed and user acceptance. These web-forms are rolled out to be used also universally for the most common ACM processes. They are a bit more difficult to maintain but can also be easily reused as templates in ACM tasks. The most important point is that the ACM processes remain the same regardless of which presentation technology (desktop, browser or mobile) is used.

Another point was that for certain user types it was necessary to hide the widgets that presented the task orientation of the work items. When a state change or some outside event would automatically delegate a task to the right next role, people would report that they had 'lost the order' while it was just in another state/folder and no longer visible to them. Because the UI is very flexible a number of perspectives with different information content were created and can be chosen by the user or their coach to avoid this.

4. BENEFITS

6.1 Cost Savings / Time Reductions

New products, new vendors, new commission structures, new task types, new partner types can now be added to the ACM setup in just a few days by the support partner through new templates. The reason is that a change management process has to be handled to test that the new models work well with existing calculations. New case templates can be created by Paneon staff manually or by extracting them by a special function from historic cases.

6.2 Increased Revenues

Revenue growth was in 2011 between 12% and 35% per MONTH.

6.3 Quality Improvements

Not applicable as operations started this way.

5. BEST PRACTICES, LEARNING POINTS AND PITFALLS

7.1 Best Practices and Learning Points

✓ Ensure that checklists of processes and their related resources are made as early as possible to schedule the data interfacing efforts timely.

✓ While it seems highly theoretical, the definition of an ontology clarifies early which data, rules and relationships are needed in the data model.

✓ Verify with management that the company culture and management style are reflected in the case/process model.

✓ Ideally, the technology should allow a smooth migration from a more hierarchical (BPM) style to a more adaptive (ACM) style.

✓ If the business does not entertain a CoE then it must provide for certain users to act as ACM coaches and supporters.

✓ Centralized CoE is more flowcharted and coaches are more adaptive.

7.2 Pitfalls

✗ Don't try to standardize forms and views to save project effort. It slows down the all-important adoption by users.

✗ Less is more. Keep the forms simple and uncluttered.

✗ Do not use rules to write application logic.

✗ Do not use programming APIs. Call SOA interface to get data.

✗ Data interfaces are the most complex part of ACM – not always SOA.

✗ Complex forms and validation logic can cause performance issues. TEST!

✗ Don't bypass change management for core structures just because the ACM cases can be adapted. A solid library of elements makes it much safer.

6. COMPETITIVE ADVANTAGES

Critical success factors:

1. Fast response to market changes through ACM
2. Innovation by simple creation of new case templates
3. Operational excellence through people empowerment
4. Customer intimacy through better collaboration/communication
5. Partners feel trusted and valued through transparency
6. Management uses dashboards to verify results and outcomes
7. Bottom-up transparency through auditable case records

Current ongoing extensions:

- Paneon management has defined a set of business objectives and principles to guide the partners and to create the links to process goals. Paneon wants to stay away from the commonly used Balanced Scorecard but rather focus on people and quality motifs.

- The recommended next step would be the creation of a business language ontology to allow communication with less ambiguity. A decision on that is outstanding by Paneon management.

- Customer satisfaction is planned to be rated across the board with voting tasks inside the case template once completed and it will send either an email or SMS to the customer who can respond with a satisfaction score.

- First tests have been performed with a Mobile version (iOS) of the ACM tasks delegation, which should become available during 2012.

- A link to Mobile contact management software is also planned to allow broader use of the partner and customer data for marketing while offline.

- Rolling Budgeting and warehouse order planning cases are being discussed.

7. TECHNOLOGY

Paneon uses the ISIS Papyrus Platform running on Intel Linux servers.

- The ACM, CRM, Correspondence and Capture Frameworks were used by Adaptive GmbH to create the solution. There was no outside programming but only method rules were defined using PQL (Papyrus Query Language). Users utilize NLR that creates PQL automatically.

8. THE TECHNOLOGY AND SERVICE PROVIDERS

ISIS Papyrus Software - http://www.isis-papyrus.com

Adaptive GmbH - http://www.adaptive.at

9. GRAPHICS

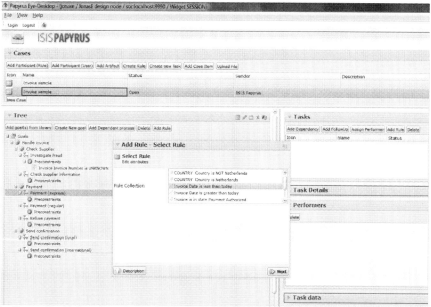

Fig 1. Case Builder GUI to add tasks and rules without BPMN

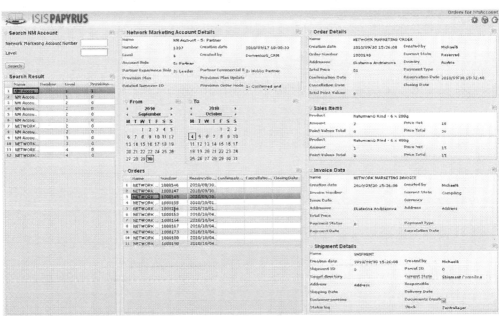

Fig 2. Team Leader Dashboard and Overview

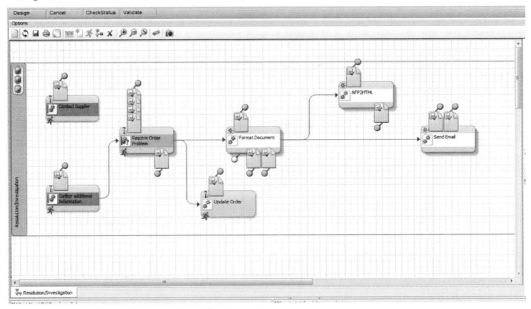

Fig. 3: BPMN case with ad-hoc (Contact Supplier) and dependent tasks

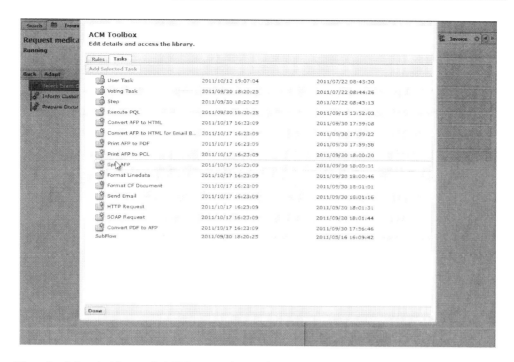

Fig. 4: Adaptation of ACM case by selecting user and system tasks in library

Fig. 5: Webshop Product listing

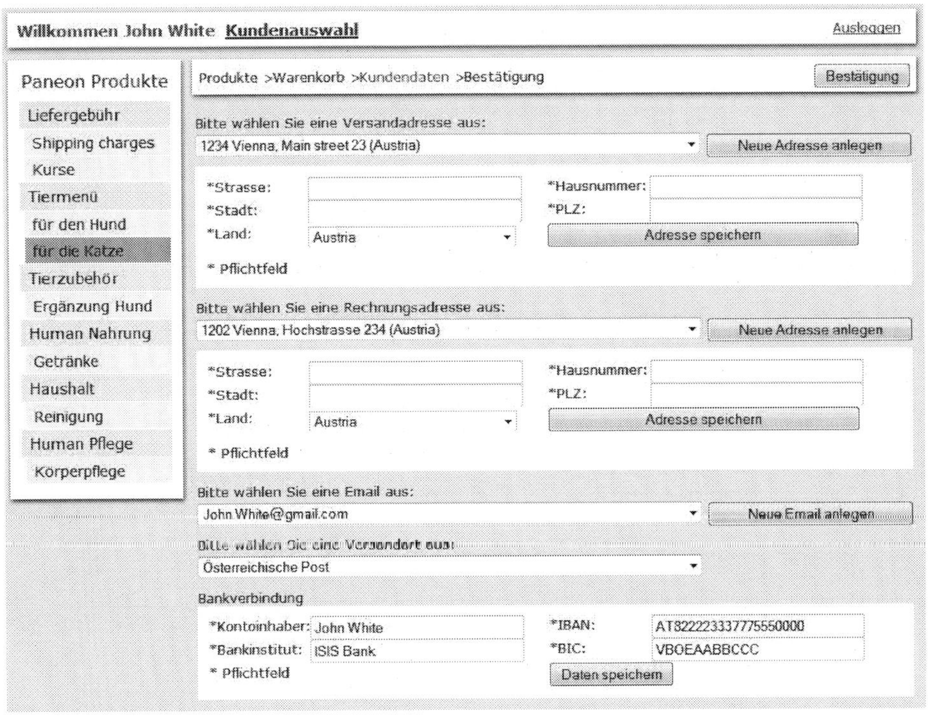

Fig. 6: Webshop Customer data entry

UWV, The Netherlands

Judges' Choice Award: Knowledge Worker Innovation

1. EXECUTIVE SUMMARY/ABSTRACT

UWV, a Dutch organization delivering employee benefits to Dutch citizens, has been using process management systems from their current vendor since 2001. The system was completely renewed and upgraded to a new version early 2012 to improve the customer experience of a UWV customer that objects to an earlier decision of UWV. These objections are handled by the 1,250 employees of the Objections and Appeals division of UWV.

According to the knowledge workers themselves, their new adaptive case management system offers them the possibility to live up to their customer's expectations. Now they can choose the optimal process path for an individual customer, helping them meet deadlines by giving them access to all necessary information in a structured and efficient way.

2. OVERVIEW

UWV is a national organization delivering employee benefits such as unemployment, health and disability cover to citizens in the Netherlands. UWV fulfills the important social task of helping people stay employed or find new employment. Its primary responsibility is to ensure citizens who do not have employment receive correct monthly allowance according to social security regulations. UWV itself employs more than 20,000 people.

UWV's objections and appeals processes are complex, with more than 300 possible process steps, multiple participants and strict legal rules that need to be followed. The objections case is opened when an allowance beneficiary (in this case study called "the customer") objects to an earlier decision of UWV via mail, phone or fax. An objections and appeals case is routed between legal advisors, administrative support, medical advisors and employment advisors that are involved in making a decision leading to the resolution of the objection. Additionally, the objector has the right to appeal the decision before an independent judge or apply for injunctive relief.

This is a large case management implementation. Annually on average more than 80,000 objections, 11,000 appeals and 2,900 higher appeals are registered at UWV and processed by 1,250 employees of the Objections and Appeals Division. Objections and appeals are handled in 15 different regional offices. The average processing time of legal cases is about thirteen weeks; if the objection is of a medical nature, cases will easily take 17 weeks. Cases that end in higher appeal can take years to complete.

3. BUSINESS CONTEXT

UWV has been using process management systems from their current vendor since 2001. The system was completely renewed and upgraded to a new version in early 2012. This new version provides the flexibility to start individual process snippets to easily add and create content, and improves monitoring and system integration capabilities. With these new case management features, UWV employees can determine the contents and process of their case in close consultation with their customers to tailor the case to the customer's needs.

The initial mission in 2001 was to be an accessible and supportive unit focused on improving the quality of processes in order to prevent disputes. Marjolijn Ketelaars, the team lead of the Process and Application team responsible for the coordination and support of these processes, explains the reasons why UWV started with case management in 2001, "We were not able to meet the time limits to process the complaints. We chose this case management solution because we wanted to reduce the wait times and ensure that decisions on cases were completed within defined time-limits."

In 2008, Marjolein Ketelaar said, "The process has inherently long waiting times as hearings must be scheduled with medical advisors who need to conduct investigations in order to reach thoroughly grounded decisions. In most cases a conclusion can only be reached after extensive further examinations. Some of the cases, in particular when they go to the appeal phase, can take up to five years. Today, more than 85 percent of the cases are completed within the time limits. The system positions us well to comply with the new law whereby we have to decide within the required 13 or 17 weeks of receiving an objection."

In 2008, the primary focus of the objections and appeals division was moved towards customer satisfaction. The new mission statement was further operationalized by the Process and Application team. When starting off the project for the new ACM system in 2011, the team put down these guiding principles:

- We obey the rules of law, policy and jurisprudence
- We place the customer principles central in the interaction with customers to improve total customer satisfaction
- When in conflict, customer satisfaction will prevail over procedural risk
- The customer's wishes with regard to the process are leading, even though that is in conflict with legal timeliness
- We are very much capable of organizing our own work

In early 2012, the new system FLEKS (flexible customer system) which operationalizes the above principles, was put into production. Ketelaars said, "FLEKS is fully adjusted to the modern society and the principles of the new world of work. It supports professionals whenever they need it, and it gives freedom wherever they want it.'

4. The Key Innovations

4.1 Business

The system operationalizes the guiding principles of customer satisfaction and case flexibility thought through by UWV's process and application department. Erik de Swart, an experienced Process and Application expert says, "System and process go hand-in-hand. By putting the customer first, we invented a different process than we would have had when primarily focusing on efficiency or lead time."

The largest impact was the deliberate choice to involve the customer in decision making regarding their process. An appeal team, consisting of a legal advisor, a medical expert, an employment advisor and sometimes an administrative help carries prime responsibility for the case. As a team they first discuss and assign a primary case responsible, usually the legal advisor. After this meeting, the case responsible calls the customer to talk the case through. The process map clearly specifies the desired outcome with the customer in mind:

- Define customer wishes: speed, information on the course of the procedure, provide single contact details and direct phone number, discuss desired communication means

- Define customer actions: the customer was able to tell his story and explain his viewpoint, the customer made his wishes clear
- Customer result: I know who my primary contact is, I have a direct phone number, I understand the procedure, I know what roles are involved, etc.
- Legal demands: Case is laid-out, state a time limit to the involved for a hearing, etc.

Obeying the customer's wishes regarding the procedure requires process flexibility. This means that system support for these processes should be very flexible, resulting in a trade-off with legal deadlines, efficiency and risk control. In this, the case responsible should pick priorities, whilst strict legal restrictions should still be monitored and sometimes even enforced by the system.

4.2 Case Handling

- The old case management system was implemented in a stringent way. For a large part, the process route was enforced by the system. Even though it was a case management system, it was by far not as adaptive as FLEKS.
- The old system already provided a case overview with view-access to all possible activities for a case. The employees had little freedom to flexibly forward the case though. An example was a request to the customer to rectify an omission. The old system forced the process on hold until the customer had rectified. In the new process, the legal advisor contacts the customer. If there is a need to move quickly because the customer risks to loose part of his regular payment, the case worker can choose to fully prepare the objection case and not lose time with waiting. Once the additional customer info comes in, the case can immediately be decided on with no time is lost.

Working with case overviews

In-case flexibility is possible through the combination of the following:

- A main case containing all individual process parts that make up a complete case. This case contains the main process from which individual process snippets can be started.

Figure 1 Case overview with vertical time-line to show process status

- An authorized employee working on a case can choose to start process snippets from this general case. By choosing a process part, the employee is presented an overview of all case activities for that process part (figure 1). The employee can choose any activity, although the activities on the time line in the middle are, according to the normal route, the most logical ones to execute. Completed activities are on the right side of the time line, future activities on the left. The overview also shows what was executed, impossible/refused (based on business rules), skipped or redone. Clicking an activity will open the attached form presenting the case data.

Data availability and case progress

In general, progressing a case means that an external party, e.g. a customer or supplier, provides his data to the company or an employee adds value to the product. This is exactly how UWV's case management system calculates the process status and decides what still needs to be done. In other words: It is not the completion of activities that forwards the case, but the availability of case data. To allow for this, an employee who works on a case fills in the data. As long as the data has not been made available (either through a user action or a system event like an integration), the task is not complete.

This also means that the user can choose to disable the case overview shown in Figure 1. The alternative is to only work with forms. Entering the data will still forward the case through the process. Once users know the process and the system better, they will prefer this mode over the case overview mode. A disadvantage of this mode is that the employee does not get feedback on completion of activities. To avoid situations in which the employee thinks he is ready, while the case still has some unconfirmed fields, UWV case designers decided to enable additional checks that notify the employee that some required data is not filled in by highlighting the form tabs containing that data: red tabs still contain required data; green tabs do not.

Case distribution

- FLEKS has much flexibility to fit the system into the distributed organization. It is used in 15 different regional offices that vary in size from three to 10 teams to handle objections and appeals. Every regional office and every team may in principle determine their own distribution mechanism. Assigned cases are accessible to the teams through work lists. The specification of these work lists is completely decoupled from the process design. In principle, every work list has the ability to access all cases in the system. However, system administration has the ability to configure work lists to only show those cases conformant to the business rules specified, for example the user's roles, the regional office, the specific team, the case priority, a specific username or individual case data identified as business rule. There is however a best practice:
- Appeal teams will usually get all cases that are assigned to them. This assignment is done by an expert who assesses the objection based on the applicable law and medical aspects. The expert may assign a case to a specific team, but will usually use the automated distribution mechanism that will distribute the case to the team with the lowest workload;
- The whole appeals team will at all times be able to open the case from the work list; if it is opened by a team member, the other members can only view it simultaneously, but not work on it.

The customer call centre is able to open any case, e.g. by social security number. Their work list is configured to open a specific form that shows the essential case information to help the customer. If the customer wants to be called back, they can leave notes which will show in the team work list.

Case authorization

Every user in the system will be able to open the case and see all activities once the case shows in his work lists (distribution). This does not mean that the user can progress the case. To progress a case requires that a process role is assigned to the user. Roles are hierarchically modelled (see Figure 2).

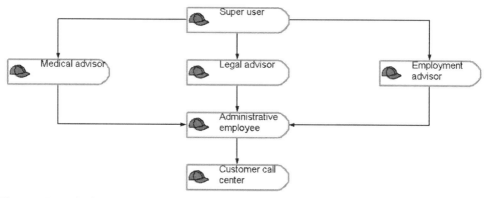

Figure 2 Role hierarchy

Based on the user's roles, restrictions will apply to a user's authorization to progress the case:

The user may only execute (add data) to an activity if he has the same or a higher role than the role specified as execute role for that activity. Roles are modelled in a role hierarchy, meaning that a user with a higher role may always execute the activities of the user with a lower role. A legal advisor, for example, may carry out all activities of an administrative employee while an administrative employee is not allowed to do the legal work. At UWV the legal advisor therefore has a hierarchically higher role than the administrative employee.

Apart from the execute role, there are also skip and redo roles. Allowing a user to redo finished activities means that the process will revert back to the status in which the data for the particular activity was still incomplete. This is done regularly in FLEKS and is part of the necessary freedom of the knowledge workers to repair mistakes or reconsider earlier decisions without the necessity to involve a system administrator to repair a "user error." In principle, this might lead to undesirable situations where, for example, letters will be sent out more than once. However, more freedom in these cases prevails. A skip for an activity will move the process status forward beyond the selected activity. In some cases this may be prevented by the case designer because system steps committing required data to back office systems must be executed. But mostly, the user is trusted to know what to do to compensate.

Medical activities within a case are only accessible from the case overview if the user has the role of the medical expert. For those activities a read role is specified. In runtime this means that the activity will only show in the case overview of the medical expert. Other users will only see an empty space for these activities because of medical privacy.

Document management and document output management

UWV still works with paper dossiers and has put out a tender to select a complete document management solution. Once in place, this will bring additional efficiency gains because the front part of the process still uses paper files. As soon as the electronic case arrives in the team, the user will collect the paper file. However, all documents created in the process are archived in and retrieved from the existing document archiving solution.

UWV's document composition and output management solution is tightly integrated with the case management system. All available data are pre-filled and, except most of the legal texts, text blocks are open for editing by the case handlers. Document templates for all letters are Microsoft Word-based and can easily be adapted by the staff.

System and case architecture

The foundations for FLEKS were laid by a project of the Objections and Appeals Process and Application team. This team consists of experienced experts who know UWV policy, process knowledge and the requirements for application support from inside out. This team also trains the regional offices to use the system.

The web-based case management portal offers:

- Direct access to cases through work lists
- The complete case information for objections, appeals, high appeals and injunctive relief cases (process, data, documents and management information)
- Portal access to important knowledge sources. An important improvement that was released with the new portal was a new index search for most of the available legal sources (both on internet and UWV internal) regarding the knowledge on the approximately 20 different labour laws that apply.
- A new knowledge base on best practices is also available, which is organized by theme and centrally maintained by the process and application experts.

The granularity of the individual process snippets, the contents of the forms and the required case interaction were also decided on by the team of process and application experts. A case in fact is a complete process application, running on the case management server and coordinating process execution and data management during the course of the process. Process parts are modelled in a graphical modelling environment. Not only is the process modeled in this environment and presented on case forms, but so is the data. Data and documents reside in several different databases and information systems and are retrieved on opening of the case. The built-in application integration framework tightly integrates into UWV's service oriented architecture, with links to UWV systems for document management and customer and employer information (see Figure 3).

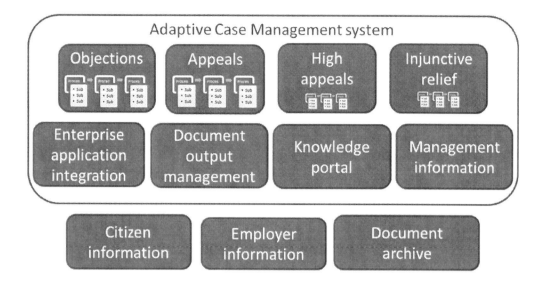

Figure 3 UWV ACM architecture

The case definition is created in a graphical modelling environment by a trained case designer and consists of:

- Sub-cases that may be retrieved either independently from a work list or as a sub-case underneath the main case.
- Sub-processes which can be re-used in different case templates. A sub-process contains all objects to show case information to the end-user: process map, activities, forms, documents, data-fields, integration calls, etc.
- Integrations: The application integration framework contains a wealth of certi-fied adapters and connectors to many systems. All integrations can be re-used from the integration library and modelled in a graphical environment with graphical integration processes and data-mapping tools.
- Document templates to create letters from within the case are maintained in a separate document output management design environment that uses Micro-soft Word to create the document templates.
- Specification of data to be used for management-information. Creation of management information reports is done in a graphical report design envi-ronment.

During execution, the case itself shows a tailored interface for all process infor-mation, process data, documents and management-information. The system's runtime flexibility is mainly determined by the granularity of the process building blocks. The larger and the more complex the process parts, the more time it will take to release a new version of that process part. Making the process parts shorter might make it more difficult for employees to keep a good overview over the complete case; sub-cases in the case should be logical process chunks to the employee.

UWV found an optimal situation by creating different case templates for one logi-cal level underneath the main process of objections. Some examples of these are "hearing", which contains all activities around hearing an employee, employer or another party, or the medical assessment in which the medical adviser assesses the medical aspects of the customer's objection.

Management information

Management information is provided on three levels: signaling in the case, monitoring the current situation and for process analysis. The monitoring and analysis capabilities are quite standard and offer insight into workload, lead times, efficiency and customer satisfaction.

The deadline signalling capabilities, however, are quite advanced. Case signalling is essential to monitor a team's commitments to the customer and to legal deadlines. These signals (up to 60 different ones for a single case) are insightfully displayed in the work lists. Every signal is automatically scored on impact and time until the deadline which together determine the case priority ("zaak gewicht" in Figure 4). Hovering over the signal will show the signal details as shown below.

Figure 4 A work list with a case signal overview

An explanation of Figure 4: Each row in this picture represents an individual case that can be opened by clicking it. The dark blue column shows the case signals: a coloured vertical bar for each active signal (colors will not be visible in the print edition). The height of the bar shows the impact of the signal. The color shows the urgency: green is safe; the closer to deep red the more urgent the deadline. For the employees progressing the case, this column usually determines case priority. The signal overview will show all current signals for the highlighted case and their expiry date.

4.3 Organization and Social

At time of publication, not all regional offices were upgraded to the new system. The first reaction from the offices that were upgraded are very positive, even though the employees needed to get used to the new system.

The most noticeable change is that the employees can more easily get to the essence of the case to service the customer. They have more flexibility to choose the optimal process path and do not have to wait for completion of activities that are currently not strictly necessary to do. The result of this is that the employees feel much more empowered; empowered to effectively apply their knowledge to the customer case and to optimize the team efficiency to deliver a high quality product to their customer in shorter time.

Another important change is that the teams are not just judged on legal timeliness anymore, but primarily on whether they honor the commitments they made to their customers. A customer satisfaction monitor is in place that scores all teams on accessibility, personal attention, customization, timeliness and clarity. The team score is also an important aspect of the individual assessment of the employees.

The fact that the team score is an important part in judging the personal performance of an employee improves the team cooperation. Team members will also be more inclined to point their colleagues on neglecting operational risks.

5. Hurdles Overcome

It must first be noted that it helped that both the process and application experts and the system development team had much experience with both the case management system and the objections and appeal processes. The focus could be put on the desired business improvements because case management principles were already clear from the system UWV had already used for a decade.

A major hurdle was the trade-off between flexibility and efficiency. The subdivision of the case into separate process parts proved not to be easy for this knowledge-intensive process. The employees need to have the complete overview to make informed decisions. The final tailored design provided an overview to not only show all sub-cases but also which parts were *not* started, which is equally important for knowledge workers to make informed decisions.

A second hurdle was the trade-off between case complexity and overview. Experienced employees know where to go to find the information. New employees need guidance. The system must provide support for both types of employees offering both a quick route and a complete overview.

6. Benefits

The system currently is still in its introduction stage and scores of the new system regarding customer satisfaction, efficiency, lead times and system usability are not available yet. However, based on the first experience we can predict some improvements.

It is inevitable that **customer satisfaction** will improve. The employees have so many possibilities to customize the process to the customer needs, and because of the fact that the teams will also be judged on their individual score on customer satisfaction, it will not be difficult to live up to these challenges.

An expected side-effect of putting the customer first is that **the average process lead time is shortened.** This is mainly caused because the customer is involved early in the procedure and can reach his contact at UWV directly to ask questions. Most customers appreciate this involvement and the cooperative approach, which makes them more eager to supply information in time, and less eager to file a higher appeal.

The **reduction of cost** was the second improvement instruction to the project team. Before the introduction of FLEKS, every team had an administrative help to organize the cases and to write and send letters. The new process does not require this role anymore and assumes that the legal advisors will write the letters. To allow for this, FLEKS contains advanced support for Microsoft Word-based document output management with the possibility to easily let the teams customize individual letter templates to their needs. In total, the cost of 20 full time employees is saved.

The **quality of UWV's decision on the appeal** has also improved. The legal advisors rely on many different sources to find the specialized information on labor law and working conditions. These sources can now more easily be combined and are accessible from within the context of the case. Moreover, the internal knowledge base is now centrally maintained and directly accessible from the case management system.

7. Best Practices, Learning Points and Pitfalls

7.1 Best Practices and Learning Points

✓ *Make sure you set your business priorities before designing your process and process system. This case demonstrates that a prime focus on customer satisfaction will create a different system than a focus on efficiency.*

✓ *Too much flexibility is inefficient. End-users need support for tasks they do not do often. If possible, provide guidance for less experienced personnel.*

✓ *Split your processes into maintainable chunks but do not let that negatively influence the user experience.*

✓ *Create a case environment that contains access to all important process information, process data and knowledge. Accessibility to all available information is key to knowledge users.*

✓ *Involve experienced business personnel that know the process, your organization and the software you use. Involve them in system specification, testing and end-user training*

✓ *Involve your software partner/vendor. Help yourself with short lines to new ideas and correct use of concepts in the software to facilitate the implementation. Help your partner/vendor improve through regular contacts with account management.*

7.2 Pitfalls

✗ *Adaptability is important. Even though case management is about operationally flexible business process management (BPM), still keep the redesign cycle in mind!*

8. Competitive Advantages

In the public sector, competitive advantage is the same as creating a good customer experience. That competitive advantage has been key throughout the improvement project of UWV. For the knowledge workers at UWV's objections and appeals division this task may be harder because they have to wipe out the memories of an earlier UWV decision that the customer objects to.

According to the knowledge workers themselves, the new system offers them the possibility to live up to their customer's expectations by allowing them to choose the optimal process path for an individual customer and by giving them access to all necessary information in a structured way.

Although the outcome of the objection to a UWV decision may not always have the desired result for the customer, UWV can now at least offer the service they promise whilst still obeying all legal rules.

9. The Technology and Service Providers

The case management system used at UWV is Perceptive Software BPMone. Case design was fully developed and deployed in BPMone and integrations are supported through BPMone Integration Framework based on Magic Software's iBOLT platform. All document output management features are delivered through Perceptive Software ModusOne. Management information reports are delivered through Oracle Discoverer.

Project delivery was a joint effort of UWV staff and Perceptive Software staff. More information on Perceptive Software is available at www.perceptivesoftware.com.

MATS Norwegian Food Safety Authority, Norway

Gold Award: Public Sector

1. EXECUTIVE SUMMARY / ABSTRACT

The Norwegian Food Safety Authority's (NFSA) overall objective is to ensure safe food and animal welfare. NFSA's area of responsibility comprises plant health, food and fodder production and handling, water supply plants, cosmetics, animal health and welfare for production animals and pets. Since 2009, about 1000 of NFSA's knowledge workers (veterinarians, biologists, engineers, other professionals) use MATS actively as a decision support system for the main bulk of their professional work; to plan, conduct and register audits. The public (farmers, restaurants, food production plants, food shops, fish exporters, plants importers, butcheries, pet owners) use MATS to register, apply, and view their own case information, resulting in 150 000 communications per year.

Each establishment or person, *NFSA client*, is viewed as a case, having a corresponding work folder in MATS. Each case is followed by NFSA over a possible time span of many years, subjected to both planned and event driven control activities (inspection, audit, sampling and document control).

MATS focuses on task support rather than workflow. Work definitions (processes, tasks, activities) share a rich domain model, and work folders can be offered as active case folders—embedding worklists, documents, and domain data. These work folders are contextual views towards the shared domain model. The folders provide access to worklists, giving knowledge workers active and dynamic task support, ensuring high-quality uniform and unified NFSA control activities.

2. OVERVIEW

NFSA's aim is to ensure safe food and drinking water, plant and animal health and animal welfare. MATS is an active task support system also providing decision support for NFSA's operational *control activities*; inspection, audit, sampling and document control. The system is the kernel of NFSA's quality system for the control activities process.

MATS also offers self-service solutions for NFSA's clients, relieving the workload for the professional knowledge workers in NFSA.

3. BUSINESS CONTEXT

NFSA was established in 2004, as the merger of The Norwegian Food Control Authority, The Norwegian Agricultural Inspection Service, The Norwegian Animal Health Authority, The Directorate of Fisheries' seafood project, and the local government Food Standards Agencies.

The development of MATS started in 2005. NFSA wanted to replace 30 legacy applications supporting parts of its core processes; case administration of applications and requests, audits/inspections, and control activities relating to importation of animals and goods. The newly formed NFSA faced four major challenges:

1. Turning a multitude of government bodies into one uniform and unified authority
2. Increasing the efficiency and quality of core processes

3. Increasing the effectiveness of services by offering the public self-service based means of reporting, applying to and addressing NFSA

4. Reducing the burden of system administration, management and maintenance.

Originating from several government bodies spread all over the country, NFSA inherited a diversity of traditions and practices. The MATS project was launched as a unification effort, to support consistent application of regulations, legally correct use of measures, and correct communications.

The MATS project both enabled and presupposed an aligned organizational development process.

4. THE KEY INNOVATIONS

Activity and task support

Traditional BPM is based on modeling the workflow from A to Z with description of all alternative paths that may occur in the process. This is ill-suited to the needs of highly qualified knowledge work, as the alternatives are so numerous and hard to foresee that the BPM charts will often turn out both unintelligible (to humans), and unfinished—or even incorrect.

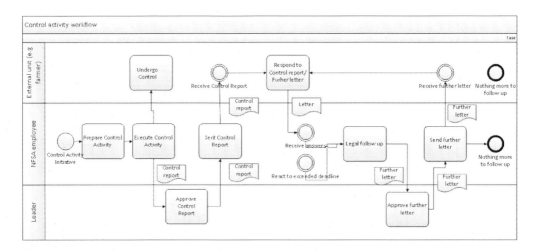

Figure 1: Sketch of the NFSA control activity process, at a high level of abstraction

We started out with models of the NFSA business processes at a high level of abstraction. At this level, the specialists in the different fields of NFSA were able to agree. As we went deeper into the matter, however, disagreements surfaced.

Instead of completing the analysis top-down, we switched to the user perspective, focusing on work performance of smaller segments, e.g. "Prepare inspection", leaving the overall workflow to the direct or indirect choices of the user, or to the state of the context. Thus, the way ahead is only partly defined, while the workflow up to the current step will be fully traceable in each particular case.

We have defined support for each activity, as a detailed and stepwise work definition with executable functionality. The resulting tasks constitute recipes for how to perform the activity and provides the functionality to get it done, allowing for flexibility on the part of the user as well as control by the system where appropriate.

In the general task template, each step may have an *include condition* determining when the step shall be included in the use of the template in performing a particular task. These include conditions may depend on context data including the connected case, environmental variables like the current user or task history.

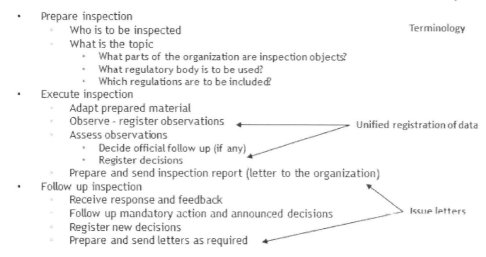

Figure 2: Disagreements emerge when going deeper into the matter

Each step may also be enhanced with conditions deciding whether it is mandatory, repeatable or presupposes the fulfillment of other steps. Thus the sequence of performance is only partially determined, and the case worker may choose whether to perform any non-mandatory step, and how many times to apply steps that are repeatable. Steps may appear or disappear as a consequence of changes made by the user or other users, or due to environmental factors.

Each available system service can be invoked from a step. Conditions and actions in the step definitions also have access to all available system functionality. By allowing a step to create new tasks, adaptive workflow can be accomplished.

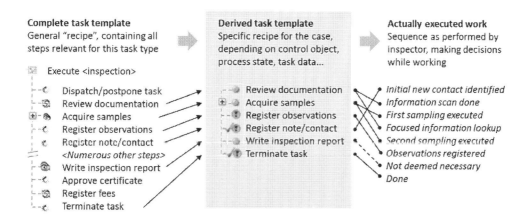

Figure 3: Activity work definition and appearance in a particular context

Task library

Tasks may be created and assigned to worklists as a result of an event, for instance the arrival of a new document in the document archive system, or the submission of an application in the self-service web client, or as a consequence of performing steps in a derived task template.

Complementing event-driven task creation, a task library is available in connection with the worklists. The inspector may opt to start any of the tasks available to him in the library, start to perform them or send them to someone else. Access to the tasks is controlled by permissions linked to actively managed user roles. Furthermore, tasks with a user supplied textual description but without task template, may be started and sent.

The case manager, e.g. an inspector, may thus start a control activity task, a general task for an informal letter, a registration task or any other task defined in the system, whenever he wants.

As activity work definitions are conceived at a sufficiently high level of abstraction for the different field experts to agree, we have been able to make few and general work definitions supporting uniform work practices, rather than numerous specific work definitions for each field.

The work definitions (task templates and task library) are managed in a separate editor, generating xml files. These work definitions are thus declarative and not implemented as part of the program code. It is in principle possible for expert users to define activity work support themselves, and to deploy these definitions in the system at runtime.

Generalized and declarative modeling

General work definitions require that the underlying business model is general enough for the use of the same functionality across different fields. One establishment may have its own water supply, keep production animals, produce nourishments for sale and have a café, whereas another may import cosmetics, export fish or be a veterinarian.

We decided to identify the *control activity objects* by their type of operation, an *operation category*. An NFSA client may thus have one or more control activity objects, typed by operation category, such as water supply, bovine husbandry or fish exportation. Each operation type is connected to the legislation governing it, related data definitions and identification types, and even to which web client forms that apply to it.

As far as possible, only the general and common parts of this were modeled using classes, object model or database structuring. The specialized parts were instead modeled by means of controlled terminology or soft typing and relations between such, as well as the use of declarative specification of data and generation of corresponding GUI, both in the internal rich client and the web client.

The operation categories are connected through relation declarations to other controlled terminologies.

The terminologies, their relations and the data definitions of the controlled objects are written in xml. The legislation down to the level of the individual section is also coded as a type hierarchy in xml, and connected with the operation categories. When the domain changes, due to new terminology, new inspection needs or new legislation, the xml definitions are updated, deployed in the system, and MATS will promptly conform. The nature of the revision may in some cases require change of the system beyond the reach or our declarative definitions, but this is rarely so.

It is possible for an NFSA expert user to add a new operation category, specify data definitions and relations between these, and forms for self-service. The new definitions may be deployed in the system at runtime, thus enabling control activities and forms for NFSA's clients without involving IT-developers. This is generally not a practical option, because it requires a thorough understanding of the structures involved, and poses strict demands on consistency. Editors for the xml-editing fit for use by non IT-developers are not yet available.

4.1 Business

Any NFSA client involved in an activity within NFSA's jurisdiction has at most one case folder in the MATS system. A case folder consists of data concerning the NFSA client registered in MATS either entered by the NFSA client itself or by NFSA personnel, or obtained from external sources.

To ensure that the same NFSA client does not have more than one case folder, the establishments are identified by the Norwegian Central Register of Establishments (Brønnøysund Register Centre) and the persons by the Norwegian Registry Office (Folkeregisteret). Identification key, names and addresses for the NFSA clients are received from these sources.

The case folder also includes information about the control activities performed by NFSA regarding the NFSA client, and all relevant documents and data.

Each case folder is used both internally by NFSA personnel and externally by NFSA clients. The two parties have access to the information about the controlled objects of the case folder and their data, but the work performed by each party can only be viewed by the party in question.

The external party submits applications and requests, and registers its activity by means of a web client. Authentication is ensured by the Norwegian common web portal for public reporting, "Altinn".

4.2 Case Handling

The general structure of a control activity such as inspection or auditing is fairly well agreed upon at the level illustrated in Figure 1. The legal actions available to NFSA personnel and principles of the Public Administrations Act (Forvaltningsloven) also apply throughout NFSA's fields of responsibility. The inspectors are subject specialists, without legal expertise. The quality of their legal decisions and selected measures is guaranteed by the task templates, the structured registration and the generation of letters to the controlled party.

MATS contains a tool for interpreting each section of an act into *requirements*, usually more specific and operational than the legal text itself. The body of requirements, *requirement base*, is created and maintained by central experts responsible for each field.

When an NFSA inspector starts a control activity in MATS, he must decide which control activity object(s) of a case folder that will be subject to control. MATS presents the acts relevant for the chosen control objects, and the inspector decides the legal foundation for this particular control. He then selects a list of corresponding requirements from the requirement base.

The inspector proceeds to the actual control activity, registering each observation with respect to the selected requirements. Every observation must be connected to a requirement, and thus to a point in the legislation. He can add requirements when needed. Based on observations, he may make a decision e.g. to close a restaurant. MATS ensures that he specifies the precise legal basis for the decision, explains how the observations constitute non-conformities, specifies what measures are to be enforced, and states the reason for selecting the measures in question. In the future, field inspections will be supported by smartphone or pad.

Based on the registered data and a structured document template, the system generates a letter, containing correctly presented inspection results as well as required elements such as information about the right to complain. The inspector may add text in specified slots, to complete the letter.

If necessary, he can go back and revise the registered data, and regenerate the letter, keeping his own added text. Only when he performs the step confirming that the letter has been sent, the system archives the letter as a journaled document, and the data and documents are then locked for editing. All documents are filed in a separate system for document handling, conforming to the Norwegian Archives Act. The archiving process and journaling is performed by MATS.

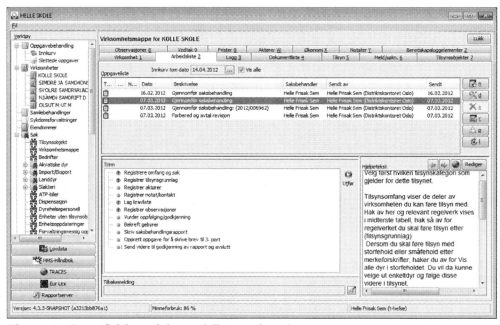

Figure 4: Case folder with worklist and task support

All information and documents registered for an NFSA client are collected and presented in the context of the relevant case folder. External identification keys for the different types of control activity objects ensure that the system is also able to present information from external sources. Control activity objects can also be connected through external sources, such as the Norwegian Land Registry (Eiendomsregisteret).

Every NFSA employee has a personal worklist. Organizational units have one or several common worklists for handling requests that are not yet allocated to a particular inspector. Any one task may appear in several worklists, and will normally be found both in the worklist of an inspector and in the worklist of the case folder connected to the task. The case folder provides an overview of the tasks pertaining to the case at hand, indicating to whom each task has been allocated.

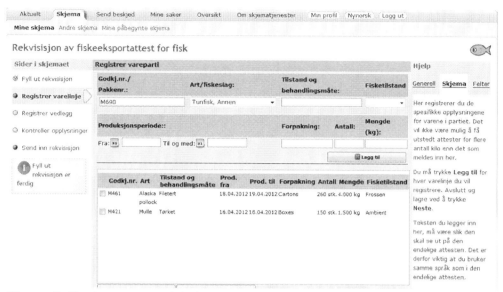

Figure 5: Task support with for the external user (registration of goods in fish export).

4.3 Organization & Social

The main assignment of the inspector is to visit the NFSA clients and cooperate with these to achieve the aims of NFSA. The legislation is a main tool in this work, providing both positive motivation and authority for the use of formal action.

The fact that the same system with the same concepts, terminology and practice is used across professions and fields, promotes discussions and facilitates co-work. This helps build one common conception of NFSA's operations, amongst NFSA employees.

The data resulting from the control activities enable powerful reporting and statistics. A uniform data basis shows exactly which legal measures have been used, down to the type of the measure and the applicable section in the legislation, as well as the non-conformity observations. For NFSA, this is useful in managing its operations, in its legislative activities and in its communications with the general public.

5. HURDLES OVERCOME

The major technical challenge was to create a system supporting unified and uniform high quality control activities in a field with great diversity and frequent changes, in particular with regard to the legislation. Our solution to this challenge was to create a domain model and a work support that is general and flexible through:

- Declarative modeling—"hard" modeling by means of programming code for the general, common and stable parts, and "soft" modeling of the data specific for each operation category by means of xml code or as data.
- Task and activity support to structure the business activities, rather than traditional BPM
- Rich case folders comprising many tasks with work support and continual collection of the results of the work, both as registered data, documents and tracing of tasks

Management

MATS is anchored at the very top of NFSA. From the start, the CEO was a member of the project board, and the project director of NFSA was the project manager. Specialists responsible for each field are involved when needed, both to give answers and to create ownership and enthusiasm. These experts became MATS ambassadors in their respective operational units.

Business

An important purpose of the project has been to establish new uniform work practices across professional and geographical borders. For a government body, it is essential to ensure fair and equal treatment in accordance with the rule of law.

MATS supports adaptive execution of NFSA control activities, tracking all observations and decisions as well as their formal basis. This is used to produce correct correspondence, as well as high quality reports and statistics.

The self-service web client represents a step forward for the customers of NFSA, supporting their own work. Task templates make it easy to file applications and requests. Self-service improves the quality of the data and takes the burden of the registration of data away from the NFSA employee. Together with the self-service invitation to inspect and improve data, this contributes to a modern, user oriented public sector.

Organization Adoption

MATS is fully established as the task and decision support tool for the control activity and impacts the whole Norwegian food industry.

The organization is involved in the development process, with a comprehensive group of NFSA employees and experts engaged, from specification to implementation in the organization. After the first of five deliveries, scrum was introduced to the project development method, reducing the time from programming to demonstration of functionality, increasing transparency and control, and simplifying prioritizing.

Since MATS focuses on NFSA's core business processes, further improvement is an ongoing activity. NFSA has established an organization unit for the product management of MATS. Forums exist for the exchange of experiences and presentations of new functionality and plans. Sections responsible for each field in NFSA take an active part in maintaining the knowledge representation of MATS.

NFSA has taken the initiative to develop an e-learning application to facilitate learning both of the system and the new ways of working.

6. BENEFITS

6.1 Cost Savings / Time Reductions

The self-service web client with task support has supplied the public with flexible forms to use in their communications with NFSA, saving time for NFSA.

The structured registration of data gives NFSA a basis for almost instant reports and statistics.

6.2 Quality Improvements

MATS has become a key factor in the development of NFSA into one unified organization.

MATS contributes to service quality, by making all relevant information available in the work context. This includes history, relevant data and documents, related external information and planned NFSA work. An overview of the relevant legislation for the case at hand, with standard but adjustable packets of requirements, further boosts the NFSA employee's freedom to work independently within boundaries that ensure uniform and correct practices.

MATS ensures that the employee connects every observation with the relevant requirement and that all required elements in the formulation of the decisions are present. Thus, the system raises the employee's awareness of correct practice while simultaneously increasing the quality of the resulting work.

The exposition of the data registered by NFSA about a client through the self-service web, gives the NFSA client the option to react if the data are incorrect, contributing to the quality of the NFSA data.

7. BEST PRACTICES, LEARNING POINTS AND PITFALLS

7.1 Best Practices and Learning Points

✓ *Workflow is neither the problem nor the solution—work performance is!*

✓ *Provide **work folders** instead of document folders: Work folders offer a particular perspective on a case, with access to worklists, task support and domain data as an enhancement to traditional documents.*

✓ *Work performance support can be provided through customized task support templates with loosely ordered task steps with associated actions and conditions for ensuring correct case handling.*

✓ *Offer the users a high degree of freedom in choosing, starting and forwarding tasks. Such freedom may reduce the needs for very detailed "exception handling" processes.*

✓ *Maximize declarative representations for covering business logic: processes and task definitions, business rules, code sets, document templates can all be separated from the programming code; they can be maintained in their own lifecycles and subject to hot-deployment.*

✓ *Hide archiving details—configure most of the recommended archiving to take place automatically.*

✓ *Engage subject matter experts in the system development effort—in the development phases as many "experts" as "system developers" contributed in the project.*

✓ *Use stepwise delivery in order to reduce risk and engage users.*

7.2 Pitfalls

✗ *Avoid simplistic top-down process thinking: by focusing on the actual work to be performed and providing task support for this, both the actual workflow and the overall processes will emerge.*

8. COMPETITIVE ADVANTAGES

For a governmental body such as NFSA, competitive advantage translates into how well it fulfills its duty maintaining fair and legally correct practices. Customer satisfaction is desirable, although not always the primary concern. The ability of NFSA to retain and motivate capable employees in the longer term is also a significant competitive challenge in the personnel marketplace.

MATS has proved to be a useful complement to the capable NFSA professional. It boosts service uniformity, adding to the confidence of the inspector during the process. Reducing the administrative burden, MATS allows more time for the hard tasks that require knowledge. Making knowledge available instead of simply automating work, MATS ACM provides a motivating work context that promotes responsibility, learning and job satisfaction.

NORWEGIAN FOOD SAFETY AUTHORITY

In this way, MATS has become a platform for further development for both the ways of working and the organization.

9. TECHNOLOGY

The task templates, worklists and task support functionality and engine, rule engine, work folder, xml terminologies and relations framework were implemented using a complete ACM framework developed for and used within the Norwegian public sector during the past 15 years. In MATS, the ACM framework was used in its Java Platform Enterprise Edition version.

10. THE TECHNOLOGY AND SERVICE PROVIDERS

Computas AS is an employee-owned Norwegian IT consulting company with around 200 consultants, which provides services and solutions for business processes and co-work. Computas AS has delivered numerous work process support applications to the Norwegian public sector and private enterprises, based on the ACM framework FrameSolutions™.

FrameSolutions™ currently has more than 100 000 users, and handles an annual cash flow of around 50 billion NOK. IT solutions based on FrameSolutions™ provide work process support and task support resulting in higher efficiency and quality in organizational processes. FrameSolutions™ is a framework for realizing bespoke process-centered case management solutions.

Fornebu Consulting is a leading Norwegian consulting firm with around 40 consultants focusing on delivering value to both the public and private through enterprise process improvement. Fornebu Consulting was NFSA's advisor with regard to initial requirement analysis and vendor/technology prequalification and selection. They also assisted NFSA with requirements engineering, knowledge acquisition and establishing organizational ownership.

This case study was assembled and authored by Helle Frisak Sem, Steinar Carlsen and Gunnar John Coll; Computas AS.

QSuper, Australia

Silver Award: Public Sector

1. EXECUTIVE SUMMARY / ABSTRACT

Organization Overview

QSuper is the superannuation fund (a retirement program in Australia) for current and former Queensland government and related entity workers. As one of Australia's largest superannuation funds, QSuper provides members with access to an extensive range of tools, information and services designed to help members grow their super.

Operating in a highly competitive and dynamic financial services environment, QSuper manages more than $30 billion in funds for over 540,000 members and is committed to working with its members so they can feel more confident they are making the best choices for their situation. QSuper Limited undertakes the daily administration of QSuper and has more than 600 employees.

Summary

QSuper's use of case management has resulted in significant benefits and ROI in terms of cost reduction, increased efficiency, improved customer experience, decreased risk and business continuity planning.

Cost reduction

QSuper staff now use only two systems, workQ and the superannuation administration system. Five systems have been decommissioned and their historic information has been migrated where required into the new system, significantly reducing business operations costs by eliminating maintenance and vendor fees.

Improved customer experience

QSuper can now provide faster, more complete responses to customer enquiries. Case management has integrated their services and information, providing a complete view of their customer.

Real-time process and business intelligence

QSuper now has comprehensive real-time management reporting and has experienced a 99 percent reduction in manual effort required to collect workflow management statistics (from 40 hours down to one half hour per week). Advanced metrics are now captured which are fed into the business intelligence platform, giving a clearer view of overall business performance.

Improved knowledge worker productivity

Customer service representatives now have a unified view of the customer to help guide their decisions when providing service while maintaining compliance. Manual and paper-based delays are removed as is the need for "swivel-chair" viewing of multiple systems.

Adjust employee workload on-the-fly

Workload management, dynamically shifting workload of employees, is now possible through real-time current and future workload reporting.

Prepared for disaster

QSuper now has greater system reliability and a robust disaster recovery capability.

Competitive advantages

QSuper now has a strategic case management platform which can be enhanced and integrates with other business systems and can re-engineer business processes to maximize competitive advantage. The case management platform supports future service improvements and efficiencies using new and emerging technologies.

Continuous improvement

A Centre of Excellence has been established to provide continued development of the business capability to support and leverage case management.

2. OVERVIEW

QSuper's use of case management has resulted in significant benefits and ROI in terms of cost reduction, increased efficiency, improved customer experience, decreased risk and business continuity planning.

Prior to using case management, only 17 percent of business processes were processed using workflow (31 out of 180) and only 35 percent of QSuper business operations staff used workflow (124 out of 338). Eight different systems were used by operations staff with numerous manual repositories for customer information, which was a mixture of paper and electronic documents.

The high level of integration between the workflow and administration records system inhibited system performance, and no business continuity capability existed in disaster situations.

Now QSuper's case management system, called workQ, handles 78 percent of business processes (140 out of 180). workQ is used across QSuper from the knowledge workers processing claims, to business operations and information technology staff, to mid and senior level management. Sixty percent of business operations staff currently use workQ (198 out of 338), with plans to roll out to 100 percent.

QSuper staff now use only two systems: workQ and the superannuation administration system. Five systems have been decommissioned and their historic information has been migrated where required into the new system, significantly reducing business operations costs by eliminating maintenance and vendor fees.

QSuper can now provide faster, more complete responses to customer enquiries. Case management has integrated their services and information. This provides a complete view of their customer over many different transactions and functions and enables visibility into where a customer's transaction is in the process and who is working on it. The system records call logging from customers, images of letters, faxes, forms and emails received from members as well as the outgoing correspondence.

QSuper now has comprehensive real-time management reporting and has experienced a 99 percent reduction in manual effort required to collect workflow management statistics (from 40 hours down to 1/2 hour per week). The old workflow had limited reporting and required significant manipulation to enable it to be analysed and used.

Now real-time reporting helps QSuper management identify pain points in business processes which can be targeted for continuous improvement. Advanced metrics are now captured which are able to be fed into the business intelligence platform, giving a clearer view of overall business performance.

Workload management, dynamically shifting workload of employees, is now possible through real-time current and future workload reporting. Previously this was not possible.

QSuper now has greater system reliability and a robust disaster recovery capability, supporting current business processes whilst maintaining efficiencies and quality assurance in the event of a major disaster.

QSuper overcame challenges such as gaining management buy-in to use agile development methodology instead of the waterfall approach which QSuper had been using. Management confidence in the agile approach increased throughout the project due to regular demonstrations of the evolving case management system.

Conflicting priorities are always a hurdle for projects. Where conflicts occurred, the business, project team and vendors worked together to maintain focus in the right places to get the best return on investment.

A Centre of Excellence has been established to provide continued development of the business capability to support and leverage the new workflow and ensure the business is well placed to meet future development and business needs.

3. BUSINESS CONTEXT

Business

- Numerous business workarounds due to obsolete processes and rules in the workflow system and a high rate of failure
- Only 35 percent of business operations staff used workflow (124 out of 338)
- Approx 17 percent of business processes were processed through workflow (31 out of 180)
- No consolidated customer view existed
- Eight different systems were used by operations staff with numerous manual repositories for customer information
- Customer information was a mixture of paper and electronic documents in multiple repositories
- High level of integration between the workflow and administration records system inhibited system performance
- No business continuity capability existed in disaster situations
- Limited visibility of re-work
- Limited visibility of business performance
- No real time workload reporting existed
- Resourcing and capacity planning was very difficult due to lack of reporting
- Performance reporting required significant manual collation of metrics

Technology

- Dependency on obsolete technology across a range of systems to manage work
- Workflow and imaging solution upgrades became unfeasible due to costs and obsolete platform
- Workflow platform degraded resulting in poor performance and availability (up to 35 percent unavailability)
- High IT maintenance costs
- No technical capability to enhance the system

4. THE KEY INNOVATIONS

4.1 Business

Customers

- Complete view of the customer now exists over many different transactions and functions
- The system records call logging from customers, images of letters, faxes, forms and emails received from members as well as the outgoing correspondence
- Customer view provides visibility of where a customer's transaction is in the process and who is working on it
- The business can now provide faster, more complete responses to customer enquiries
- Staff can confirm with customers that they have received their letters, faxes, forms and emails and can advise them of the progress of the case

Vendors

- Business process and agile development methodology was adopted very successfully into the business in partnership with OpenText Business Process Solutions
- True partnership with OpenText Business Process Solutions through on-site and off-site support
- OpenText Business Process Solutions worked well with project team, business units and other vendors
- OpenText Business Process Solutions executive visits to QSuper demonstrated commitment to QSuper as a customer even though QSuper is an organization of only 700 people
- OpenText Business Process Solutions has included QSuper code in their version testing prior to release of new product versions
- OpenText Business Process Solutions worked closely with the vendor of our core superannuation administration system to optimize processes, data and document transfer between the workflow and the superannuation administration systems
- Business process and agile development methodology will be adopted for future QSuper projects wherever possible

4.2 Case Handling

Before the project

- No technology environment assisting the unstructured knowledge work portions of the workflow
- Only 35 percent of business operations staff used workflow (124 out of 338)
- 31 transaction types were handled through workflow
- Approx 17 percent of business processes were processed through workflow (31 out of 180)
- Though desired goals & outcomes were the same, cases were handled differently across separate business units depending on whether or not workflow had been enabled in the area
- Paper-based transaction types had minimal case management requiring many manual processes and manual collection of performance metrics
- Case management across different business units was handled through emails and paper-based forms

- There was limited visibility of what stage a case was at in the process
- Limited visibility of re-work

After the project
- 60 percent of business operations staff use workflow, with plans to roll out to 100 percent (198 out of 338)
- 140 transaction types are handled through workflow
- Approx 78 percent of business processes now handled through workflow (140 out of 180)
- Business units are able to process cases in a consistent and efficient manner
- Focused around case elements that are important to helping the knowledge worker advance the case as well as using process snippets where automation can be invoked
- The system has high availability and transaction processing times have reduced significantly
- All business units, including the contact centre, have full visibility of cases and the stages they are at
- Business units no longer use email to manage cases across business units, as all case management is contained within the workflow system by creation of linked cases
- Re-work is highly visible due to cases being automatically routed back to the original user

Case template

Current business processes were mapped using BPMN.
- Upon comparison of these process maps it became evident that a generic workflow and a generic case template could be used to cover all processes.
- A generic workflow and case template was developed, with enough flexibility to cater to different needs of business units.
- Usability consultants were contracted to design the screen layout
- The final layout aligned to the business process followed by the user, which has resulted in more efficient processing of the case

Key roles
- Indexer—allocate the work type and attach the work to a client
- Processor—check the work for completeness, process the work, quality check other processors' work
- Supervisor—allocate work to processors, monitor escalate queue, team lead, management reporting
- Manager—management reporting
- Business Admin—assign roles and business units for users within their business area
- Information & Communications Technology (ICT)—system administrator, provide operational support

Roles management
- workQ users are created/removed through ICT service requests to ensure alignment of user details across other business systems
- Roles are assigned by each business area's Business Admin users
- A user can have multiple roles across one or many business units
- Roles are controlled at the business unit level, allowing greater flexibility and faster turnaround times for role and business unit change requests

Master folders

A master folder is used to hold high-level business entity ("client") information (IDs, name, address, etc) for:

- Members
- Employers
- Products (Superannuation Funds)
- Organisations (QSuper, QInvest)

Case folders

Case folders are created for incoming work and the allocation across QSuper business units. Cases are linked to the relevant "client" master folder and flow through a simple 6 step configurable workflow:

- Index—who is this for and what type of work is it
- Completeness—have I got all the right information to do the work
- Process—do the work
- Quality—check the work
- Approve—additional check for high value transactions
- Finalise—close the work

All work types use this 'generic' workflow. A work type can be configured to route through the required steps for that work type based on a percentage of cases to be routed or a transaction dollar amount.

During the workflow, cases can be:

- Pended awaiting additional information from the customer or another business unit, or
- Escalated to a supervisor for technical assistance
- Cases can be pended awaiting correspondence or waiting action by another business unit (through the linked case functionality):
- Pended cases auto-wake when a new document is indexed/attached to the case. A notification is automatically sent to the person who sent the case to pend so they have instant visibility of it.
- Pended cases auto-wake when any linked cases are completed

Case use

Usability consultants assisted with design of the case layout (UI), resulting in a layout which balanced productivity and intuitiveness. Different personas were created, for example contact centre and processor.

Throughout the lifecycle of a case, a case manager is able to:

- View client information
- View all cases and related documents both incoming and outgoing for a client
- View all documents against the master folder for a client
- Add notes to the case in a discussion format
- Add documents to the case
- Create and send email from the case
- View the process history (who has worked on it and when)
- Trigger a new case from the open case which can be linked for visibility of dependent cases

5.   4.3 Organization & Social

Employees

Employees now use only two systems (workflow and the superannuation administration system). Five systems have been decommissioned and their historic information has been migrated where required into the new workflow system.

Workflow has integrated the services and information these fragmented systems provided in the past, making processing easier with all information at hand

Employees now have greater workflow system reliability and a robust disaster recovery capability, supporting current business processes whilst maintaining efficiencies and quality assurance in the event of a major disaster

Workflow has the ability to change to support changing business needs and can be supported by business users instead of vendor resources

Changes to the old workflow, where attempted, had proven difficult and costly and therefore at times were not implemented

Employees can now see all transactions currently being worked on for a member and also a history of previous actions/transactions/calls, etc.

Work has been made easier and faster to process enabling employees to serve our members more efficiently

Workflow now includes comprehensive real-time management reporting functions. The old workflow had limited reporting and required significant manipulation to enable it to be analysed and used.

Workload management is now possible through real-time current and future workload reporting. Previously this was not possible.

Centre of Excellence

A Support Framework was established to provide continued development of the business capability to support and leverage the new workflow and ensure the business is well placed to meet future development and business as usual (BAU) needs. The centre of excellence includes the following key groups:

Control board

A control board has been created from business and ICT representatives.

The board will have a business focus, as opposed to systems focus, and is accountable for the delivery outcomes of work packages executed for workflow delivery.

Delivery arm

A delivery team has been assembled to provide continuous development capability of workflow across programs of work and BAU. The team was assembled from the project team and has the ability to expand/contract based on workloads. The delivery arm consists of a core team of agile delivery specialists.

> Key responsibilities are:
> - Development as agreed through the control board
> - Technical alignment into logical development packages
> - Project management of delivery
> - Commercial engagement and relationship management with vendor in support of workQ development delivery

Operational support

Operational support services ensure that the workflow solution is kept up and running as well as working to agreed service standards. These services have been aligned with established ICT and business unit operational support procedures. Key responsibilities are:

- Service desk
- Systems application support
- Production incident root cause analysis and resolution
- Production enhancement management in conjunction with the delivery arm
- Vendor contract management and renewals
- License management and renewals
- Infrastructure management

6. HURDLES OVERCOME

Management

Under agile development, detailed user requirements were not available up front. This differed from the waterfall approach which QSuper adhered to previously. Management buy-in was sought and confidence in the agile approach increased throughout the project due to regular demonstrations of the evolving workflow system.

Governance approach differed using the agile approach. Some governance processes were adjusted/streamlined to enabled faster and continuous improvement throughout the project.

OpenText Business Process Solutions and QSuper progressed on the journey together, optimizing what was leveraged out of the product to best meet the needs of the organization.

Business

Previously, all development projects were run using waterfall methods under which the business needed to get every last document and requirement to the project team before development commenced. Under the agile approach detailed requirements were not required. Instead, regular business consultation was undertaken as the solution evolved. After a few early solution demonstrations, the business could see their suggestions being included and the solution evolving before their eyes. They became more relaxed and confident that the final solution would meet their needs and cater for changing requirements.

Conflicting priorities are always a hurdle for projects. Where conflicts occurred, the business, project team and vendors worked together. Detailed effort was focused in the right places to get the best return on investment.

Accommodation issues were overcome with a flexible vendor arrangement, where OpenText Business Process Solutions staff worked from different locations.

The Brisbane floods in January 2011 caused significant disruption with the closure of QSuper offices. At short notice, OpenText Business Process Solutions provided equipment and premises to overcome this hurdle. QSuper project staff relocated to OpenText Business Process Solutions' Melbourne offices at no extra cost to QSuper, thus ensuring that critical path project activities remained on schedule.

The introduction of sophisticated management reporting triggered the need for appropriate management strategies to best leverage the new reporting tools and training on how to deal with the increased visibility of performance metrics.

Organization Adoption

- Business process design and agile developments were new to organization

- Standardization of tools across workforce management and customer-centric personas

7. BENEFITS

6.1 Cost Savings / Time Reductions

Benefit	Measure	Result
Decreased business risk due to failures of the legacy workflow system.	Avoided costs for manual processing and loss of information with workflow failure. High availability of new workflow system with disaster recovery in place.	Risk mitigated ROI of 1.08
Increased efficiencies due to greater system reliability and enhanced business capabilities.	System availability measures. Level of staff effort supporting/maintaining workflow system.	System availability increased to 99 percent from as low as 65 percent
Decreased costs due to decommissioning of the legacy workflow system.	Level of vendor costs to maintain and support the legacy workflow system.	Avoided costs System can now scale for continuous improvement Cost effective system scales across more business units and users.
Business continuity enablement	High availability of new workflow system.	Disaster recovery in place Paperless office with email, fax and paper documents electronically imported to workflow system, enabling work to continue from any site
Improved member experience with faster and more complete responses to members.	Level of staff effort on processing claims. Increased efficiency across processes and business unit engagements.	15 percent reduction in average cycle time of high volume transactions 38 percent reduction in effort required to manage cases across business units (40 hours down to 25 hours per week)
Increased efficiency of management reporting	Level of staff effort collecting team management statistics Increased efficiencies due to real time management reporting	99 percent reduction in manual effort required to collect workflow management statistics (40 hours down to 1/2 hour per week)

6.2 *Quality Improvements*

- Awareness by employees of their errors identified during quality checks through re-work process, enabling targeted training and a reduction in occurrence of errors
- Better informed decision making by staff due to improved visibility and awareness of customer case management

8. Best Practices, Learning Points and Pitfalls

7.1 *Best Practices and Learning Points*

- ✓ *Use of agile methodology. Although it was the first application of an agile method in QSuper, it was well received and understood by project team members and business contributors alike and was considered an appropriate method to use*
- ✓ *Use of trial implementations to manage risk. Trial implementations were found to be an effective and efficient approach to managing implementation risk and enabling timing of tasks to be refined prior to actual implementation.*
- ✓ *'Big Bang' approach to implementation would not have been appropriate. Use of an incremental staged implementation approach was successful. Defects are caught early and rectified for future stages of the implementation.*
- ✓ *Develop a post implementation change support network. The level of effectiveness of the business transition and support phase for project releases was dependent upon the establishment of a "fit for purpose" support network which was responsive to business needs.*
- ✓ *Adopt a process-centric design approach. While a primary objective of the project was to replace the existing technology, extensive effort was invested in process redesign to ensure the fit of changes within existing business processes and procedures. This avoided last minute and unplanned needs for business support to close any gaps.*
- ✓ *Testing processes and practices including collaboration between internal groups, the tools used, etc., point towards an improved testing practice in QSuper. The level of software quality achieved in the project illustrated the potential of an agile method to improve overall testing outcomes.*

7.2 *Pitfalls*

- ✗ *Most difficult development work was around the workflow integration with other business systems. Need to ensure sufficient resources and time is allocated to any integration development.*

9. Competitive Advantages

QSuper now has a strategic case management platform which can be enhanced and integrates with other business systems:

- A base has been established to enable the re-engineering of business processes to maximize competitive advantage
- A technology base has been established to extend further service improvements and efficiencies, using new and emerging technologies.
- A single customer view has been established, improving services and customer experience.
- Advanced management reporting implemented, identifying pain points in business processes which can be targeted for continuous improvement.

Advance metrics are now captured which are able to be fed into the business intelligence platform, giving a clearer view of overall business performance.

Extend workflow solution

Extend foundation capability through other projects, including:

- Integration with internal capability and external providers for customer correspondence capture, generation and delivery
- Integration with additional document management repository
- Integration with self-service web platform for managing exceptions, recording activities, exposing member information
- Integration with business intelligence platform
- Extend to other business units/functions

Continuous improvement

Extend capability of workflow solution to all processing areas to improve case management, including:

- Refine and leverage capability
- Extend optical character recognition (OCR) capability into areas with high volumes of simple paper forms that are going to remain inbound, with goal of reducing data entry
- Re-engineer correspondence to provide tailored correspondence/forms and channels with customers
- Integrate workflow solution with call recording platform (links in member view to recorded calls)
- Integrate workflow solution with call centre telephone network using Computer Telephony Integration (CTI) technology (auto screen pop of customer's view and screen capture of system actions to link with phone recording)
- Cater for SMS channel and preferred customer contact method and channels
- Improved workforce management
- Refine rules, roles and user skill profiles to enable improved work allocation methods and more management reporting
- Enhance rules and reporting to provide improved analytical capability, including simulation as well as resource forecasting, management and optimisation
- Update customer view to better summarise information and offerings to meet strategic needs
- Government initiatives
- Integrate with Enterprise Application Integration (EAI) platform

10. TECHNOLOGY

Infrastructure overview

QSuper's technology roadmap strongly embraces server virtualisation using VMware technologies and Microsoft server platform. QSuper leveraged these technologies to underpin the installation of workflow solution:

Case management

- OpenText Case360
- OpenText Filestore360
- Core Superannuation Administration
- Acurity
- SwiftView Convert (PCL to PDF conversion)
- Fax integration into workflow
- FaxIP (messageManager)

- Email integration into workflow
- Microsoft Exchange (email)
- TinyMCE (browser-based rich text editor)
- Scanning paper-based documents into workflow
- Scanning software (Kofax)
- Scanning hardware (Fujitsu)
- Advanced management reporting.
- OpenText managerView
- Tableau

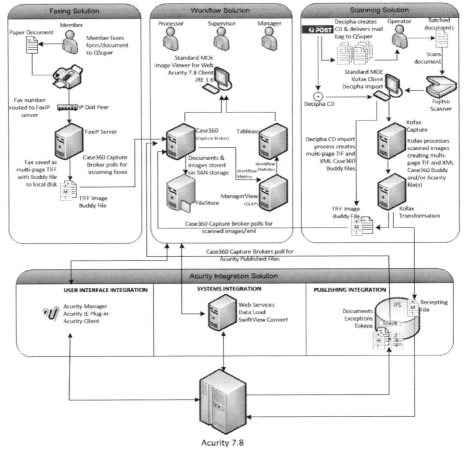

Infrastructure View Illustration

11. BENEFITS

QSuper currently operates the production environment using three OpenText Case360 servers behind F5 load balancers, active/passive Microsoft SQL 2008 cluster and clustered Microsoft Windows file servers for OpenText Filestore. Benefits of this environment are:

- OpenText Case360's built in cluster (multi-server awareness) provides QSuper with a workflow solution that is highly available, robust and scalable.
- The virtual servers are automatically re-balanced amongst the physical host servers by the VMware technologies ensuring overall system performance.

- This configuration allows QSuper to apply patches/work on individual components whilst maintaining solution availability.
- It also allows a server snap-shot as a backup prior to making certain changes, especially those at the operating system level.
- Due to the simplicity of the OpenText Case360 deployment, QSuper has leveraged VMware server cloning and within 30 minutes has built and made operational additional cluster nodes.

The infrastructure design also provides for future up-scaling of the solution to include handling of online forms and process orchestration for external administration systems. This can be achieved by adding in additional OpenText Case 360 node(s) into the cluster (if required) and/or changing the workload percentage handled by each node. This effectively provides dedicated nodes servicing end-users (web server) and other nodes dedicated to handling workflow processing (application server).

12. THE TECHNOLOGY AND SERVICE PROVIDERS

OpenText Business Process Solutions (BPS)

OpenText BPS provides process management, case management, and business architecture solutions that increase efficiency and effectiveness through a highly individualized user experience that empowers the people that do the work. OpenText BPS is supported by a strong global partner network including SAP®, Microsoft® and Oracle®. OpenText BPS's industry leadership has been recognized by global IT analyst firms including Gartner, Forrester Research, IDC and others.

Visit www.OpenTextBPS.com or the blog www.BecauseProcessMatters.com.

The following technologies also formulate the overall solution:

Infrastructure Component	Product	Vendor
Server Hardware	IBM 3850x5	IBM http://www.ibm.com/au/en/
Storage Hardware	DS3512 SAN	IBM http://www.ibm.com/au/en/
Server Operating System	Microsoft Server 2008 R2 64 bit	Data#3 (reseller) http://www.microsoft.com/en-au/default.aspx
Database	Microsoft SQL 2008	Data#3 (reseller) http://www.microsoft.com/en-au/default.aspx
Server Virtualisation	vmware ESX	Technology Effect (reseller) http://www.vmware.com/ap
Application Service Layer	JBoss EAP	Redhat http://www.redhat.com/
Document Scanning	Kofax Capture & Transformation	OpenText (reseller) http://www.kofax.com/
Scanning Hardware	Fujitsu FI-6670, Fujitsu FI-6230	Proscan (reseller) http://www.proscan.com.au/

Document Conversion	SwiftView Convert+PDF	SwiftView http://www.swiftview.com/
Browser rich text editor	TinyMCE	ephox (reseller) http://www.ephox.com/
Faxing	messageManager FaxIP	OpenText (previously message manager solutions) http://www.mmanager.com/
Superannuation Administration System Integration	Acurity Web Services Acurity Manager	Financial Synergy http://www.financialsynergy.com.au/

State Agency that Manages Services for Children and Families, USA

Special Mention: Public Sector

1. EXECUTIVE SUMMARY / ABSTRACT

The State Agency ("the Agency") helps process Daycare and Foster Care applications by collecting and reviewing criminal history review data. The Agency was experiencing increased workloads and mounting storage needs, and the processing of applications was manually-intensive and inefficient. The goal of the case management solution was to implement an automated workflow system to minimize the physical handling of the applications and streamline the overall business processes. The solution enables users—Criminal History Raters, Criminal History Reporting staff, Criminal History Analysts, and Record Keepers—to securely and reliably expedite application processing while meeting legal requirements for processing background checks, enabling validation and audits. The case management platform provides an integrated system that supports processing, maintenance, and distribution of criminal history reviews so that state staff can respond accurately and efficiently. It also provides interoperability with the applications from other agencies and departments.

2. OVERVIEW

The Agency is responsible for promoting the safety and well-being of children and vulnerable adults. In addition to providing programs for foster care, adoption and child protective services, the Agency oversees and monitors child care facilities, subsidies, resources and referrals. The Agency also handles all elements of the state's juvenile justice programs. It works closely with stakeholders and providers to help ensure availability of adequate youth development services and programs at the local level.

In response to new regulations, the Agency needed rapid, repeatable and auditable processes for criminal history reviews that helped ensure compliance in processing applications for foster parents, adoptive parents, daycare operators or workers. The Agency created an integrated case management platform. Through this solution, agency staff members can expedite criminal history reviews while meeting legal requirements for processing background checks and streamlining validation and audits.

3. BUSINESS CONTEXT

Protecting the welfare of children

The State enacted an act to prevent placement of children in homes with convicted violent felons. This made it a legal requirement to fingerprint foster and adoptive parent applicants. A short time later, another act extended this requirement to mandate fingerprinting of employees and operators working in or running a day care facility.

In response, the Agency created a unit to collect and review the criminal history of anyone who applied to be a foster parent, adoptive parent, daycare operator or worker and report back out to the agency. Initially, the unit's processes were paper-intensive and highly manual. For example, it sent actual fingerprint cards for review.

When legal requirements for criminal background checks were extended, the unit faced increased workloads and mounting storage needs. The Agency sought a document handling and automated workflow solution to minimize the physical handling of both foster care and day care applications, help ensure regulatory compliance and accelerate the criminal history review process.

Reducing regulatory risk with repeatable and auditable processes

The Agency began the initial phase of the criminal history background review system. The project team built an integrated solution that supports document imaging and automated electronic workflow for storing and retrieving documents. The solution also provided interoperability with applications from other agencies and departments.

Essentially, the system supported a case management approach to document retention and workflow focused around applicants for positions that involved working with children. All applicant-specific documents received or created were digitized and became part of an electronic workflow. For example, when an individual was fingerprinted as part of the application process, the system enabled electronic capture and transmission of the fingerprint record to the Justice Department to search their agency files for any criminal record of charges or convictions in the state or nationally. As a result, a process step that previously took two or three days to complete was reduced to near-real time.

Using the highly secure and reliable system, staff members (including criminal history raters, reporters, analysts and record keepers) could process applications more quickly and accurately. The system helped ensure they were meeting legal requirements for handling background checks and facilitated validation and audits.

The system also generates outbound correspondence per agency policies. For example, clearance letters for applicants with no criminal history are generated automatically. If in any search a criminal record is found, applicants will receive summary information about the charges or convictions.

Adapting to process and organizational changes

Years after, the Agency needed to respond to internal and external process and organizational changes. For instance, the Justice Department enhanced its ability to capture and send a digital record of applicant fingerprints to the Federal Bureau of Investigation (FBI), cutting weeks off the time required for a criminal history search. Before, when requests were made by mail, the process took three to four weeks; this was converted to minutes.

In addition, the agency workflow required lawyers in the State's investigation department to review each applicant's file. However, because most of the reviews involved routine legal questions, the Agency wanted to automatically process applicant cases that fell within typical parameters, so that only one investigator is needed to handle exceptions to the norm.

Enhancing system agility

As the Agency faced growing case loads, it became apparent that additional efficiencies were needed. While the system automated transaction-based case management processes quite well, the system needed to accommodate more unstructured tasks. This unstructured activity accounted for a significant portion of staff member workload. For example, rap sheet information from the Justice Department and the FBI is often fragmented and incomplete. Correspondence with the jurisdictions to collect missing history is fluid and events can occur during collection of history, such as another arrest.

The Agency began looking for more dynamic case management technologies to better adapt to changes in legal requirements, types or categories of positions, regulations, or business rules. The agency embarked on Phase II of the solution, which offers a wide range of configurable, automated capabilities out-of-the box to help improve overall productivity. For example, Phase II is being designed to automatically generate and track routine correspondence (such as clearance letters and applicant record updates) while streamlining non-routine correspondence (such as criminal summary letters and agency data).

4. THE KEY INNOVATIONS

4.1 Business

The Agency has improved child welfare by enhancing synergies across agencies through a common approach, common technology, and greater integration.

4.2 Case Handling

The collection and review of criminal history is outcome oriented to address the unstructured and ad-hoc nature of reviews:

- Following up on rap sheet information from the Justice Department and the FBI that is often fragmented and incomplete
- Corresponding with Jurisdictions to collect missing history
- Responding to events that occur during the collection of history (e.g. another arrest)
- Sending clearance letters that require no intervention (no criminal activity found)
- Updating applicant records updates

The earlier implementation of the system provided advantages such as:

- Virtual and immediate access to electronic files facilitated by the electronic capture of applicant information, including rap sheets, final letter/memo, responses from district courts/attorneys
- Efficient, automated distribution of work, with facility for 'out-of-office' assignment
- Automated workflow with minimum user intervention, including automated letter/memo generation

Phase II leverages a framework and reusable components for similar solutions. Features include the ability to:

- Streamline generation and tracking of correspondence to Jurisdictions
- Streamline production of criminal summary letters and data for agencies and facilities
- Execute lights-out production of clearance letters
- Streamlines applicant record updates (transactional processes)
- Provide basic output management

The Agency saw an opportunity to extend efficiencies in deploying case management solutions. With the configurability of the case management technology, the Agency expects to significantly accelerate deployment of the technology underlying any new business process change. With the solution, almost all adaptations to the system required coding changes and took significant IT time to develop and maintain. In contrast, IT will have many opportunities to adapt Phase II to changing business needs through configuration changes, not always having to resort to code changes.

4.3 Organization & Social

A major component of Phase II is work management. The enhanced user interface, or dashboard, will help focus case worker attention on new and follow-up activities scheduled for each day and provide access to a holistic view of each case. In addition, the case workers will be able to create their own status alerts to new tasks that must be completed based on responses to inquires or unexpected events. Consider a situation where a new charge is brought against an applicant who is already being evaluated by the Agency. When notified of the arrest, the case worker can instruct the system to send a reminder to follow up within a specified number of days.

Planning the day's activities will be much easier. Instead of having to review a report about pending cases and next steps, staff members will see on their desktops only those work items that need their current attention. Instead of having to go out and grab all the information required to complete these work items, the system will offer rapid access to a case file with all relevant content. There is no need to waste productive time figuring out what to do each day or hunting for documents in different systems.

5. HURDLES OVERCOME

5.1 Management

The project work was executed using two project teams. One team was staffed by external team members, and the other team was staffed by Agency employees and contract staff. While the Agency team was all located at the central IT office, the external team was distributed. In light of the dynamic case requirements of this solution, the ability of the teams to communicate effectively was identified as a major potential hurdle. The project managers agreed to create a communication plan that would be used throughout the project. The plan included communication paths used for the developers, managers and users. By following this plan, the project teams were able to stay informed of each member's activities. The managers were kept abreast of the project status, and they were able to proactively react to most issues before they became risks. The users and upper management on both teams were kept up to date on the project status and issues.

5.2 Business

Another hurdle has been the ability to get the users to trade the amount of user-friendly options that they've been accustomed to for greater configurability. The existing application had a highly-customized user interface, which was built over the last seven years to make the application as user-friendly as possible. This required a lot of custom coding. One of the major advantages of using the new case management platform is that the developer has a framework that allows for more rapid development. This configurable case-based framework reduces the cost of development and long-term maintenance of the application. However, the framework does not provide the amount of UI options that the users currently have available. The function could be added through custom coding, but that would increase the development time. In the short term, it has been a challenge to meet the user's request without expanding the scope of the project. Going forward, the solution will be improved to meet the all the users' UI requests.

6. BENEFITS

6.1 Cost Savings / Time Reductions

Before implementing the system, the application review process took 11 weeks. The system streamlined the process to a little over one hour.

6.2 *Quality Improvements*

The system allows for more accurate reviews and background checks to help agencies place children in safe settings, while meeting legislative and compliance requirements.

7. BEST PRACTICES AND LEARNING POINTS

- ✓ *Take an iterative approach—Discovery, Construction iterations (3), Acceptance testing*
- ✓ *Collaborate between IT team and business*
- ✓ *Implement via time-boxed construction*
- ✓ *Approach with light-weight requirements and design*

8. TECHNOLOGY

The solution is built on IBM's advanced case management platform. This solution focuses on the tenets of:

- Aligning information to make better decisions. The solution leverages a persistable case object infrastructure implemented in the content engine that inherits the full breadth of enterprise content management services. It captures and activates criminal history information in the context of a case, providing a 360 degree view for all applicants. This information is stored and available for audits.

- Supporting the way people work. The solution provides runtime task flexibility. This enables support for the knowledge worker—Criminal History Raters, Criminal History Reporting staff, Criminal History Analysts, and Record Keepers—to address the dynamic, unpredictable, ad-hoc, and collaborative activities in processing applications and ensuring legal compliance.

- Optimizing case outcomes. The solution provides comprehensive real-time and persisted analytics of structured and unstructured data. This enables Agency personnel to have visibility into cases to provide guidance to ensure the optimal processing of reviews.

- Enabling business control. The solution development platform fosters collaboration between business and IT. It is business-driven, enabling the agility and flexibility to adapt to regulatory changes and realize faster time-to-value.

9. THE TECHNOLOGY AND SERVICE PROVIDERS

Enterprise Content Management (ECM) solutions from IBM help companies realize the value of content for better insight and business outcomes. IBM ECM can help companies transform the way they do business by enabling them to put enterprise content in motion—capturing, activating, socializing, analyzing and governing it throughout the entire lifecycle. With industry-specific IBM ECM solutions, companies can capture, manage and share content throughout its lifecycle, helping ensure compliance, reduce costs and maximize productivity. The IBM ECM portfolio includes a wide array of capabilities that integrate with existing systems to help organizations maximize the value of information, including document capture and imaging, social content management, advanced case management, information lifecycle governance, and content analytics. More than 13,000 global companies, organizations and government organizations rely on IBM ECM software to improve performance and remain competitive through innovation.

IBM services for ECM enable organizations to meet their business requirements by helping ensure optimal system performance and assisting with future expansion and enhancement of ECM investments.

Touchstone Health, USA
Finalist: Production Case Management

1. EXECUTIVE SUMMARY / ABSTRACT

Touchstone Health faced a momentous challenge with their current Appeals and Grievances (A&G) process. Touchstone was managing 1,500 A&G cases per month through a largely manual case management process. In addition, regulatory compliance requirements required timely and auditable records be provided to avoid potential fines.

The primary users, the A&G case managers, were dealing with a highly manual process that required data gathering from multiple systems and departments. They had to manually reconcile all reporting, and manually generate and track the required correspondence and deadlines. Additionally, the case managers often lost visibility and control when assigning cases throughout the organization.

Touchstone Health adopted a new Adaptive Case Management approach that greatly improved the productivity of the company's knowledge workers and ensured compliance to regulatory requirements. The ACM approach provided an automated system that ensures all correspondence is automatically sent and meets regulatory timing requirements. The approach has saved eight hours of manual work weekly on reporting reconciliation alone, saves countless hours on the generation and tracking of correspondence, and the case manager only has to learn and access one system for all relevant data and documents.

Adaptive workflow was used to allow the case manager to determine what personnel to obtain data from and these assignees could in turn also sub-delegate the work. The system dynamically adapted on a case-by-case basis, providing flexibility without losing the control and visibility of typical structured workflow.

Touchstone Health believes exponential gains in productivity, visibility and reporting will set the industry standard for A&G systems.

2. OVERVIEW

Touchstone Health is a $200M Health Plan/Insurance provider that is currently serving approximately 20,000 members. Founded in 1998, this HMO works with Medicare, and operates primarily in the NYC area. By law, members of health insurance providers (e.g. HMO, PPO and Medical Savings Account plans) have the right to appeal any decision made by the provider. For example, if Medicare does not pay for an item or service that has been given, or if an item or service thought necessary is denied, members may appeal. Members may also submit grievances expressing dissatisfaction with any aspect of the operations, activities or behavior of a Medicare health plan, or its providers, regardless of whether remedial action is requested. Providers who do not strictly follow the laws involving A&G's are subject to regulatory fines. In 2007, United Healthcare paid $12 Million to 36 states for improperly processing Appeals and Grievances. In 2009, Arizona regulators fined another health provider, Health Net, $236,500. On average, providers allocate $2.50 per member per month to process A&G's.

Annual costs for a company such as Touchstone can easily reach as much as $600,000. The fact that Touchstone was managing 1,500 A&G cases per month, through a largely manual case management process, resulted in the company deciding that they needed to automate. Automating A&G processes cuts 20%-30 percent in operational costs, which is a $120K-$180K annual savings. Additionally, automation adds a layer of governance that helps health insurance providers to avoid future regulatory fines of this nature.

The BPM technology selected to implement the automated A&G system added the extra benefit of handling unstructured activities – a crucial element of Touchstone's A&G processes. Touchstone's CIO also saw the value of the BPM solution provider's experience designing and developing process-driven applications.

3. BUSINESS CONTEXT

Before implementing the ACM approach to automate their A&G process, Touchstone Health was managing 1,500 A&G cases per month through a largely manual case management process. A&G case managers had to gather data from multiple systems and multiple departments. They had to manually reconcile all reporting, and manually generate and track the required correspondence and deadlines. The case managers often lost visibility and control when assigning cases throughout the organization. The outdated system being used did not meet the necessary requirements, and did not allow case managers to effectively and efficiently handle complaints or questions submitted by providers and beneficiaries.

4. THE KEY INNOVATIONS

The impact that resulted from Touchstone's A&G process automation was widespread. The automation greatly improved the productivity of the A&G case managers, while ensuring compliance with regulatory requirements. The approach has saved eight hours of manual work weekly on reporting reconciliation alone. Additionally, countless hours are saved on the generation and tracking of correspondence. Now, instead of A&G case managers having to gather data from multiple systems and multiple departments, they only need to learn and access one system for all relevant data and documents.

The automation ensures adherence to CMS regulatory requirements on reporting, auditing and correspondence timelines. It has also reduced the learning curve and skill level needed for processing A&G's, by consolidating all required systems into a single case management tool (SDS Document Management, Claims Data, Enrollment Data and A&G Data). The automation has improved overall case handling, allowing the case manager to retain control of the case, while tasking others for input to the case.

4.1 Business

The A&G process automation has greatly improved the experiences of not only the A&G stakeholders, but also the providers and beneficiaries who are contacting Touchstone with a question or complaint. Now, when a call comes in, the A&G case manager opens the *one and only* system necessary to use, and notes all relevant details of the case. This determines what personnel they need to obtain data from. The automation makes it possible for these assignees, in turn, to sub-delegate the work as well. Keeping everything in one system makes it much easier to train A&G case managers, decreases the number of mistakes, and reduces the skill level needed to complete the job. The automated system dynamically adapts on a case-by-case basis – this provides flexibility, while allowing the case manager to maintain control and visibility. An overview of the system is shown in the below graphic. This is the one and only system case managers need to open when a call comes in. The top third of the graphic shows where work is initiated, the second section contains structured work items, while the bottom third consists of dynamic tasks.

Appeals & Grievances Menu

4.2 Case Handling

Prior to automation, when a call came in with a complaint or question from a provider or beneficiary, A&G case managers would have to gather data from multiple systems and multiple departments in order to handle the claim. It was very difficult to keep track of each claim and handle it efficiently and effectively. Everything was done manually.

After the project, cases are much more streamlined and easy to handle. The case manager opens the system to input basic information about the claim. The system then determines where and who the necessary information should come from. The claim can easily be tracked in the system all the way through to completion.

4.3 Organization & Social

The A&G process automation has had a huge impact on Touchstone employees. The jobs of the A&G case managers have been simplified significantly. The training method for case managers is more efficient, as case managers now only have to learn one system. Before automation, the case manager would be required to sift and sort through many different systems to try to determine what information was needed to process the claim, and where they had to go to get this information. Now, it is far easier to determine and locate this information, as everything is consolidated into one system. The manager simply has to open the system (that all employees now use) when a call comes in, and insert some basic information. The system then will inform the case manager where they must go to get the necessary information for the next step. Since only one system is used, delegating work has never been easier. It's all contained in one spot, allowing anyone to easily track where in the process the claim is, who is in charge of each task, when the task was assigned to them, etc. The graphic below is an illustration of how a claim can be easily tracked. To see where in the process a claim is, basic information is input, and all case details are immediately pulled up.

5. HURDLES OVERCOME

Management

During the automation process, challenges arose, as expected. From a management perspective, this was the first endeavor of this type for the company. This meant there was an uncertainty of what was needed, which dictated that all initial requirements gathering be done in person. These initial requirements were gathered in several one-day group sessions, with a BPM solution provider account executive traveling to NY to attend the first several meetings in person. Once the initial meetings were completed, subsequent webcasts were conducted. Since Touchstone had never dealt with anything like this before, the team had to have many reviews in order to stay on track.

Business

From a business perspective, the BPM solution provider established "safeguard" clauses to determine responsibility with the client. Many reviews were conducted to stay on track. A project schedule was developed in MS Project, and then shared with Touchstone through Smartsheet. This allowed for information sharing, and kept everyone on the same page. There was a "traffic light" indicator for task status, to bring Touchstone's attention to overdue tasks. The BPM solution provider ensured that their part was always complete and ready, so Touchstone would never have to be waiting on them. Weekly status calls were held, where the Smartsheet schedule was reviewed, and the team reviewed action items from the previous week to ensure all team members were on track. The weekly calls also ensured documentation captured changes and updates.

Organization Adoption

There were challenges in organization adoption during the automation process, largely because Touchstone had never dealt with anything like this before, and required a lot of guidance. Since they have a very small IT department, they needed a lot of help. Periodic reviews of the application were provided, to minimize post-UAT (user acceptance testing) changes. Mentoring was also a big factor facilitating organizational adoption – the client resource developed a small part of the application in order to help them get some experience and comfort level with the tool.

6. BENEFITS

6.1 Cost Savings / Time Reductions

The ACM approach has saved eight hours of manual work weekly on reporting reconciliation alone. The approach has also saved countless hours on the generation and tracking of correspondence, and the case manager only has to learn and access one system for all relevant data and documents.

6.3 Quality Improvements

Overall, case handling has been greatly improved by using the BPM solution – this allows the case manager to retain control of the task, while tasking others for input to the case, and improves processing time significantly. The automation also ensures adherence to CMS regulatory requirements. The automation has reduced the learning curve and skill level needed for processing A&G's by consolidating all required systems into a single case management tool.

7. BEST PRACTICES, LEARNING POINTS AND PITFALLS

7.1 Best Practices and Learning Points

✓ Doing a walk through with the actual case managers to understand the existing way the process was being done was very helpful in designing a new system (keeping what was important about the current way the process was being done but eliminating the issues/limitations of the current approach).

✓ Prototyping the screens early in the development process really helped the users visualize the system and help speed the implementation and minimize changes.

✓ Frequent (weekly) reviews of the application with all key stakeholders as it was being implemented allowed for more rapid development, drove shorter testing cycles and minimized post delivery modifications due to functional defects or functional shortcomings.

7.2 Pitfalls

✗ Engaging the other vendors utilized in the process earlier. While the BPM system is the core and primary solution, two other vendors played a role in the complete system. It would have been better to bring them into the design process from the beginning, even though they each had only a relatively small part of the total application.

✗ Documenting the requirements was important, but starting the prototyping sooner would have likely yielded an even more rapid deployment.

8. COMPETITIVE ADVANTAGES

Touchstone believes the exponential gains in productivity, visibility and reporting achieved by the A&G process automation will set the industry standard for A&G systems. Touchstone plans to sustain competitive advantage by automating more processes (in the short-term), and eventually taking the automation to other companies (in the long-term).

9. TECHNOLOGY

A dynamic BPM solution was used to implement an automated A&G system to increase productivity and meet regulatory requirements. The solution, while filling all major BPM criteria of the project, had the extra benefit of handling unstructured activities, a crucial element of Touchstone's A&G processes.

10. THE TECHNOLOGY AND SERVICE PROVIDERS

HandySoft provided business process management (BPM) software (BizFlow), application development, and customer support for this project. HandySoft is a leading global provider of BPM, Tasking and Compliance software and solutions for government and business organizations. BizFlow® is the first and only BPM Suite on the market to seamlessly integrate and automate dynamic tasks, case management, content collaboration, and structured processes along with Process Intelligence and RIA capabilities to drive visibility, control and productivity across all work that happens within an organization. For more information, visit www.handysoft.com.

Appendix

Author Appendix

STEINAR CARLSEN
Chief Engineer, Computas AS, Norway
Dr. Steinar Carlsen is a recognized Norwegian expert within business processes and workflow technology. He is a senior advisor specializing in adaptive case management, business process management, knowledge management, social technologies, with more than 20 years of experience in different approaches to the modelling of work processes. His focus is on realizing work support systems, as well as baselining "organizational implementation/enactment". Steinar has a background from applied research within business process modelling, enterprise modelling, enterprise architecture and requirements engineering. Steinar is the product owner of FrameSolutions™ - Computas AS' framework for realizing operational ACM solutions.

LUIS CASTILLO, PHD
Chief Technology Officer, IActive US Corp.
With a background of near 20 years of research on Artificial Intelligence, 17 of which he has served as Associate Professor at the University of Granada in Spain, Luis is now part of IActive and Cognocare and he is driving the development of the Artificial Intelligence engine that constitutes the basis of Cognocare. During that time and after many public research projects and private research contracts with leading companies, he has devoted his efforts to bring academic research into real world applications and to introduce several types of Artificial Intelligence technologies (planning, scheduling, machine learning) into commercial products within the family of Adaptive Case Management, leading to two patents currently being processed in US.

GUNNAR JOHN COLL
Senior Advisor, VP, Computas AS
Gunnar John Coll represents a behavioural approach to technology, organization and knowledge. He assists customers in corporate process initiatives, including knowledge management and organizational learning. His main area of work is where business process and human competence meet with new technology, to answer the need for change. He provides perspectives, facilitates and manages initiatives in close cooperation with customer's key personnel. Gunnar has more than 25 years of experience in IT projects related to organizational processes. Due to his combined background as a psychologist and an IT professional, he provides a complementary perspective on system development and organizational adoption.

LAYNA FISCHER
Publisher, Future Strategies Inc., USA
Ms Fischer is the Chief Editor and Publisher of Future Strategies Inc., the official publishers to WfMC.org. She was also Executive Director of WfMC and BPMI (now merged with OMG) and continues to work closely with these organizations to promote industry awareness of BPM and Workflow.

Future Strategies Inc. (www.FutStrat.com) publishes unique books and papers on business process management and workflow, specializing in dissemination of information about BPM and workflow technology and electronic commerce. As such, the company contracts and works closely with individual authors and corporations worldwide and also manages the renowned annual Global Awards for Excellence in BPM and Workflow and the new annual Adaptive Case Management Awards.

Future Strategies Inc., is the publisher of the business book series *New Tools for New Times*, the annual *Excellence in Practice* series of award-winning case studies and the annual *BPM and Workflow Handbook* series, published in collaboration with the WfMC. Ms. Fischer was a senior editor of a leading international computer publication for four years and has been involved in international computer journalism and publishing for over 20 years.

KEITH HARRISON-BRONINSKI
CTO, *Role Modellers*

Keith Harrison-Broninski is CTO of Role Modellers, a Gartner BPM Cool Vendor 2012. The company mission is to develop understanding and support of human-driven processes - the field that Keith pioneered. Its software product, the Human Interaction Management System (HIMS) HumanEdj, provides unique software support for collaborative, adaptive human work.

Keith has been regarded as an IT and business thought leader since publication of his 2005 book "Human Interactions: The Heart And Soul Of Business Process Management". Building on 20 years of research and insights from varied disciplines, his theory of Human Interaction Management (HIM) provides a new way to describe and support collaborative human work. Keith speaks regularly about HIM and the associated change management methodology Goal-Oriented Organization Design (GOOD) in keynotes to business, IT and academic audiences at national conferences, most recently in Poland, India, the Netherlands, the UK, Finland and Portugal.

More information about HumanEdj is available at www.rolemodellers.com and about Keith at http://keith.harrison-broninski.info.

FRANK MICHAEL KRAFT
CEO, *AdaPro GmbH*

Frank Michael Kraft has twenty years of experience as a systems analyst and software architect for custom and standard software (ERP) for business processes.

AdaPro focuses on supporting companies to set up a strategy for adaptive processes that covers standard processes, workflows and Adaptive Case Management. Adaptive processes do not stand on their own, but have to be integrated into existing system- and model landscapes in a blended approach to protect previous investments while at the same time extending the capabilities of process management to become more adaptive. AdaPro follows an evolutionary approach that allows for small steps on the way to adaptive processes.

In a former role at SAP AG, he defined the architecture for the model-driven development of the business processes of two hundred business objects as part of the business process platform that is the foundation for SAP Business ByDesign. These business objects cover the application areas of supplier relationship management, customer relationship management, logistics planning and execution, production, project management, human resources, and financials. Frank was responsible for the governance process for the business process management (BPM) models, and he conducted many thousands of model reviews, which included the design of many thousands of service operations as part of the service-oriented architecture. A special focus of Frank's work was the flexibility and adaptability of the modeled business processes, for which he developed innovative concepts. He is an inventor with various patents in the area of business process integration and design and flexibility. Recently, he was member of the BPMN 2.0 specification team and contributed in the area of choreography modeling, where he also published scientific articles.

ALBERTO MANUEL
CEO of *Process Sphere, Portugal*

Alberto Manuel has over 10 years of hands-on experience helping companies to improve, redesign and implement business process, in order to become more agile and lean over and over again, working as a mentor, coach and consultant helping companies to reach successful outcomes.

Previously, for seven years, he was committed to R&D of consumer goods products and improving manufacturing operations.

He is involved with the BPM community helping to bring innovation to this field of practice. He is Vice President of the *Association of Business Process Management Professionals - Portuguese Chapter*, member of the task force on Process Mining, and various working groups of the Workflow Management Coalition and World Wide Web Consortium. His blog is at http://ultrabpm.wordpress.com

JOHN T. MATTHIAS, J.D., PMP
Principal Court Management Consultant, National Center for State Courts

Mr. Matthias has worked as a management consultant and business analyst in courts and justice agencies in 35 states, as a city prosecutor, and as program manager of a commercial case management system product. His experience in 75 projects spans caseflow management, CMS needs assessment, requirement definition, performance measurement, and business process redesign. He has contributed to Future Trends in State Courts, and a variety of his reports and publications are available at www.ncsc.org and www.ctc2011.org.

DERMOT MCCAULEY
Vice President of BPM and Case Management, Kofax, Inc.

Dermot McCauley is Vice President of BPM and Case Management at Kofax, Inc. Prior to its acquisition by Kofax in 2011, Dermot had held a number of executive team roles at Singularity, a leading BPM and Case Management software supplier. Before joining Singularity in 2003, he held President and General Manager roles in publicly quoted high-growth technology companies in the U.S. and Europe, including Cambridge Technology Partners (CTP) and Rare Medium Group. An executive in his own successful start-up that was purchased by CTP in 1995, Dermot has previously worked for JPMorgan Chase, Dun & Bradstreet, and Sema. Dermot holds a Mathematics degree from Imperial College, London.

HAJO NORMANN
BPM/SOA Lead ASG, Accenture GmBH

Since 13 years Hajo Normann motivates, designs and implements solutions successfully at various customers and worked on choosing the right mix of tools, on setting up a successful modernization, sourcing & vendor strategy and sharing SOA/BPM principles, design guidelines and best practices. Solutions created at customers involve the relationship between EA and BPM, finding the right mix of rigid and adaptive processes and creating reusable functionality through generated and standardized services with the help of a SOA Service Factory. Hajo is Oracle ACE Director and a frequent speaker at Conferences. He is co-author of an article on ACM in the German "ComputerWoche", of the German publication "Industrialized SOA" and of 3 patterns in Thomas Erl's bestselling book "SOA Design Patterns". His blog is at http://hajonormann.wordpress.com/

NATHANIEL PALMER
Chief BPM Strategist of SRA International and Executive Director, Workflow Management Coalition

A noted author, practitioner and one of the early originators of Adaptive Case Management, Nathaniel Palmer has been the Chief Architect to some of the world's largest BPM, SOA and ACM projects, involving investments of $200 Million or more. He is the BPM Practice Director at SRA International, as well as the Executive Director of the Workflow Management Coalition. Previously he was Director, Business Consulting for Perot Systems Corp, and spent over a decade with Delphi Group serving as Vice President and Chief Technology Officer. He frequently tops the lists of the most recognized names in his field, and was the first individual named as Laureate in Workflow.

He is a regular speaker at leading BPM forums and industry user groups. He has served on the boards of Align, COMNET, eDOC Journal, Infonomics, AIIM New England, and the Governor of Massachusetts' IT Advisory Board.

MAX J. PUCHER
Chief Technology Officer, ISIS Papyrus Europe AG, Austria

Max J. Pucher has a 38-year background in enterprise IT and has given the future of BPM substantial coverage in his writing and speaking. He is co-author of 'Mastering the Unpredictable,' the first book in 2009 to discuss Adaptive Case Management. His passion is designing software technology that empowers humans in the enterprise arena. His blog 'Welcome To The Real (IT) World' on the future of process and business management is read by over 3000 expert followers http://www.adaptive-process.com.

Because of his belief in social networking concepts he joined forces in 2010 with the co-founder of ACT! Mike Muhney. Together they founded VIPorbit Software International, Inc. to offer Mobile Cloud solutions with VIPorbit®, the only full-featured Mobile Contact Manager designed for the iPhone.

HELLE FRISAK SEM
Chief Architect, Computas AS, Norway

Dr. Helle Frisak Sem is a Chief Architect in Computas, specializing in solution architecture and requirements engineering. With more than 20 years of experience, Helle leads functional teams towards the realization of operational ACM solutions, in collaboration with customer and user. She is a senior advisor in knowledge management, work process support, enterprise modelling, estimation of software projects and user interface design. From a background in research and education, Helle combines deep technical knowledge with experience on how customers' problems may be met by an operational solution. Helle is the functional architect behind the MATS solution described in this book, and over the last 15 years she has been a main contributor to FrameSolutions™ - Computas AS' framework for realizing operational ACM solutions.

KEITH SWENSON
Vice President of R&D, Fujitsu America Inc., USA

Keith Swenson is Vice President of Research and Development at Fujitsu America Inc. and is the Chief Software Architect for the Interstage family of products. He is known for having been a pioneer in collaboration software and web services, and has helped the development of many workflow and BPM standards. He is currently the Chairman of the Technical Committee of the Workflow Management Coalition. In the past, he led development of collaboration software MS2, Netscape, Ashton Tate and Fujitsu. In 2004 he was awarded the Marvin L. Manheim Award for outstanding contributions in the field of workflow. His blog is at http://kswenson.wordpress.com.

CHARLES WEBSTER
President of EHR Workflow Inc.

Charles Webster, MD, MSIE, MSIS has degrees in Accountancy, Industrial Engineering, Artificial Intelligence, and Medicine. He designed one of the first undergraduate and graduate programs in medical informatics and was Chief Medical Informatics Officer for an electronic health record vendor. Dr. Webster is currently President of EHR Workflow Inc., providing process engineering services to healthcare. He's been a judge for the Global Awards for Excellence in Adaptive Case Management and is a member of the IEEE Task Force on Process Mining. He blogs at http://chuckwebster.com and tweets at @EHRworkflow.

Glossary of Terms
Adaptive Case Management

To have a meaningful discussion, we must start with clear definitions.

- **activity**—A description of a piece of work that forms one logical step within a process. It is the basic unit of work within a process. Presumably, work could be subdivided into units smaller than a given activity, but it is not meaningful for the organization to track the work to that level of detail. Synonyms include node, step, and task.
- **adaptive case management (ACM)**—A productive system that deploys not only the organization and process structure, but it becomes the system of record for the business data entities and content involved. All processes are completely transparent, as per access authorization, and fully auditable. It enables nontechnical business users in virtual organizations to seamlessly create/consolidate structured and unstructured processes from basic predefined business entities, content, social interactions, and business rules. It moves the process knowledge gathering from the template analysis/modeling/ simulation phase into the process execution phase in the lifecycle. It collects actionable knowledge—without an intermediate analysis phase—based on process patterns created by business users. ACM differs from business process management (BPM) and from human interaction management (HIM) in that the case information is the focus and the thing around which the other artifacts are organized. And it is the case information that persists for the long term.
- **ad hoc process**—See emergent process.
- **agile methodology**—To move quickly and lightly. In reference to solution development, it is a method where many short iterations are used, with many quick (internal) releases, so that the nontechnical customer of a solution can be more actively involved in guiding the course of development. The agile approach to development is known to produce solutions that better meet the needs of the customer, and it also allows for greater responsiveness to external changes in requirements.
- **analytics**- A mechanism for collecting and processing statistics. Process analytics will gather and process statistics about the running of processes in such a way that it is useful for evaluating how well the process is running.
- **best practice**—An approach to achieving a particular outcome that is believed to be more effective than any other approach in a particular condition or circumstance.
- **business operations platform (BOP)**— A next-generation technology platform oriented toward continuously designing, executing, monitoring, changing, and optimizing critical business processes proposed by Fingar (2009).
- **business process**— A set of one or more linked activities which collectively realize a business objective or policy goal, normally within the context of an organizational structure defining functional roles and relationships.

- **business process execution language (BPEL)**—A standard executable language, based on XML, for describing a process that uses web service calls to communicate with the outside world.
- **business process management (BPM)**—The practice of developing, running, performance measuring, and simulating business processes to effect the continued improvement of those processes. Business process management is concerned with the lifecycle of the process definition. BPM differs from adaptive case management (ACM) and from human interaction management (HIM) in that its focus is the process, and it uses the process as an organizing paradigm around which data, roles, and communication are organized. Process models are prepared in advance for particular situations, and the performance can be measured and monitored so that over time the process will be improved.
- **business process management suite/soft ware/system (BPMS)**—A soft ware system designed to support business process management. The acronym BPMS is used to distinguish the technology product from the management practice of BPM.
- **business process modeling notation (BPMN)**—A standard set of graphical shapes and conventions with associated meanings that can be used in modeling a business process.
- **business process orientation (BPO)**—A concept that suggests that organizations could enhance their overall performance by viewing all the activities as linked together into a process that ultimately produces a good or service.
- **business rules engine (BRE)**—A soft ware system for managing and evaluating a complex set of rules in a business processing environment. A business rule is a small piece of logic that is separated from the application logic so that it may be managed separately from the application code. Rules are oft en expressed in a language that is more accessible to non-programmers.
- **case**—The name given to the specific situation, set of circumstances, or initiative that requires a set of actions to achieve an acceptable outcome or objective. Each case has a subject that is the focus of the actions—such as a person, a lawsuit, or an insurance claim—and is driven by the evolving circumstances of the subject.
- **case file**—Contains all of the case information and processes, and it coordinates communications necessary to accomplish the goal for a particular case. A case file can contain information of any type including documents, images, video, etc.
- **case management**—A method or practice of coordinating work by organizing all of the relevant information into one place—called a case. The case becomes the focal point for assessing the situation, initiating activities and processes, as well as keeping a history record of what has transpired. Beyond this generic definition, case management has specific meanings in the medical care, legal, and social services fields. For this book, we see case management as a technique that could be used in any field of human endeavor.
- **case owner**—A person (or group of people) who is responsible for the outcome of a case. The case owner can change any aspect of a case and is actively involved in achieving the goals of the case.

- **clinical pathway**—a method that medical professionals use to standardize patient care based on accepted practice guidelines.
- **commercial-off -the-shelf (COTS)**—Describes software or hardware products that are ready-made and available for sale to the general public. This term is used to distinguish such product from custom software and hardware made specifically for a purpose that is presumed to be more expensive to produce and maintain.
- **crowdsourcing**—Identify evolving trends and best practices through continuous analysis of social interactions and conversations[2]
- **customer relationship management (CRM)**—Technology to manage a company's interactions with customers and sales prospects.
- **dynamic case management**—support real-time, incremental and progressive case-handling in response to changing events by leveraging collaborative and information-intensive BPM.[2]
- **emergent process**—A process that is not predictable. Emergent processes have a sensitive dependence upon external factors outside of the control of the process context, which is why they cannot be fixed according to their internal state. Workers involved in an emergent process will experience it as planning and working alternately or at the same time, such that the plan is evolved as the work evolves. Synonyms include *ad hoc* process and unstructured process.
- **enterprise content management (ECM)**—Strategies, methods, and tools used to capture, manage, store, preserve, and deliver content and documents related to organizational processes. ECM strategies and tools allow the management of an organization's unstructured information, wherever that information exists.
- **enterprise resource planning (ERP)**—Computer system used to manage resources including tangible assets, financial resources, materials, and human resources.
- **extended relationship management (XRM)**—a discipline of mapping and maintaining relationships between any type of asset in very flexible ways, for the purpose of leveraging those relationships in business rules or business processes.
- **goal-oriented organization design (GOOD)**—The change management methodology associated with human interaction management (HIM), which defines 3 standard Stages: Design (scope definition, business motiation modeling, benefits definition), Delivery (requirements management, stakeholder management, operational transition, risk management) and Optimization (marketing & communications, benefits realization). Each Stage has associated Roles, Activities and Deliverables.
- **human interaction management (HIM)**—The practice of describing, executing and managing collaborative human activity according to 5 standard principles (effective teams, structured communication, knowledge management, time management and dynamic planning) so as to achieve optimal results. HIM differs from business process management (BPM) and adaptive case management (ACM) in that its focus is definition of goals, assignment of associated responsibilities, and management of

---

[2] Forrester Research, USA

the resulting knowledge. Templates describing Stages, Roles, Activities and Deliverables are used to generate executable Plans that evolve during usage and may be re-used as new templates.

- **knowledge work**—A type of work where the course of events is decided on a case-by-case basis. It normally requires a person with detailed knowledge who can weigh many factors and anticipate potential outcomes to determine the course for a specific case. Knowledge work almost always involves an emergent ACM/BPM process or HIM Plan template.

- **knowledge workers**—People who have a high degree of expertise, education, or experience and the primary purpose of their job involves the creation, distribution, or application of knowledge. Knowledge workers do not necessarily work in knowledge intensive industries.

- **lifecycle**—This book uses lifecycle only in regard to the work of creating a solution. The development lifecycle of a solution might start with definition of requirements, development of a process definition, development of forms, testing, deployment of the solution into production, use of the solution by many people, and finally the shutting down of the solution. The lifecycle of a solution may involve monitoring the running process instances and improving those process definitions over time. Note: A solution has a lifecycle that takes it from start to finish; a case has a process or processes that take it from start to finish.

- **model**—A simplified summary of reality designed to aid further study. In the business process field, a process model is a simplified or complete process definition created to study the proposed process before execution time.

- **node**—See activity.

- **online transaction processing (OLTP)**—A class of systems where time-sensitive, transaction-related data are processed immediately and are always kept current.

- **organizational agility**—That quality of an organization associated with sensing opportunity or threat, prioritizing its potential responses, and acting efficiently and effectively.

- **predictable process**—process that is repeatable and is run the same way a number of times. Synonyms include definable process, repeatable process, and structured process.

- **process definition**—A representation of a business process in a form that supports automated manipulation, such as modeling or enactment by a process management system. The process definition consists of a network of activities and their relationships, criteria to indicate the start and termination of the process, and information about the individual activities, such as participants, associated IT applications, and data. Synonyms include process diagram and workflow.

- **process diagram**—A visual explanation of a process definition. Synonyms include process definition, process model, and process flowchart.

- **process flowchart**—See process diagram.

- **process instance**—A data structure that represents a particular instance of running of a process. It has associated context information that can be used and manipulated by the process. A process instance plays a role in a business process management suite (BPMS) that is very similar to but not exactly the same as a case in a case management system. A particular case may have more than one process instance associated with it.

- **process model**—A simplified or complete process definition created to study the proposed process before execution time. Synonyms include process diagram.
- **records management**—Management of the information created, received, and maintained as evidence and information by an organization in pursuance of legal obligations or in the transaction of business.
- **role**—An association of particular a user, or users, with a particular set of responsibilities in a particular context. In this case, responsibility means the expectation to perform particular activities for that context. routine work— Work that is predictable and usually repeatable. Its predictability allows routine work to be planned to a large extent before the work is started. As the name implies, routine work is considered normal, regular, and it is not exceptional.
- **scientific management**— An early twentieth century school of management that aimed to improve the physical efficiency of an individual worker by carefully recording precisely what must be done for a particular task, and then training workers to replicate that precisely. It is based on the work of Frederick Winslow Taylor (1856–1915).
- **scrum**—An agile software development methodology emphasizing iteration and incremental development. Originally referred to as the *rugby approach.*
- **service-oriented architecture (SOA)**—An approach to system design where the software functionality is deployed to a specific logical location (a service) and programs requiring that soft ware functionality make use of communications protocols to access the service remotely. SOA has oft en been discussed together with business process management (BPM), but this connection is coincidental. While BPM might benefit from SOA the way that any program/system would, there is no inherent connection between managing business processes and the system architecture that supports them.
- **social business**—An organization that has put in place the strategies, technologies and processes to systematically engage all the individuals of its ecosystem (employees, customers, partners, suppliers) to maximize the co-created value.
- **social BPM**—Leverage social networking tools and techniques to extend the reach and impact of process improvement efforts.
- **social network analysis**—Pinpoint historical activity patterns within social networks through the statistical mining of complex behavioural data sets.
- **social process guidance**—Apply crowdsourcing and social network analysis techniques to deliver real-time contextual advice and guidance for completing a process task or activity.
- **social software**—A class of software systems that allows users to communicate, collaborate, and interact in many flexible ways. Generally, such software allows users to form their own relationships with other users and then exchange messages, write notes, and share media in different ways.

- **solution**—A package of artefacts (configurations, forms, process definitions, templates, and information) that have been prepared in advance to help users address particular kinds of recurring situations. A solution may embody best practices for a particular kind of situation.
- **sphere**—a collection of people or other assets. Inclusion in a sphere can be based on business rules or can be a nested collection of other spheres. Spheres can represent nodes in a network of relationships or process flow in a workflow system
- **step**—See activity.
- **straight-through processing (STP)**—The practice of completely automating a process and eliminating all manual human tasks. This term is typically used in the financial industry.
- **subject (of a case)**—An entity that is the focus of actions performed in the context of a case. For example, a person, a lawsuit, or an insurance claim.
- **task**—See activity.
- **template**—The general concept of something that is prepared in advance approximately for a particular purpose with the anticipation that it will be modified during use to more exactly fit the situation. A process template does not define a process in the way that a process definition does.
- **unstructured process**—See emergent process.
- **work**—Exertion or effort directed to produce or accomplish something. Organizations exist to achieve goals and work is the means to achieve those goals. The smallest recorded unit of work is an activity. Activities are combined into procedures and processes.
- **workflow**—The automation of a business process, in whole or part, during which documents, information, or tasks are passed from one participant to another for action according to a set of procedural rules. Synonyms include process definition.

These definitions are licensed under Creative Commons—you are free to copy and use them in any way that helps the pursuit of knowledge. It is not strictly necessary to reference this glossary, but we would appreciate a link back to this book. The bulk of this glossary is derived from the work done by Keith Swenson at http://social-biz.org/glossary and was originally assembled for inclusion in Mastering the Unpredictable[3]."

Accreditation guide: "How Knowledge Workers Get Things Done" 2012 published by Future Strategies Inc. Lighthouse Point, FL. www.FutStrat.com

---

[3] Mastering the Unpredictable: How Adaptive Case Management Will Revolutionize the Way That Knowledge Workers Get Things Done, published by Meghan-Kiffer Press, April 2010

WfMC Structure and Membership Information

What is the Workflow Management Coalition?

The Workflow Management Coalition, founded in August 1993, is a non-profit, international organization of workflow vendors, users, analysts and university/research groups. The Coalition's mission is to promote and develop the use of workflow through the establishment of standards for software terminology, interoperability and connectivity among BPM and workflow products. Comprising more than 250 members worldwide, the Coalition is the primary standards body for this software market.

Workflow Standards Framework

The Coalition has developed a framework for the establishment of workflow standards. This framework includes five categories of interoperability and communication standards that will allow multiple workflow products to coexist and interoperate within a user's environment. Technical details are included in the white paper entitled, "The Work of the Coalition," available at www.wfmc.org.

Achievements

The initial work of the Coalition focused on publishing the Reference Model and Glossary, defining a common architecture and terminology for the industry. A major milestone was achieved with the publication of the first versions of the Workflow API (WAPI) specification, covering the Workflow Client Application Interface, and the Workflow Interoperability specification.

In addition to a series of successful tutorials industry wide, the WfMC spent many hours over 2009 helping to drive awareness, understanding and adoption of XPDL, now the standard means for business process definition in over 80 BPM products. As a result, it has been cited as the most deployed BPM standard by a number of industry analysts, and continues to receive a growing amount of media attention.

Workflow Management Coalition Structure

The Coalition is divided into three major committees, the Technical Committee, the External Relations Committee, and the Steering Committee. Small working groups exist within each committee for the purpose of defining workflow terminology, interoperability and connectivity standards, conformance requirements, and for assisting in the communication of this information to the workflow user community.

The Coalition's major committees meet three times per calendar year for three days at a time, with meetings usually alternating between a North American and a European location. The working group meetings are held during these three days, and as necessary throughout the year.

Coalition membership is open to all interested parties involved in the creation, analysis or deployment of workflow software systems. Membership is governed by a Document of Understanding, which outlines meeting regulations, voting rights etc. Membership material is available at www.wfmc.org.

Coalition Working Groups

The Coalition has established a number of Working Groups, each working on a particular area of specification. The working groups are loosely structured around the "Workflow Reference Model" which provides the framework for the

Coalition's standards program. The Reference Model identifies the common characteristics of workflow systems and defines five discrete functional interfaces through which a workflow management system interacts with its environment—users, computer tools and applications, other software services, etc. Working groups meet individually, and also under the umbrella of the Technical Committee, which is responsible for overall technical direction and coordination.

WORKFLOW REFERENCE MODEL DIAGRAM

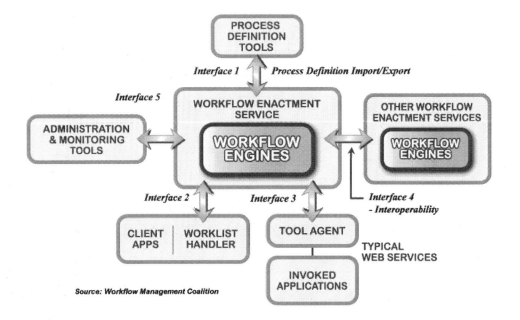

WHY YOU SHOULD JOIN

1. Gain Access to Members-Only Research and Q&A Forums
2. Participate in Members-Only "Brown Bag" Networking Sessions and Industry Speaker Series
3. Receive Free Admission to Business Process Focused Events and Programs (a Benefit Worth $1,000s Annually)
4. Access to the Industry's Largest Research Library on Business Process Modeling, Workflow, BPMS
5. Assistance in Product Certification and Conformance, as well as Requirements Analysis and Procurement Strategy

Being a member of the Workflow Management Coalition gives you the unique opportunity to participate in the creation of standards for the workflow industry as they are developing. Your contributions to our community ensure that progress continues in the adoption of royalty-free workflow and process standards.

MEMBERSHIP CATEGORIES

	Full Member	**Associate Member**	**Individual Member**
Annual fee	$3500	$1500	$500
Hold office	Software Vendors, IT & Professional Services Firms, Government, Non-Profit & Commercial	Government or Non-Profit (incl. academic); Any Commercial Firm Not Selling Software or IT Services	All open to all organizations; limited to observing roles, not eligible for officer or committee participation
Limitations	Eligible for All Offices & Committees	Eligible for All Offices & Committees	Observer Only
Events/ Research	Full Admission to WfMC Events (up to 3 individuals) and Full Access to the WfMC Research Library (up to 3 log-ons)	Full Access to the WfMC Research Library (single log-on) and Free Admission to All WfMC Events	Full Access to the WfMC Research Library (single log-on) and Free Admission to Select WfMC Events
Promotional Benefits	Logo on All WfMC Pages; Free Use of WfMC Banner Serving; Detailed Company Profile in WfMC Publications	Listed on WfMC Members List and Within Member Directory	N/A

ADDITIONAL BENEFITS OF MEMBERSHIP

This corporate category offers exclusive visibility in this sector at events and seminars across the world, enhancing your customers' perception of you as an industry authority, on our web site, in the annual BPM Handbook, by speaking opportunities, access to the Members Only area of our web site, attending the Coalition meetings and most importantly within the workgroups whereby through discussion and personal involvement, using your voting power, you can contribute actively to the development of standards and interfaces.

Full member benefits include:

- Financial incentives: 50 percent discount all "brochure-ware" (such as our annual CDROM Companion to the BPM and Workflow Handbook, advertising on our sister-site www.e-workflow.org), $500 credit toward next year's fee for at least 60 percent per year meeting attendance or if you serve as an officer of the WfMC.
- Web Visibility: your logo on all WfMC pages, inclusion in the WfMC web banner network, a detailed company profile in online member directory as well as in all WfMC publications.
- User RFIs: (Requests for Information) is an exclusive privilege to all full members. We often have queries from user organizations looking for specific workflow solutions. These valuable leads can result in real business benefits for your organization.
- Publicity: full members may choose to have their company logos including collaterals displayed along with WfMC material at conferences / expos we attend. You may also list corporate events and press releases (re-

lating to WfMC issues) on the relevant pages on the website, and have a company entry in the annual Coalition Workflow Handbook

- Speaking Opportunities: We frequently receive calls for speakers at industry events because many of our members are recognized experts in their fields. These opportunities are forwarded to Full Members for their direct response to the respective conference organizers.

ASSOCIATE MEMBERSHIP

Associate and Academic Membership is appropriate for those (such as IT user organizations) who need to keep abreast of workflow developments, but who are not workflow vendors. It allows voting on decision-making issues, including the publication of standards and interfaces but does not permit anything near the amount of visibility or incentives provided to a Full Member. You may include up to three active members from your organization on your application.

INDIVIDUAL MEMBERSHIP

Individual Membership is appropriate for self-employed persons or small user companies. Employees of workflow vendors, academic institutions or analyst organizations are not typically eligible for this category. Individual membership is held in one person's name only, is not a corporate membership, and is not transferable within the company. If three or more people within a company wish to participate in the WfMC, it would be cost-effective to upgrade to corporate Associate Membership whereby all employees worldwide are granted membership status.

HOW TO JOIN

Complete the form on the Coalition's website at www.wfmc.org, or contact the Coalition Secretariat. All members are required to sign the Coalition's "Document of Understanding" which sets out the contractual rights and obligations between members and the Coalition.

THE SECRETARIAT

Workflow Management Coalition (WfMC.org)
Nathaniel Palmer, Executive Director,
+1-781-923-1411 (t), +1-781-735-0491 (f)
nathaniel@wfmc.org

Index

Additional Resources

NON-PROFIT ASSOCIATIONS AND RELATED STANDARDS RESEARCH ONLINE

- AIIM (Association for Information and Image Management)
  http://www.aiim.org
- BPM and Workflow online news, research, forums
  http://bpm.com
- BPM Research at Stevens Institute of Technology
  http://www.bpm-research.com
- Business Process Management Initiative
  http://www.bpmi.org *see* Object Management Group
- IEEE (Electrical and Electronics Engineers, Inc.)
  http://www.ieee.org
- Institute for Information Management (IIM)
  http://www.iim.org
- ISO (International Organization for Standardization)
  http://www.iso.ch
- Object Management Group
  http://www.omg.org
- Open Document Management Association
  http://nfocentrale.net/dmware
- Organization for the Advancement of Structured Information Standards
  http://www.oasis-open.org
- Society for Human Resource Management
  http://www.shrm.org
- Society for Information Management
  http://www.simnet.org
- Wesley J. Howe School of Technology Management
  http://howe.stevens.edu/research/research-centers/business-process-innovation
- Workflow And Reengineering International Association (WARIA)
  http://www.waria.com
- Workflow Management Coalition (WfMC)
  http://www.wfmc.org
- Workflow Portal
  http://www.e-workflow.org

More Unique Books from
Future Strategies, Publishers (www.FutStrat.com)

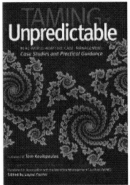

TAMING THE UNPREDICTABLE

http://futstrat.com/books/eip11.php

The core element of Adaptive Case Management (ACM) is the support for real-time decision-making by knowledge workers.

Taming the Unpredictable presents the logical starting point for understanding how to take advantage of ACM. This book goes beyond talking about concepts, and delivers actionable advice for embarking on your own journey of ACM-driven transformation.

Retail #49.95 (see discount on website)

DELIVERING BPM EXCELLENCE

http://futstrat.com/books/Delivering_BPM.php

Business Process Management in Practice

The companies whose case studies are featured in this book have proven excellence in their creative and successful deployment of advanced BPM concepts. These companies focused on excelling in *innovation, implementation* and *impact* when installing BPM and workflow technologies. The positive impact to their corporations includes increased revenues, more productive and satisfied employees, product enhancements, better customer service and quality improvements.
$39.95 (see discount on website)

BPMN 2.0 Handbook SECOND EDITION
(see two-BPM book bundle offer on website: get BPMN Reference Guide Free)
http://futstrat.com/books/bpmnhandbook2.php

Updated and expanded with exciting new content!

Authored by members of WfMC, OMG and other key participants in the development of BPMN 2.0, the BPMN 2.0 Handbook brings together worldwide thought-leaders and experts in this space. Exclusive and unique contributions examine a variety of aspects that start with an introduction of what's new in BPMN 2.0, and look closely at interchange, analytics, conformance, optimization, simulation and more. **Retail $75.00**

BPMN MODELING AND REFERENCE GUIDE

(see two-BPM book bundle offer on website: get BPMN Reference Guide Free)

http://www.futstrat.com/books/BPMN-Guide.php

Understanding and Using BPMN
How to develop rigorous yet understandable graphical representations of business processes.

Business Process Modeling Notation (BPMN) is a standard, graphical modeling representation for business processes. It provides an easy to use, flow-charting notation that is independent of the implementation environment.
Retail $39.95

BPM & WORKFLOW HANDBOOK: BUSINESS INTELLIGENCE
HTTP://FUTSTRAT.COM/BOOKS/HANDBOOK10.PHP

Linking business intelligence and business process management creates stronger operational business intelligence. Users seek more intelligent business process capabilities in order to remain competitive within their fields and industries. BPM vendors realize they need to improve their business processes, rules and event management offerings with greater intelligence or analytics capabilities.
Retail $75.00 (see discount offer on website)

BPM & WORKFLOW HANDBOOK: HUMAN-CENTRIC BPM

http://www.futstrat.com/books/handbook08.php

Spotlight on Human-Centric BPM

Human-centric business process management (BPM) has become the product and service differentiator. The topic now captures substantial mindshare and market share in the human-centric BPM space as leading vendors have strengthened their human-centric business processes. Our spotlight this year examines challenges in human-driven workflow and its integration across the enterprise.
Retail $95.00 (see discount on website)

DELIVERING THE CUSTOMER-CENTRIC ORGANIZATION

http://futstrat.com/books/Customer-Centric.php
The ability to successfully manage the customer value chain across the life cycle of a customer is the key to the survival of any company today. Business processes must react to changing and diverse customer needs and interactions to ensure efficient and effective outcomes.

This important book looks at the shifting nature of consumers and the workplace, and how BPM and associated emergent technologies will play a part in shaping the companies of the future.**Retail $39.95**

Social BPM

http://futstrat.com/books/handbook11.php
Work, Planning, and Collaboration Under the Impact of Social Technology

Today we see the transformation of both the look and feel of BPM technologies along the lines of social media, as well as the increasing adoption of social tools and techniques democratizing process development and design. It is along these two trend lines; the evolution of system interfaces and the increased engagement of stakeholders in process improvement, that Social BPM has taken shape.
Retail $59.95 (see discount offer on website)

Get 25% Discount on ALL Books in our Store.

Please use the discount code **SPEC25** to get 25% discount on ALL books in our store; both Print and Digital Editions (two discount codes cannot be used together).
http://store.futstrat.com/servlet/Catalog